Just Living Together

Implications of Cohabitation on Families, Children, and Social Policy

The Pennsylvania State University
Family Studies Symposia Series

Just Living Together

Implications of Cohabitation on Families, Children, and Social Policy

Edited by

Alan Booth
Ann C. Crouter
The Pennsylvania State University

Camera ready copy for this book was provided by the author.

Lawrence Erlbaum Associates, Inc., Publishers
10 Industrial Avenue
Mahwah, NJ 07430

Cover design by Kathryn Houghtaling Lacey

Library of Congress Cataloging-in-Publication Data

Just living together: implications of cohabitation for children,
families, and social policy / edited by Alan Booth,
    Ann C. Crouter.
       p. cm.

Includes bibliographical references and index.
ISBN 0-8058-3963-1 (hardcover : alk. paper)
1. Unmarried couples–Congresses. 2. Family–Congresses.
    3. Family policy–Congresses. 4. Child development–
    Congresses. I. Booth, Alan, 1935– II.Crouter, Ann C.
HQ803.5 .J87   2001
306.73'5–dc21

                        2001033989
                             CIP

Books published by Lawrence Erlbaum Associates are printed
on acid-free paper, and their bindings are chosen for strength
and durability.

Printed in the United States of America
10 9 8 7 6 5 4 3 2 1

Contents

CONTENTS   vii

Preface

Recent demographic trends signal that the time has come for family researchers and policymakers to take a serious look at cohabitation. The rise in the number of couples in the United States who opt to cohabit outside of marriage has risen markedly over the last several decades. Forty-one percent of women between the ages of 15 and 44, have cohabited, and 7% of women in this age bracket are currently cohabiting. For some, cohabitation is a prelude to marriage. Other couples opt to live together after dissolving a previous marriage and may do so for months or even years. For a growing number of men and women, cohabitation is not linked to marriage in any way but is a long-term substitute for formal marriage and may involve having children. Although cohabitation is on the rise, family scholars have been somewhat slow to focus on this evolving family form. Indeed, little is known about the conditions that give rise to cohabitation and the consequences of this family form for cohabiting adults and their children. Understanding the meaning of cohabitation across racial and ethnic groups, for men, women, and children, and for the quality of family relationships is a crucial prerequisite to developing social policy in this area.

The chapters in this volume are based on the presentations and discussions from a national symposium entitled "Just Living Together: Implications of Cohabitation for Children, Families, and Social Policy," held at the Pennsylvania State University, October 30–31, 2000, as the eighth in a series of annual interdisciplinary symposia focused on family issues. The book is divided into four sections, each dealing with a different aspect of cohabitation. The first section addresses the big picture question, "What are the historical and cross-cultural foundations of cohabitation?" British demographer Kathleen Kiernan addresses this issue by using a variety of survey data sets that encompass variations across European nations. Her chapter is complemented by the comments of demographer Nancy Landale, sociologist Julie Brines, and human development scholar Andrea Hunter who widen the comparative framework to encompass some of the ethnic and racial diversity in North America and Latin America.

The second section focuses specifically on North America and asks, "What is the role of cohabitation in contemporary North American family structure?" The lead chapter by demographers Pamela Smock and Sanjiv Gupta provides a detailed picture of the circumstances that appear to give rise to cohabitation, including comparative data on Quebec, where cohabitation is strikingly high, and the rest of Canada. Chapters by Rukmalie Jayakody and Natasha Cabrera, an interdisciplinary team, Rebekah Levine Coley, a developmental researcher, and Celine Le Bourdais, a demographer from Quebec, take different angles on this issue. Two key issues that emerge in their chapters is the need to think about cohabitation in a more process-oriented way and the importance of comparing cohabiting families not only to married families but to other family forms, including mother-headed, postdivorce families and families in which mothers have never married.

In the third section, the focus turns to the question, "What is the long- and short-term impact of cohabitation on child well-being?" Demographer Wendy Manning addresses this important but neglected question with the most comprehensive review to date of the available evidence. The authors of the three chapters that follow Manning's all take quite different approaches to this issue. Ariel Kalil, a developmental scholar, underscores the importance of looking at individual differences in children and underscores how the implications of cohabitation may vary depending on children's developmental stage. Demographer Susan Brown presents research showing that children living in cohabiting families appear more similar to children residing with single mothers both in terms of poverty and well-being. Bruce Ellis, a developmental scholar with bioevolutionary interests, reviews some of the provocative new evidence that suggests that a girl's onset of puberty may be sped up if her mother cohabits with a male who is not the girl's biological parent.

The final section addresses how cohabiting couples are affected by current policies and what policy innovations could be introduced to support these couples. Wendell Primus and Jennifer Beeson, of the Center on Budget and Policy Priorities, lay out the current programs available to cohabiting couples and explicate the situations under which the presence of a cohabiting partner alters the benefits families receive. This overview is amplified and critiqued in chapters by legal scholar Margaret Mahoney, economist Anne Winkler, and Ron Haskins of the Senate Subcommittee on Human Resources, Committee on Ways and Means.

Together, these chapters represent one of the first systematic efforts to focus on cohabitation. As such, they provide a road map for future research, program development, and policymaking in this area and an important resource for people interested in learning about variations in the ways families of today are choosing to organize themselves. In an effort to integrate the themes that cut across the four focal areas and suggest profitable directions for future activity in this area, Penn State colleagues Lynette Hofer and Dawn Stauffer have contributed a closing commentary chapter that pulls the volume together.

Acknowledgments

We are grateful to many organizations and people for their assistance in both developing the symposium and pulling together this edited volume. We are indebted to the National Institute of Child Health and Human Development for their support of the symposium series. We thank many units at Penn State for their assistance, including the Population Research Institute, the Consortium for Children, Youth, and Families, the Prevention Research Center, the College of Agricultural Sciences, the Center for Human Development and Family Research in Diverse Contexts, Dickinson School of Law, the Departments of Human Development and Family Studies, Psychology, Sociology, Economics, and Labor Studies and Industrial Relations, the Crime, Law, and Justice Program, and the Women's Studies Program.

A lively, interdisciplinary group of scholars from across the Penn State campus meets with us each year to generate topics for the next symposia. We are grateful for their rich reservoir of ideas and their enthusiasm. We are also grateful for the intellectual guidance and support of Christine Bachrach, our program officer at NICHD. The contributions of Cassie Johnstonbaugh, Erin Lesser, Diane Mattern, Kris McNeel, Sherry Yocum, and Kim Zimmerman in assisting with the administration of the symposium were invaluable. Special thanks to our colleagues Robert Shoen, Sal Oropesa, Mark Greenberg, and Rukmalie Jayakody for presiding over the four sessions and for steering discussion in stimulating directions.

—*Alan Booth*
—*Ann C. Crouter*

I

What Are the Historical and Cross-Cultural Foundations of Cohabitation?

1

Cohabitation in Western Europe: Trends, Issues, and Implications

Kathleen Kiernan
London School of Economics and Political Science

In many Western European nations, few developments in family life have been quite as dramatic as the recent rises in unmarried cohabitation and having children outside of marriage. Although cohabitation is often regarded as a recent development, it includes a range of living arrangements some of which are novel whereas others are more traditional. Prior to the 1970s, cohabiting unions were largely statistically invisible and may well have been socially invisible outside of the local community or milieu. In some European countries, there were subgroups of the population who were more prone to cohabitation than others: the poor; those whose marriages had broken up but were unable to obtain a divorce; certain groups of rural dwellers; and groups who were ideologically opposed to marriage.

Although there are few statistical data on how common cohabitation was in the past, there is evidence from parish register data for Britain, that stable, nonmarital procreative unions in earlier periods, going back several centuries, often attained the status of legal marriage (Laslett, Oosterveen, & Smith, 1980). Moreover, cohabitation after a marriage breaks down and between marriages is unlikely to be a recent development as common sense alone would suggest that in periods when divorces were less easy to obtain people might well choose to cohabit. Booth, in his studies of the laboring population in London, noted that those who were most likely to cohabitate were older, formerly married persons. He noted "more license is granted by public opinion to the evasion of laws of marriage by those who have found it a failure, than is allowed to those who relations to each other have not yet assumed a permanent form" (Booth, 1902, cited in Gillis, 1985, p. 232).

Similarly, in other European countries there are a number of historical sources from around the beginning of the 20th century that suggest that the phenomenon was sufficiently visible to attract some comment. In Sweden, according to Trost (1988), there were two types of cohabitation: one known as "marriage of conscience" practiced by a group of intellectuals as a protest against the fact that only church marriages were permitted at that time (their protests led to the introduction of civil marriage in 1909) and the second known as "Stockholm marriages," which were found among poor people who could not afford to marry. These unions were probably akin to those observed in poorer sections of British, French, and German

3

urban society (on Britain see Roberts, 1973; on France see Villeneuve-Gokalp, 1991; and on Germany, see Abrams, 1993).

A NEW FORM OF COHABITATION

It is likely that cohabitation following marital breakdown persisted throughout the 20th century, and postmarital cohabitation was the most prevalent form of cohabitation in the 1950s and 1960s. For example, in Britain among women marrying in the latter half of the 1960s, only 6% of never married women reported having lived with their husband prior to marriage compared with one in four women who were remarrying (General Household Survey, 1989). Moreover, with the growth in divorce that has occurred across European nations, "postmarital" cohabitation has become even more prevalent with the divorced cohabiting either in preference to, or as a prelude to, remarriage.

Whether the poor continued to enter into informal unions is unknown, although in France there is some evidence that this continued to be the case (see Villeneuve-Gokalp, 1991). However, given the growing popularity of marriage and, in particular, youthful marriage that occurred in the 1950s and 1960s, it is likely that informal unions among single people were rare during these decades. A so-called golden age of marriage prevailed in Western European nations from the 1950s up to the early 1970s (Festy, 1980), when marriage was youthful and almost universal. This pattern of marriage receded during the 1970s. Marriage rates declined and the average age at marriage increased. This situation continues unabated to the present time. It is a new type of cohabitation that is implicated in the marriage bust that has occurred across European nations. A form of cohabitation came to the fore in the 1970s and has escalated during the 1980s and 1990s, whereby young people live together as a prelude to, or as an alternative to marriage.

European researchers have also attempted to discover where in the social structure cohabitation first took hold. Who were the initiators of this new form of cohabitation? For Norway, the results are inconclusive (Blom, 1994; Ramsoy, 1994). Some analyses suggest that it began among university students, others that it began among the poor (a legacy of the past). Similarly, in France there is evidence (Villeneuve-Gokalp, 1991) that cohabitation developed first among upper class children and university students and then spread down, but initially it was more common among the lower social groups, particularly the unemployed. In Sweden, the rise in cohabitation was initially observed among the working classes (B. Hoem, 1992). But Bernhardt and Hoem (1985) also observed that in the case of working-class women, cohabitation was a setting for having children, whereas among the daughters of salaried workers, it was a relatively long-lasting childless phase. In Britain, cohabitation was embraced so rapidly across the social spectrum that it is difficult from the extant data to clearly identify the initiators (Kiernan, 1989). The speed with which this new phenomenon took hold in many countries may account for the lack of a clear answer to who initiated this change.

A PARTNERSHIP TRANSITION?

It has been suggested by several scholars that many European societies may be going through a transition in the way that men and women become couples or partners (see Prinz, 1995, for a review). Most scholars draw on the experience of the Swedish population, which is the nation that has gone furthest in these developments, from which a number of stages can be identified (J. Hoem & Hoem, 1988). Simplifying, in the first stage, cohabitation emerges as a deviant or avant-garde phenomenon practiced by a small group of the single population, while the great majority of the population marries directly. In the second stage, cohabitation functions as either a prelude to or a probationary period where the strength of the relationship may be tested prior to committing to marriage and is predominantly a childless phase. In the third stage, cohabitation becomes socially acceptable as an alternative to marriage and becoming a parent is no longer restricted to marriage. Finally, in the fourth stage, cohabitation and marriage become indistinguishable with children being born and reared within both, and the partnership transition could be said to be complete. Sweden and Denmark are countries that have made the transition to this fourth stage. These stages may vary in duration, but once a society has reached a particular stage it is unlikely that there will be a return to an earlier stage. Also, once a certain stage has been reached, all the previous types of cohabiting unions can co-exist. Such stages also have parallels at the level of the individual. At any given time, cohabitation may have different meanings for the men and women involved (Manting, 1996), for example, it may be viewed as an alternative to being single, or as a precursor to marriage, or as a substitute for marriage. Moreover, how a couple perceives their cohabitation may change over time and the perception may also vary between the partners. Dissecting cohabitation in this way highlights the diversity of the phenomenon and suggests that more so than marriage it is a process rather than an event. Additionally, the inconstancy of cohabitation poses challenges for the analysis as well as the understanding of this development in family life.

In this chapter, we examine data on cohabitation and childbearing outside marriage for a range of European countries to ascertain the extent and depth of these changes and we also examine the policy responses to these developments.

THE RISE OF COHABITATION

Until recently, European-wide data on cohabitation tended to be scarce and generally emanated from ad hoc surveys that made comparative analyses problematic, as sample sizes, coverage, and definitions can vary. However, during the 1990s more information from standardized questionnaires became available from Eurostat (the Statistical Office of the European Communities) and from a series of Fertility and Family Surveys (FFS) carried out in the main in the first half of the 1990s under the auspices of the UN Economic Commission for Europe (ECE) (United Nations, 1992).

The Incidence of Cohabitation

Our analysis of data from Eurobarometer surveys carried out in the 15-member States of the European Union in 1996 provides a perspective on the incidence of cohabiting and marital unions across a range of nations (Kiernan, 2000a). Eurobarometer surveys are primarily opinion surveys covering a range of topics relevant to the European Union (EU), which contain some very basic demographic information on the respondents including information on marital status in which "living as married" is one of the categories; the others being the more conventional ones of single, married, divorced, separated, and widowed. Such marital status distributions are not as accurate as those obtained in dedicated family and fertility surveys but they probably reflect the relative position of different European countries in these categories (European Commission, 1996).

Figure 1.1 shows the proportions of women aged 25 to 29 years in the 15 EU countries who were cohabiting, married, single, or separated/divorced/widowed at the time of the survey in 1996. In these data, never married and postmarital cohabitants cannot be differentiated but it is reasonable to assume that at these younger ages the former is likely to be the most prevalent. It is clear from Fig. 1.1 that there is a good deal of diversity across European states in the incidence of cohabitation. Cohabitation is strikingly most common in the Nordic countries of Denmark, Sweden, and Finland, and France also has relatively high proportions cohabiting. There is also a middle group of countries, which includes the Netherlands and Belgium, Great Britain, West and East Germany, and Austria with mid-levels of cohabitation. Data for the United States (Raley, 2000) and Australia (McDonald, 2000) suggest that they too would fall into this middle group. At the other extreme is the set of southern European countries and Ireland, where cohabitation is seemingly much rarer with only a tiny minority cohabiting.

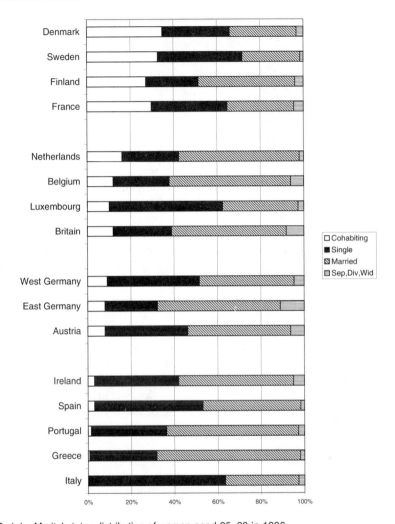

FIG. 1.1 Marital status distribution of women aged 25–29 in 1996.

Type of First Partnership

The UN ECE Fertility and Family surveys carried out in the main during the first half of the 1990s included a full partnership history that incorporated dates of marriages and any other coresidential heterosexual intimate relationships. Such histories permis more in depth examinations of partnership formation and dissolution than can be gleaned from vital registration data or cross-sectional surveys that only include current status information.

These data are used to examine cohabitation patterns across a range of European nations. From Table 1.1, which shows for two recent cohorts of women the proportions who entered their first partnership at marriage, we see that in many European nations there have been large increases in the proportions of couples cohabiting, and nowadays cohabitation rather than marriage marks the formation of a union. It is clear from these data that the younger women, those aged 25 to 29, were much less likely to have commenced their first partnership at marriage compared with the older women. There are marked reductions to be seen in the proportions of women who married directly without cohabiting in most countries. For example, in France one in two of the older women but only one in five of the younger women married directly; a pattern that is repeated across many of the nations. The main exceptions are Sweden and the southern European countries. In Sweden, cohabiting rather than marrying was already well established among the older women, whereas in Italy and Spain there are indications of a rise in cohabitation. However, in the latter two countries for the majority of women marriage still heralds the start of first partnership, which is in contrast with the Scandinavian and western European nations where it is a minority practice.

It is also the case that in many European countries, cohabiting unions have simply replaced the marriages of yesteryear, in that compared with the recent past there has been little change in the proportions of men and women who have formed a residential partnership by their mid-20s, whereas in other countries, most noticeably the southern European states, cohabitation is only part of the story in the decline in marriage rates (Billari et al., 2000; Kiernan, 1999a). Here, young people have been spending longer periods of time as solos than in the recent past; living with their parents (in the main), on their own or sharing with others (European Commission, 1998).

Duration of Cohabiting Unions

In many countries, cohabitation has eclipsed marriage as the marker for entry into first union but subsequently, many of these unions convert into marriages and others dissolve. Life table estimates of the proportions of cohabitations that had converted into marriages or dissolved by 5 years for a range of European countries, which are shown in Table 1.2 suggest that there is some variation in the propensity to marry across nations and age groups. Sweden exhibits the lowest conversion to marriage with only one in three cohabitations having become marriages within 5 years of the start of the partnership, whereas in most other countries one in two cohabitations had converted into marriages by the fifth anniversary of the union. In several countries, there are indications of a decline in the propensity to marry over time, most noticeably in Norway and France (particularly in the early years of the union), whereas in other countries there is little sign of change, for example, in West Germany. Turning to the extent to which cohabit-

Table 1.1
Type of First Partnership Among Women With a First Partnership According to Age Group at the Time of the Survey

	Age group 25–29			Age-group 35–39		
	Married directly	Cohabited and Married	Cohabited	Married directly	Cohabited and Married	Cohabited
Sweden[a]	7	41	52	8	62	30
Norway[b]	24	40	35	62	30	7
Finland	17	43	40	31	46	23
France	21	34	45	55	33	12
Great Britain	37	33	31	72	18	10
Austria	19	41	40	30	42	28
Switzerland	19	44	37	30	52	18
West Germany	16	38	46	38	33	29
East Germany	15	35	50	21	26	53
Spain	80	8	12	91	4	5
Italy	86	8	6	91	5	4

[a] Sweden birth cohorts 54 and 64. [b] Norway birth cohorts 50 and 60.

Table 1.2
Proportions (Derived From Life Table Analysis) of First Cohabiting Unions That Had Converted to Marriages or Dissolved by 2 and 5 Years of Start of Union by Age of Woman

	Married		Dissolved	
	2 Years	5 Years	2 Years	5 Years
Sweden				
1964[a]	8	34	16	37
1954	19	44	10	24
Norway				
1960[a]	27	56	16	35
1950	64	81	8	29
Finland				
25–29	33	60	11	31
35–39	45	66	8	21
France				
25–29	37	63	9	31
35–39	58	78	6	17
Great Britain				
25–29	34	58	14	36
35–39	29	50	21	41
Austria				
25–29	26	54	7	26
35–39	31	50	6	18
Switzerland				
25–29	36	67	14	38
35–39	37	70	9	26
West Germany				
25–29	30	57	14	36
35–39	32	51	7	17
East Germany				
25–29	26	42	8	27
35–39	20	26	6	15

[a] Birth cohorts.

ing unions dissolve, Table 1.2 shows that in most countries amongst those aged 25 to 29 years, between one quarter and one third had dissolved by the fifth anniversary of the start of the union.

Who Cohabits?

As well as cross-national variation in union formation behavior, there is also variation within nations and between subgroups of the population (see Carmichael, 1995, for a review). There is now robust evidence that in most nations younger generations are more prone to cohabit than were older generations, and growing evidence that the more secular members of a society and those who had experienced parental divorce during childhood are also more likely to cohabit. There is also evidence that those residing in metropolitan areas are more prone to cohabit. Being in full-time education also tends to inhibit union formation but the association between level of educational qualifications and employment status with cohabitation is less clear cut and tends to vary across nations.

Drawing on data collected in the UN ECE Family and Fertility Surveys, I examine two of the factors associated with the propensity to cohabit, namely religious observance and experience of parental divorce. Table 1.3 shows the proportions of women under age 40 who married directly according to whether they attended church on some occasions versus those who reported that they practically never did. The last column shows that there was some variation in the proportions responding in this way, with nonattendance being rare in Italy and more common in East Germany and Sweden. However, within a given country it is seen that those who married directly were more likely to attend church than their contemporaries who had commenced their first partnership with cohabitation. Thus, across Europe cohabitation appears to be associated with the more secular groups within a population and other research has also shown this to be the case when cohabitation was rare as well as when cohabitation became more popular (for a detailed discussion see Lesthaeghe & Moors, 1996).

The other background factor examined was whether there had been experience of parental separation or divorce. There is evidence for Great Britain and the United States (e.g., Kiernan, 1992; Thornton, 1991) that children who experience parental divorce are more likely to cohabit and have children outside of marriage. The UN ECE Fertility and Family Surveys' included a question on whether the parents of the respondents had ever separated or divorced and the age at which this happened, which allowed us to examine whether this was the case in other European countries. Table 1.4 shows the proportions of women who had married directly according to whether they had experienced parental divorce during childhood. It is clear that in all these countries the proportions marrying directly is invariably higher among those who did not experience parental divorce during childhood than among those who did. This applies in northern European, western European, and southern European countries and in countries where marrying di-

Table 1.3
Proportions Married Directly According to Some Church Attendance Versus None Among Women Who Had a Partnership and Were Aged 20–39 Years at the Time of the Survey

	Some Church Attendance	Never Attends Church	% Reporting Never Attended Church
Sweden	12	4	66
Norway	50	23	67
Finland	25	14	35
Great Britain[a]	59	41	45
Switzerland	31	14	41
West Germany	32	16	43
East Germany	23	14	77
Spain	90	80	53
Italy	90	81	9

[a] France and Austria did not include this question. Great Britain nearest equivalent data used.

Table 1.4
**Percent Married Directly by Experience of Parental Separation or
Divorce at Age 16 or Under Among Women Aged 20–39 Years at
the Time of the Survey**

	Parental Divorce		% with Parental Divorce
	Yes	No	
Country			
Sweden	3	7	14
Finland [a]	16	21	8
France	20	37	15
Austria	8	25	13
Switzerland	16	24	14
West Germany	17	26	14
East Germany	12	18	21
Spain	67	86	6
Italy	65	88	4

[a] Finland did not ask age at parental divorce. Norway and Great Britain did not include a question on parental divorce.

rectly is rare and cohabitation normative as in Sweden and in countries where marrying directly is normative and cohabitation is relatively rare such as Italy. All these differences were statistically significant at the 5% level or less. The preference for cohabiting among children who experienced a parental separation or divorce may well represent reluctance on the part of young people with such an experience to make a permanent commitment, such as that enshrined in legal marriage. Alternatively, given the experience of parental separation they may want to be more certain about committing to a permanent relationship and may take longer in the search for their ideal partner or in testing the strength of the relationship via cohabitation before committing to marriage.

PARTNERSHIP DISSOLUTION

Across Europe, divorce has increased since the late 1960s and early 1970s up into the 1980s, at which time rates tended to stabilize, but there continues to be cross-national variation in the extent of divorce (Council of Europe, 1999). Moreover, with the rise in cohabitation data on divorce are increasingly likely to be underestimates of the extent of partnership breakdown. We have examined the issue of partnership dissolution using the data from the partnership histories collected in the FFS for those countries that had medium to high levels of cohabitation. A central interest was an assessment of the relative fragility of the different types of first union: direct marriage, cohabitations that converted into marriage, and cohabiting unions that had not converted into a marriage by the time of the survey (Kiernan, 2000b).

Premarital Cohabitation and Marital Dissolution

The data were analyzed taking into account competing risks. We addressed a number of questions. First, we inquired whether marriages were more likely to breakdown if they are preceded by a period of cohabitation. Cox proportional hazard models were used with the survival time being the duration of marriage to dissolution or censoring at the time of the survey. Whether cohabitation preceded marriage or not was treated as a fixed covariate. We also included a control for age at first marriage and two background factors; namely, whether parental divorce had been experienced during childhood and whether the respondent was or not a non or infrequent attendee at church. The first column in Table 1.5 shows the relative risks of marriage breakdown for those who cohabited prior to marriage relative to those who married directly, column 2 includes a control for age at first marriage, experience of parental divorce and whether the woman attended church or not. In some countries, there is evidence that those who cohabit prior to marriage compared with those who don't have a higher risk of marital dissolution (France, Germany, and Sweden) and other countries this is less the case (Norway, Finland, Austria, Switzerland).

Duration of Premarital Cohabitation and Marital Dissolution

A subsidiary inquiry was whether length of cohabitation prior to marriage had any bearing on dissolution risks. For example, short-duration cohabitations may have different impacts than longer periods of cohabitation, in that short cohabitations may be more likely to include people with a greater commitment to marriage than those who cohabit more long term. Table 1.6 shows for a selection of countries the relative risks of marital dissolution according to duration of premarital cohabitation. The reference category is those who cohabited for 1 to 6 months prior to marriage. The evidence from this simple analysis suggests that in these countries

Table 1.5

Relative Risk of Marital Dissolution in First Marriage (Which Is a First Partnership) According to Whether Woman Cohabited Prior to Marriage or Not Among Women Aged 20 to 39 Years at the Time of the Survey

Country	Model 1	Model 2
Sweden	1.40	1.58*
Norway[a]	0.90	0.95
Finland	1.14	1.16
France[a]	1.52**	1.63**
Austria[a]	1.23	1.24
Switzerland	1.41*	1.28*
West Germany	1.62**	1.42**
East Germany	1.32*	1.38*

Note. Relative risks derived from Cox models. Model 1 has no controls, Model 2 includes controls for age at first marriage, church attendance, and experience of parental divorce.

[a] Norway had no information on parental divorce and France and Austria had no question on religion.

***$p < 0.0001$. **$p < 0.01$. *$p < .0.05$.

there is little variation in the relative risk of marital breakdown according to length of premarital cohabitation.

Type of First Partnership and Partnership Dissolution

The second question addressed was to what extent the risk of breakdown varied across our three different types of first union. In this analysis, the clock starts at onset of first partnership and marriage is included as a time-varying covariate and the two states of married are distinguished; namely, married at start of partner-

Table 1.6
Relative Risk of Marital Dissolution in First Marriage (Which Is a First Partnership) According to Whether Woman Cohabited Prior to Marriage and Duration of Cohabitation Prior to Marriage Among Women Aged 20 to 39 Years at the Time of the Survey

Duration of Cohabitation	France	Switzerland	Austria	West Germany	East Germany	Sweden
None	0.60*	0.65*	0.69[+]	0.72	0.89	0.71
1–6 months (reference category)	1.00	1.00	1.00	1.00	1.00	1.00
7–12 months	0.78	1.08	0.68	1.66	1.29	1.33
13–24 months	0.74	0.84	1.11	1.17	1.25	1.10
25–36 months	1.24	0.94	0.53[+]	0.97	1.53	0.96
37–60 months	1.11	0.60	0.80	1.10	1.32	1.07
61 or more months	0.66	1.17	0.61	1.28	0.67	0.72

Note. Relative risks derived from Cox models.
$*p < 0.05.$ $^{+}p < 0.10.$

ship, and married later or not married by the time of the survey. Age at first partnership and the two background factors, parental divorce and degree of religious observance, were also included in the analysis. Table 1.7 shows the relative risk of partnership breakdown for the three types of designated first partnership. Model 1 provides the gross risk and Model 2 includes controls for age at first partnership, church attendance, and experience of parental divorce. It is clear that across all the countries, continuing cohabiting unions had the highest risk of breakdown, with a level of risk that was substantially higher than that observed for direct marriages and converted unions. The story for unions that had converted into marriages was more varied. Focusing on Model 2 in Table 1.7, one can see evidence of an elevated risk of breakdown for these unions in France, West and East Germany, and to a lesser extent in Sweden, while in remaining countries there is little difference in the risk of dissolution of converted unions compared with direct marriages. From these analyses, there is robust crossnational evidence that

Table 1.7

Relative Risk of Partnership Dissolution According to Type of First Partnership for Women Aged 20 to 39 Years at the Time of the Survey

Country	Model 1			Model 2		
	Married Directly	Cohabited Married	Cohabitation Only	Married Directly	Cohabited Married	Cohabitation Only
Sweden	1.00	1.61*	4.48***	1.00	1.50+	3.96***
Norway[a]	1.00	0.86	5.28***	1.00	0.85	4.92***
Finland	1.00	1.02	3.22***	1.00	1.12	3.44***
France[a]	1.00	1.47**	5.77***	1.00	1.49**	6.04***
Austria[a]	1.00	1.11	3.50***	1.00	1.01	3.08***
Switzerland	1.00	1.30+	6.06***	1.00	1.11	4.84***
West Germany	1.00	1.59**	3.18***	1.00	1.38*	3.07***
East Germany	1.00	1.35*	1.44**	1.00	1.35*	1.55***

Note. Relative risks derived from Cox proportional hazard models with marriage included as a time varying covariate. Model 1 no controls, Model 2 controls for age at first partnership, church attendance, and experience of parental divorce.
[a] Norway had no information on parental divorce and France and Austria had no question on religion.
***$p < 0.0001$. **$p < 0.01$. *$p < 0.05$. +$p < 0.10$.

cohabiting unions that had not converted to marriages were the most fragile unions, but that the role of premarital cohabitation in union dissolution may be more variable across nations.

THE RISE OF NONMARITAL CHILDBEARING

Alongside the rise in cohabitation, there have been striking increases in the levels of nonmarital childbearing, two developments that are intimately related. It is clear from Fig. 1.2 that in recent decades across most European states, as in the United States, there have been noteworthy increases in the proportions of births

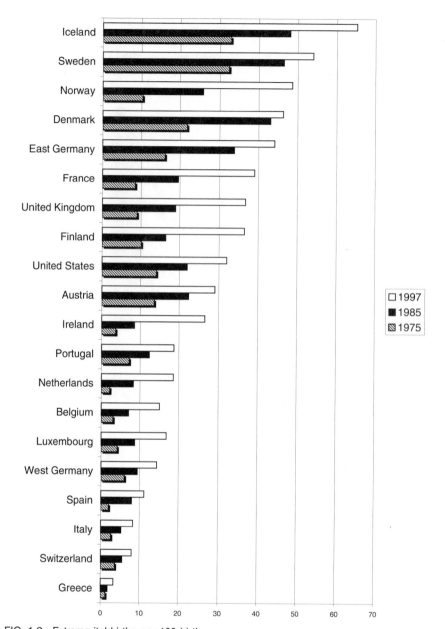

FIG. 1.2 Extramarital births per 100 births.

occurring outside of legal marriage, but there also continues to be marked variation in the extent of nonmarital childbearing across nations. As seen in Fig. 1.1, at
one extreme are the Nordic countries where well over 40% of births in 1997 were
outside marriage and at the other extreme are the southern European countries of
Italy and Greece where, along with Switzerland, 10% or fewer births occurred
outside marriage. Between these two extremes, two broad groupings can be dis-
cerned. A set of countries with ratios between 10% and 20%, including the geo-
graphically close Benelux countries and West Germany, and a set with 25% or
more, which encompasses Ireland (which has experienced one of the most notable
changes—up from 8% in 1985 to 27% in 1997), the United Kingdom and France
(with remarkably similar trends), and Austria and Finland. In 1975, only 5 of the
19 European countries represented here had nonmarital birth ratios of more than
10%, in 1985 this had increased to 10 and by 1997 stood at 16. In 1975, Sweden
and Iceland were dramatic outliers, with one in three births already being born
outside of marriage, this is much less the case today.

   Undoubtedly, an important engine driving the rise in nonmarital childbearing
is the rise in cohabitation that has occurred, particularly since the beginning of the
1980s, in many European countries. However, as discussed earlier, there is a good
deal of diversity across European states in the incidence of cohabitation. In Europe, levels of cohabitation and childbearing outside marriage tend to be in accord, with countries with high levels of cohabitation having higher rates of
nonmarital childbearing and vice versa. However, there are exceptions. Britain
and Ireland have higher levels of childbearing outside marriage than one would
expect from cohabitation estimates alone and the Netherlands and West Germany
have lower rates of nonmarital childbearing than might be anticipated from their
levels of cohabitation. This suggests that norms about marriage being the conventional setting for having children may be stronger in some countries than others.

Partnership Context of First Birth

The union and fertility histories collected in the UN ECE FFS surveys allowed
examination of the partnership context of first birth. Table 1.8 shows the proportions of women in the various countries who made the transition to motherhood in
one of four settings: before they had any coresidential partnership; within their
first partnership, which was a cohabitation; within first marriage; and after their
first partnership (either a cohabitation or a marriage).

   There are a number of findings that stand out. It is clearly the case for almost
all these European countries that it is normative to become a mother in the first
partnership. Having a child prior to a partnership is a minor practice in many
countries, including those with high levels of nonmarital childbearing and those
with low levels (Table 1.8). For example, the overall proportion of women who
had a child prior to any union was only 7% in Sweden and 6% in France. The
extent of out-of-partnership births is somewhat higher in Norway and notably

Table 1.8
Percentage of Women With Different Partnership Contexts at First Birth According to Age of Woman

Country	Before Any Partnership	In First Cohabiting Union	In First Marriage	After First Partnership Ended	Percent With First Birth by Survey
Norway[b]					
25–29	12	28	53	8	68
35–39	13	7	75	4	91
20–45	12	18	65	5	62
Sweden[a]					
25–29	6	53	23	19	66
35–39	6	53	30	12	92
20–45	7	51	29	13	74
Austria					
25–29	21	29	47	3	70
35–39	20	20	53	7	91
20–45	20	22	53	5	73
Switzerland					
25–29	4	8	78	10	45
35–39	5	8	76	11	83
20–45	5	7	77	11	66
West Germany					
25–29	11	17	64	8	38
35–39	11	8	73	8	75
20–39	10	13	70	7	45
France					
25–29	9	22	62	7	56
35–39	5	11	80	4	91
20–45	6	14	74	6	71
Great Britain					
25–29	15	17	59	8	54
35–39	4	4	82	9	80
20–45	9	9	75	8	65
Italy					
25–29	4	5	90	1	36
35–39	5	3	90	1	83
20–45	5	3	90	1	61
Spain					
25–29	8	6	85	-	47
35–39	4	3	92	1	92
20–45	5	3	90	1	65

[a] Norway 1950 and 1960 cohorts: 35–39 and 25–29 equivalent.

[b] Sweden 1954 and 1964 cohorts: 35–39 and 25–29 equivalent.

higher in Austria, but Austria is a special case because it has a long history of marriage following a first birth (Prinz, 1995). There is also evidence (Kiernan, 1999a) that the proportions of births occurring prior to a first partnership have hardly changed over recent cohorts, and the general direction in most countries has been for the proportion to decrease. The major exception to this trend is Great Britain where the proportion has more than doubled. In Spain and Italy, and to a lesser extent Switzerland, first marriage continues to be the preeminent context for first births, whereas in the remaining countries, the picture is less clear-cut. However, in most of the countries, there is a discernible movement away from having a child within marriage to having a child within a cohabiting union.

Characteristics According to Type of First Partnership

Table 1.9 shows the average age at first birth among women according to the partnership context of their first birth. It is clear from this table, and not unsurprising to find, that the group of women who have their first child after a first partnership had ended have the highest mean age at first birth, being around 27 years in most of the countries. At the other end of the spectrum, having a child prior to any coresidential partnership, in most countries these women have the youngest average age at childbearing, and in most cases this falls within the 20 to 21 age range, which is typically some 2 years younger on average than that observed for women who have their first child within their first partnership.

The story is less clear-cut when one compares the average ages of first birth among those who were in cohabiting and marital unions. Any comparison or interpretation is of course complicated by the fact that in countries where there have been recent increases in the propensity to have children in cohabiting unions as opposed to marital unions, other things being equal, women who have children within a cohabiting union are likely to be selected for relative youthfulness. Table 1.9 shows that in most countries, cohabiting women have their first child on average at a younger age than those in marital unions: The extreme example is Great Britain where there is a 2.3 year difference in the average age at birth, but the same tendency exists in Sweden, Norway, and Austria where there is more than 1 year's difference in the average age at first birth for these two groups of women. Table 1.8 showed that in Sweden there had been little change over recent cohorts in the extent to which women were having their first child in cohabiting unions as compared with marital unions but this was less the case in Britain and Norway where there have been marked increases over time in the proportions having a child in a cohabiting union. In most of the other countries, the tendency is for cohabiting women to have their first child at a younger age than married women as in Spain, Switzerland, and France but in the case of Italy and West Germany there are only small differences between these two groups of women.

Table 1.9

Average Age at First Birth According to Partnership Context of First Birth
Women Aged 20 to 45 Years

Country	Before Any Partnership	In First Cohabiting Union	In First Marriage	After First Partnership Ended	All Mothers	Number in Sample
Norway[a]	20.7	22.2	23.4	26.9	23.1	2,590
Sweden[a]	20.6	22.9	24.5	26.8	23.7	2,812
Austria	21.0	22.1	23.3	26.7	22.7	2,758
Switzerland	20.1	24.9	25.4	28.9	25.5	2,198
West Germany[b]	20.4	23.9	24.1	26.9	23.9	1,247
France	20.3	23.2	23.8	27.4	23.7	2,502
Great Britain	19.1	21.4	23.7	27.6	23.5	1,629
Italy	22.4	24.0	24.2	29.1	24.1	2,457
Spain	21.3	23.2	24.0	26.9	23.9	2,243

[a] Norway and Sweden specific cohorts. [b] West Germany age range 20-39.

Child Within a Cohabiting Union

The totality of nonmarital births includes children born outside a union and those born within cohabiting unions. Mothers who have children on their own subsequently form partnerships. For example, in most of the European countries in our study between 20% and 30% of the mothers had partnered by the time the child was age 1, and by the time the child was age 5, typically one in two of the mothers had entered a marital or cohabiting union. Mothers who have a child within a cohabiting union also marry. Here we examine the extent to which these unions convert into marriages or to put it in older day parlance, to what extent are children born outside a marital union legitimated by the subsequent marriage of their parents?

Table 1.10 shows life table estimates of the proportions of women who had legalized their union by 1, 3, and 5 years after the birth of their baby. It is apparent that there is some variation across nations in the extent to which cohabiting unions are converted into marriages. Great Britain exhibits the lowest proportion at around 33% and the high conversion set includes Switzerland, Austria, Italy, and Sweden with around 70% or more having married. One can also examine the pace at which the cohabiting unions were converted into marriages. By the first anniversary of

Table 1.10
Proportions Marrying and Life-Table Estimates of Duration to Marriage Among Women Aged 20–45 Years Who Had Their First Child in a Cohabiting Union

Country	Proportions married	% married Within 1 months	% married within 3 years	% married within 5 years	Number in sample
Norway[a]	57	31	60	66	457
Sweden[a]	69	20	44	56	1425
Austria	73	21	55	69	606
Switzerland	78	39	68	75	151
West Germany[b]	56	27	49	55	162
France	47	25	33	45	565
Great Britain	36	18	30	39	150
Italy	70	34	55	70	86
Spain	45	21	37	46	67

[a]Norway and Sweden specific cohorts. [b]West Germany age range 20-39.

the birth of the child, between 17% and 39% of the women had married and the pace of conversion tends to gather speed in the first few years after the birth and then slows down. For example, in many countries the proportions of women marrying between the first and third anniversary of the birth of their baby almost doubled but between the third and fifth anniversary the pace of conversion to marriage slows down.

Why women choose to marry rather than continue to cohabit or what triggers marriage are questions to which there are few answers. The UN ECE FFS did not collect information on why people chose to marry rather than to continue to cohabit after they had a child. However, some relevant information was collected in a 1993 Eurobarometer survey carried out in the then 12-member states of the EU. In this survey, respondents were asked about their level of agreement to a list of 11 reasons for getting married (Malpas & Lambert, 1993). The top response related to committing oneself to being faithful to a partner, with 62% completely agreeing with this statement, and the next important reason, with 51% in complete agreement, was "it was the best way to guarantee the rights of the children. In third place was "to prove to other person that you really love him/her" with 41% completely agreeing with this statement. Thus, one might infer that commitment and the rights of children are important elements in the impetus to marry. These are responses for all groups, but the ordering of the importance of the responses did not vary significantly according to gender, marital status, or a past history of cohabitation. Similarly, in a recent British study (Haskey, 1999), the two main reasons given for marrying among those who had cohabited with their future spouse were to do with strengthening the relationship and children. In the final section of this chapter, I will examine the position of children in out-of-wedlock families.

PARENTAL SEPARATION

The final topic we explored was whether children born into cohabiting unions as compared with those born to married parents were more or less likely to see the separation of their parents, and whether parental marriage after the birth makes any difference. We used life table analysis to estimate the survival probabilities of partnerships where the clock started with the birth of the child not with the onset of the union. Life tables were estimated for women who had a marital birth and among those who had a nonmarital birth, marriage was included as a time-varying covariate. Table 1.11 shows the proportions of unions surviving 3 and 5 years after the birth of their first child for all marital unions and cohabiting unions and for the two subsets of cohabiting unions, those that had converted into marriages by the time of the survey and those that had not.

In all the countries included in our analysis, children born within marriage were less likely to see their parents separate than those born in a cohabiting union. Within the set of cohabiting unions, those that had not been converted into marriages were the most fragile, with at least one in five of these unions having dis-

Table 1.11
Life Table Estimates of Percentage of Unions Surviving 3 and 5 Years After the Birth of First Child Among Women Aged 20–45 Years According to Type of First Partnership

Country	Percent Surviving 36 Months	Percent Surviving 60 Months	Number in the Risk Set
Norway[a]			
Married	97	94	1,677
Cohabitation	87	82	456
-cohabited/married	98	95	131
-cohabited only	79	71	325
Sweden[a]			
Married	96	93	817
Cohabitation	90	84	1,424
-cohabited/married	97	94	493
-cohabited only	84	75	931
Austria			
Married	97	94	2,161
Cohabitation	92	86	670
-cohabited/married	98	96	246
-cohabited only	86	71	424
Switzerland			
Married	97	95	2,191
Cohabitation	82	73	166
-cohabited/married	95	86	65
-cohabited only	64	53	101
West Germany[b]			
Married	95	91	873
Cohabitation	92	85	161
-cohabited/married	97	91	45
-cohabited only	89	80	116
France			
Married	97	95	1,522
Cohabitation	85	78	258
-cohabited/married	94	90	90
-cohabited only	81	70	168
Great Britain			
Married	96	92	1,242
Cohabitation	71	57	149
-cohabited/married	90	75	43
-cohabited only	61	48	106
Italy			
Married	99	98	2,677
Cohabitation	95	91	90
-cohabited/married	-	-	31
-cohabited only	93	82	59
Spain			
Married	99	98	1,540
Cohabitation	79	67	74
-cohabited/married	-	-	16
-cohabited only	71	51	58

[a] Norway and Sweden specific cohorts. [b] West Germany age range 20-39.

solved by the time the child was 5 years old. Among children born within marriage or cohabiting unions that subsequently converted to marriages, there was little difference in the chances of them seeing the break-up of their parents marriage by their fifth birthday in Sweden, Norway, Austria, and West Germany; with less than one in ten of these children having experienced parental separation. However, in Switzerland and more noticeably in Great Britain, children born into marital unions were more likely to see their parents remain together until their fifth birthday than those children born into a cohabiting union that converted into a marriage.

POLICY BACKGROUND AND RESPONSES

The rise in cohabitation and childbearing outside marriage raises important questions about the hegemony of legal marriage and the assumptions on which public policies are built. Different European countries have responded in different ways to these developments. The position with respect to children has been discussed and codified in recent years and is much less controversial than the position of cohabiting couples.

Cohabitation

In the past, ties between spouses were deemed to be of sufficient importance that marriages were included within the scope of vital registration systems. With the rise of cohabitation, this public acknowledgment has been eroded and consequently raises policy questions about the links between partners and unmarried parents and their children with respect to the public domains of life. Many European countries are recognizing that changes in union behavior are underway and that marriage law, practices, and values and the assumptions on which public policies are built are being evaluated.

To date, there have been a variety of policy responses to the emergence of cohabitation in different European countries. At the beginning of 1998, the Netherlands, a country with intermediate levels of cohabitation and low rates of nonmarital childbearing, instituted the formal registration of partnerships for both heterosexual and homosexual couples, which made legally registered cohabitation functionally equivalent to marriage, except cohabiting couples do not have the right to adopt. In the early 1990s, Denmark had instituted the legal registration of homosexual partnerships but the Netherlands was the first country in Europe to formalize heterosexual cohabitation. However, Registered Partnerships in the Netherlands were primarily instituted to meet the needs of gay couples who did not have the option of marriage (Schrama, 1999). In September 2000 a new bill was passed (which will take effect in 2001) that will allow gay couples to convert their current registered same-sex partnerships to fully-fledged marriages so the registration of heterosexual cohabitation may be short-lived.

In France, which in terms of cohabitation levels is the most Nordic in that the rise of cohabitation and nonmarital childbearing has followed a similar trend to the developments in the Nordic countries, the government instituted Civil Solidarity Pacts (PACS) in October 1999 (without a good deal of preceding controversy). PACS allows homosexual and heterosexual couples to enter legal agreements that will give unmarried couples (coresiding for a minimum of 3 years) broadly equivalent inheritance, tax, health, and tenants rights as those now held by married couples. In France, the PACS were originally conceived as meeting the demands of gay organizations for a form of legally recognized marriage ceremony. However, to avoid homophobic attacks from the right wing, the government broadened the idea to include heterosexuals (Thery, 2000).

In Sweden, Finland, and Denmark, a more pragmatic approach to cohabiting couples has been taken. Over time, family law has come to be applied to married and cohabiting couples in the same way, recognizing that legislation developed to meet the needs of married couples is also suited to the needs of unmarried couples (Bradley, 1996). Norway established a commission to examine the issue. The commission reported in late 1999 that it accepted the need for a law regulating heterosexual cohabitation where this was "marriage-like"; that is, where there are children or where the relationship had lasted for 2 or more years (Noack, 2000). In Britain, the Lord Chancellor's Department reported on issues pertaining to cohabitation in 2000 but the main focus was on property issues. In Germany, the protection of the family enshrined in the constitution applies only to marriage and not to "marriage-like partnerships" (Ditch, Barnes, & Bradshaw, 1996), which implies a principled commitment not to accord equal status to married and cohabiting relationships, although private law could be changed. So, just as the phenomenon of cohabitation is diverse and complex, the responses to date have been equally variable, suggesting that there are few simple, straightforward solutions to this development in family life.

Children Born Outside Marriage

Across European nations, the legal position of children born outside marriage has historically tended to reflect social attitudes to nonmarital childbearing, attitudes that have varied over time and space and from one social or cultural group to another. Over the course of the 20th century, there have been shifts toward improving the legal position of children born outside marriage, but the speed of change and the extent of changes has been quite variable across nations. For example, as early as 1917 the Swedish government banned the use of the term *illegitimate* in all official documents, whereas it was some 70 years later in 1987 that such legislation was enacted in England and Wales. Progress has tended to be slower in terms of, for example, children's rights to inherit from their father. In Sweden, it was not until 1969 that children born within and outside marriage had the same rights, whereas Norway was a forerunner in tackling this issue with rights of inheritance being granted in 1916 (Eekelaar & Katz, 1980). In all the nations included in our analysis, married couples have automatic parental rights and responsibilities as soon as the child is born; and unmarried mothers, whether they are cohabiting or not, automatically have the same rights and responsibilities as married mothers, but the position of cohabiting fathers is less clear cut. In all the countries, when paternity has been established, unmarried fathers have a financial duty to maintain their children but they have no automatic rights over their children, although in most countries fathers can establish parental responsibility by making some form of formal declaration (European Observatory on National Family Policies, 1996). However, there is some variation with respect to guardianship and custody (Millar & Warman, 1996). Guardianship (analogous terminology includes care or parental responsibility) refers to the right to make decisions regarding the rearing of the child, while custody (residence or control) refers to the right to make everyday decisions concerning the child and the provision of day-to-day care. After the parental relationship has been formalized, the current situation in Sweden, France, Norway, and Great Britain is that both parents can share parental obligations and rights equally, as do married couples. In Austria and Spain, both parents can share parental rights and responsibilities but only with the agreement and ratification of the courts, and in Germany and Italy, at the discretion of the courts, the father can gain some rights to guardianship but not necessarily to custody. Given that cohabitation does not automatically confer the rights of married fatherhood, if couples separate the situation is the same as if the couple had never lived together. Generally speaking, across European nations issues surrounding children born outside marriage and their position vis-a-vis their parents has been discussed and codified in recent years and the public policy debate has moved from a focus on the obligations and responsibilities arising from marriage to the obligations and responsibilities of parenthood (Millar & Warman, 1996).

Thus, European nations have moved to a position whereby children born within and outside marriage are increasingly equably treated in the realm of public policy but there is much more ambivalence about the rights and responsibilities of men and women in cohabiting unions per se.

CONCLUSION

Comparative data on union and fertility behavior has shown there to be marked variation across European nations in the ways men and women are forming partnerships and the extent to which children are born within and outside marriage. In southern European countries, marriage is still the preeminent marker for entry into first union; whereas in most west and northern European countries, cohabitation has eclipsed marriage as the marker for first partnership, and in the Nordic countries, there is evidence that long-term cohabitation has become more prevalent. Within Europe, there continues to be marked differences in the level of nonmarital childbearing and the saliency of marriage as the context for having children. Marriage is still a preeminent setting for having a child in the southern European countries and the middle European countries of Switzerland and West Germany but this is much less the case in the Nordic countries, with Sweden being the only country with more first births born within cohabiting unions than marital unions. Across all the European countries included in this study, there have been temporal increases in the propensity to cohabit and have children outside of marriage, albeit from different levels. However, as yet, there is no substantial evidence to suggest that a movement to a Swedish model of partnership behavior is imminent in most European countries. In summary, one might conclude that there is not just one but several European perspectives on cohabitation and nonmarital childbearing behavior both in terms of behavior and public policy responses.

ACKNOWLEDGMENTS

The Economic and Social Research Council (United Kingdom) provided the funding for this project. The ESRC Data Archive supplied the British Household Panel Survey and the Eurobarometer data. The Fertility and Family Survey data were supplied by the Population Activities Unit at the UN Economic Commission for Europe at Geneva. Thanks are also due to the Advisory Group of the FFS program of comparative research for permission granted to use the FFS data in this study. This paper draws on a range of papers including Kiernan (1999 a, b) and Kiernan (2000 a, b) and Kiernan (2001).

REFERENCES

Abrams, L. (1993). Concubinage, cohabitation and the law: Class and gender relations in nineteenth-century Germany. *Gender and History*, *5*, 81–100.

Bernhardt, E., & Hoem, B. (1985). Cohabitation and social background: Trends observed for Swedish women born between 1936 and 1960. *European Journal of Population*, *1*, 375–395.

Billari, F., Castiglioni, M., & Castro Martin, T. (2000, May). *Household and union formation in a Mediterranean fashion: Italy and Spain*. Paper presented at the FFS Conference Brussels.

Blom, S. (1994). Marriage and cohabitation in a changing society: Experience of Norwegian men and women born in 1945 and 1960. *European Journal of Population, #10*, 143–173.

30 KIERNAN

Bradley, D. (1996). *Family law and political culture: Scandinavian laws in comparative perspective.* London: Sweet & Maxwell.

Carmichael, G. (1995). Consensual partnering in the more developed countries. *Journal of the Australian Population Association, 12,* 51–86.

Council of Europe. (1999). *Recent demographic developments in Europe.* Strasbourg: Author.

Ditch, J., Barnes, H., & Bradshaw, J. (1996). *A synthesis of national family policies 1995.* Brussels: Commission of the European Communities.

Eekelaar, J., & Katz, S. (Eds.). (1980). *Marriage and cohabitation in contemporary societies.* Toronto: Butterworth.

European Commission. (1996). *Eurobarometer No. 44* (ESRC Data Archive). Essex, England: Author.

European Commission. (1998). *Social portrait of Europe.* Luxembourg: Office for Official Publications of the European Communities.

European Observatory on Family Policies. (1996). *A synthesis of national family policies, 1995.* Brussels: European Commission.

Festy, P. (1980). On the new context of marriage in Western Europe. *Population and Development Review, 6,* 311–315.

General Household Survey Report (1989). OPCS, HMSO.

Gillis, J. (1985). *For better or worse: British marriages 1600 to the present.* Oxford: Oxford University Press.

Haskey, J. (1999). Cohabitational and marital histories of adults in Great Britain. *Population Trends, 96,* 13–24.

Hoem, B. (1992). Recent changes in family formation in Sweden. *Stockholm Research Report in Demography, 71,* 1–29.

Hoem, J., & Hoem, B. (1988). The Swedish family: Aspects of contemporary developments, *Journal of Family Issues, 9,* 397–424.

Kiernan, K. (1989). The family: Fission or fusion. In H. Joshi (Ed.), *The changing population of Britain* (pp. 27–41). Oxford: Basil Blackwell.

Kiernan, K. (1992). The impact of family disruption in childhood on transitions made in young adult life. *Population Studies, 46,* 213–234.

Kiernan, K. (1999a). Cohabitation in western Europe. *Population Trends, 96,* 25–32.

Kiernan K. (1999b). Childbearing outside marriage in western Europe. *Population Trends, 98,* 11–20.

Kiernan K. (2000a). European perspectives on union formation. In L. Waite, C. Bachrach, M. Hindin, E. Thomson, & A. Thornton (Eds.), *Ties that bind: Perspectives on marriage and cohabitation* (pp. 40–58). Hawthorne: Aldine de Gruyter.

Kiernan K. (2000b). *The State of European unions: An analysis of FFS data on partnership formation and dissolution.* Paper presented at the FFS Flagship Conference (May).

Laslett, P., Oosterveen, K., & Smith, R. M. (1980). *Bastardy and its comparative history.* London: Edward Arnold.

Lesthaeghe, R., & Moors, G. (1996). Living arrangements, socio-economic position, and values among young adults: A pattern of description for France, West Germany, Belgium, and the Netherlands. In D. Coleman (Ed.), *Europe's population in the 1990s* (pp. 163–221). Oxford: Oxford University Press.

Malpas, N., & Lambert, P-Y. (1993). *Europeans and the family.* Brussels: Commission of the European Communities.

Manting, D. (1996). The changing meaning of cohabitation. *European Sociological Review, 12,* 53–65.

McDonald, P. (2000). Family relationships in Australia: The conservative–liberal–radical debate. *Review of Population and Social Policy, 9,* 1–24.

Millar, J., & Warman, A. (1996). *Family obligations in Europe.* London: Family Policy Studies Centre.

Noack, T. (2000, April). *The case of Norway.* Paper presented at Symposium entitled "Trends in Cohabitation: Demography, Law and Policy." Wolfson College, Oxford.

Prinz, C. (1995). *Cohabiting, married single* Aldershot: Avebury

Raley, K. (2000). Recent trends and differentials in marriage and cohabitation: The United States. In L. Waite, C. Bachrach, M. Hindin, E. Thomson, & A. Thornton (Eds.), *Ties that bind: Perspectives on marriage and cohabitation* (pp. 40-58). New York: Aldine de Gruyter.

Ramsoy, N. R. (1994). Non-marital cohabitation and change in norms: The case of Norway. *Acta Sociologica, 37,* 23–37.

Roberts, R. (1973). *The classic slum: Salford life in the first quarter of the century.* London: Pelican.

Schrama, W. M. (1999). Registered partnerships in the Netherlands. *International Journal of Law, Policy and the Family, 13,* 315–327.

Thery, I. (2000). *Marriage and cohabitation in France.* Paper presented at Symposium entitled "Trends in Cohabitation: Demography, Law and Policy." Wolfson College, Oxford.

Thornton, A. (1991). Influence of marital history of parents on the marital and cohabitational experiences of children. *American Journal of Sociology, 96,* 868–894.

Trost, J. (1978). A renewed social institution: Non-marital cohabitation. *Acta Sociologica, 21,* 303–315.

United Nations. (1992). *Questionnaire and codebook fertility and family surveys in countries of the ECE region.* New York: Author.

Villeneuve-Gokalp, C. (1991). From marriage to informal union: Recent changes in the behaviour of French couples. *Population (an English Selection), 3,* 81–111.

2

Contemporary Cohabitation: Food for Thought

Nancy S. Landale
The Pennsylvania State University

In 1982, John Hajnal wrote an influential article in which he argued that the preindustrial family system of northwest Europe was distinct from that in most of the rest of the world, especially Asia (Hajnal, 1982). Northwestern Europeans were considered to be unique because of several features of their family formation system, namely the late age at marriage for both men and women, the establishment of independent households at marriage, and the high proportion of households containing unrelated young adult servants. These features of family formation have been attributed to the existence of a stem family system, an arrangement in which land is left to a single heir. Under such a system, non-heirs must gain access to an independent livelihood prior to marriage and heirs must wait to marry until their father is ready to relinquish control of the land. Because land was relatively scarce in preindustrial northwest Europe, the stem family system led to a pattern of late age at marriage and high rates of permanent celibacy (Hajnal, 1965). In contrast, most other regions of the world had a joint household system, in which households often contained more than one married couple and newlywed couples typically lived with the groom's parents. The joint household system was conducive to early marriage because newlywed couples could draw on the resources of a larger family unit.

It is clear from the historical record that a unique marriage pattern existed in preindustrial northwest Europe. However, some family scholars (e.g., Goody, 1996) argue that classification of the family formation systems of the past into two discrete types may oversimplify reality. For example, under the European pattern of separate residence, it was not uncommon for newlywed couples to set up households adjacent to one set of parents and to continue to engage in complex economic and noneconomic relations with them. Under the joint household system, important aspects of family life sometimes took place within subgroups within the household rather than the household as a whole. For example, shared food consumption is often considered a defining feature of household membership. However, under the joint household system married couples and their children sometimes prepared and consumed their meals apart from other household members. These examples suggest that classifying household systems of the past into two separate categories may mask important ambiguities in their defining features and overstate the differences between them. Accordingly, Goody (1996) argued for the utility of thinking about systems of household formation broadly in terms of a set of variables, some of which are present in certain settings and some of which are not.

The focus of this volume is contemporary family formation patterns rather than family systems of the past. However, the issue of how to think about comparisons between family formation systems raises several questions that must be answered in thinking about this topic. First, is contemporary cohabitation in Europe and the United States a new and unique phenomenon—or does it share important similarities with cohabitation at other times and in other places? And second, how clear are the boundaries between cohabitation and other union types? Are various union statuses (e.g., single, cohabiting, married) truly distinct in terms of the nature of family relations? In this chapter, I address these themes in the context of a discussion of Kiernan's chapter.

A NEW FORM OF COHABITATION?

Kiernan restricts her focus to western Europe and provides an excellent descriptive analysis of the role of cohabitation in family formation and variation in that role across western European countries. The analysis provides careful documentation of a number of important conclusions:

1. There is considerable diversity across western European countries in the prevalence of cohabitation as a first union type.
2. With the exception of Spain and Italy, a higher proportion of western European women currently cohabit at the outset of their first union than enter marriage directly.
3. Cohabitation is generally brief, and the vast majority of cohabiting couples either marry or dissolve their union within 5 years.
4. Cohabiting unions that have not been converted to marriage have a high risk of dissolution.
5. A growing proportion of first births are occurring within cohabiting unions.

Kiernan argues that contemporary cohabitation in western Europe is "a new type of cohabitation that is implicated in the marriage bust that has occurred across European nations." In making this assertion, Kiernan is referring to comparisons between current and past cohabitation within western Europe, but the statement raises a larger concern that has not been addressed in the literature. As in the debate about preindustrial household formation systems, one must ask whether it is more fruitful to view contemporary cohabitation in the United States and western Europe as largely a distinct phenomenon—or to view it as a phenomenon that may share similarities with cohabitation in other settings. The latter implies a broader search for the conditions under which cohabitation arises and the distinguishing features of cohabiting unions. My goal here is not to answer this question, but rather to provide food for thought. First, it must be remembered that virtually all human societies attempt to regulate union formation through marriage customs and/or law because the family is "the part of institutional system through which the creation, nurture, and socialization of the next generation is mainly accomplished" (Davis, 1985, p. 7). Nonetheless, despite a social preference for marriage, other types of unions are common in many settings. Davis (1985) outlined five common types of unions and how they differ. According to Davis, *marriage* is a union in which sexual relations are expected, the partners share a common residence, there is a division of labor, children are expected, permanence is assumed, and there is public recognition of the union. *Common-law marriage* shares all of those features, except public recognition. What are commonly know as *consensual unions* include sexual relations, a common residence, a division of labor, and the expectation of children. It is less clear whether permanence is assumed by the parties involved. *Cohabitation* involves sexual relations and a shared residence, but other features of the arrangement are ambiguous. Finally, what Davis calls *liasons* are unions in which the only clear feature is sexual involvement.

This classification system identifies two types of unions that involve coresidence without legal or common-law marriage: consensual unions and cohabitation. Although such "informal unions" were relatively rare in western Europe before the 1970s (Kiernan, chap. 1, this volume), in many parts of the world they have been common for a long period of time. For example, in Latin America and the Caribbean, consensual unions have existed alongside marriage since the European conquest (De Vos, 2000; Greene & Rao, 1995). The roots of this practice presumably can be found in the status inequality between the European colonizers and the indigenous women. European males did not consider indigenous women to be appropriate marriage partners because of their skin color and their relatively low socioeconomic standing. However, consensual unions continued apart from their origins in status inequality between mates. Throughout the 20th century, informal unions were common among relatively impoverished, poorly educated men and women. The weak bargaining power of low-status women relative to their male counterparts may have continued to encourage this pattern (Parrado & Tienda, 1997; Siman de Betancourt, 1988), but other contributing factors are the economic marginality of low-status males (Blake, 1961), a lack of concern with property rights related to inheritance (Fitzpatrick, 1981), and female economic independence (Blumberg, 1975; Steward et al., 1956).

At first glance, the informal unions found in Latin America and the Caribbean seem to be entirely distinct from cohabitation in western Europe and the United States today. Yet, it is important to remember that union patterns have continued to evolve in response to current circumstances in the former region as well as the latter, and many similar social changes have occurred in both areas of the world. For example, in western Europe and the United States—and Latin America and the Caribbean—union formation now takes place in the context of relatively high

levels of female independence due to increased education and labor force participation, and considerable control over reproduction via modern contraceptive methods (Parrado & Tienda, 1997). In both settings, economic marginality among males
is a widespread problem in some social strata. These and other conditions have
contributed to a growing separation between union formation and childbearing,
which may be related to a loosening of social control over the union formation
process. They have also contributed to a reduction in at least some of the benefits of
legal marriage. I think it is important that we further investigate the commonalities
in the conditions giving rise to cohabitation (and consensual unions) across different areas of the world. Such an investigation will further the understanding of potentially complex relationships between structural conditions, history, and culture
in union formation patterns.

THE FLUIDITY OF UNION STATUS

There are also similarities in the nature of cohabiting unions across many areas of
the world. Kiernan demonstrates that in western Europe, relatively few cohabiting couples remain in informal unions for long: Within 5 years of union formation, the great majority of cohabitors either marry or go their separate ways. Furthermore, rates of union dissolution are much higher for cohabiting unions than
for marriages. Yet, despite its instability, cohabitation is increasingly a setting into
which western European children are born. In chapter 1 (this volume), Kiernan
notes that "the inconstancy of cohabitation poses challenges for the analysis as
well as our understanding of this development in family life."

   Studies of cohabitation and consensual unions in other settings echo Kiernan's
observations. Research focusing on Latin America, the Caribbean, and Sub-Saharan Africa concludes that informal unions are less stable than marriages (Parrado
& Tienda, 1997; Pilon, 1994; Quilodran, 1985, 1991; Vazquez Calzada, 1988). In
each of these regions, childbearing was a common feature of informal unions historically and continues to be so today. Coupled with Kiernan's findings, this suggests that the boundary between what has traditionally been defined as a consensual union and what we now call cohabitation is increasingly hazy. The fact that
informal unions are highly unstable and reproduction takes place within them also
indicates that informal unions are linked to female family headship.

   Taken together, these patterns suggest that informal unions are part of a very
fluid process of union formation and dissolution in which the boundaries between
various union statuses are increasingly unclear. They also suggest that studies
might benefit from looking more deeply at the content of unions of various types
and the extent to which changes in union status represent changes in that content.

   As an example, one important aspect of unions that may vary by union type is
the extent to which the economic resources of male and female partners are pooled.
Given the higher level of uncertainty about the permanence of the union in co-

habitation compared to marriage, one might expect a lower level of resource pooling in cohabiting unions. This, in turn, might have implications for the well-being of women and children.

I recently fielded a study (with co-investigators Oropesa and Dávila) in which the mothers of Puerto Rican infants in both the United States and Puerto Rico were asked about their union status and various aspects of their relationships with their partners. Called the Puerto Rican Maternal and Infant Health Study (PRMIHS), the study entailed in-person interviews with 2,763 mothers of infants sampled from the 1994 and 1995 birth and infant death records of six U.S. vital statistics reporting areas (Connecticut, Florida, Massachusetts, New Jersey, New York City, Pennsylvania) and the Commonwealth of Puerto Rico. Roughly two thirds of the interviews (1,946) were with mothers of infants sampled from the computerized birth certificate files maintained by the states and Puerto Rico. The weighted birth sample is representative of 1994-1995 births to Puerto Rican women residing in the study area. By extension, the birth sample represents Puerto Rican mothers of infants born in the specified area and period of time (see Landale, Oropesa, & Gorman, 2000, for further details about the study design).

Here, I focus on the information provided by the 574 mothers of infants drawn into the birth sample in Puerto Rico. About 14% of those mothers were not living with the baby's father at the time of the birth. An additional 31% were living with the baby's father informally and 55% were married to the baby's father. We asked the mothers who were living in informal unions or marriages about the economic contributions of their partner around the time of the birth. Mothers in informal unions were slightly less likely to have received economic support from their partner than mothers in marriages—87% compared to 94%. Mothers who received support were then asked to indicate which of the following response categories best described how the partner provided that support:

- Paid for all expenses himself without involving you
- Gave you a weekly or monthly allowance to pay for expenses
- Gave money or bought things, but not on a regular schedule
- Contributed his money to a "common pot" or "common fund" that you both could use
- Something else

Table 2.1 shows the distribution of responses to the question on partner contributions by union status. Clear differences by union type in the handling of finances are evident. The most striking contrast between cohabiting and married women is in the percentage whose partners contributed their money to a common pot or common fund that both could use. Slightly more than half of married women (52%) reported that their partner contributed his money to a common fund, compared to 25% of cohabiting women. The partners of cohabiting women were more likely to contribute in ways that gave them greater autonomy than resource pool-

Table 2.1
How Partner Provides Economic Support, Cohabiting and Married
Mothers in Puerto Rico

	Cohabiting	Married
Pays all expenses himself (%)	27.5	22.4
Gives an allowance (%)	27.8	15.1
Gives money or buys things irregularly (%)	15.5	7.7
Contributes to common pot (%)	24.8	51.6
Other (%)	4.5	3.2
	100.1	100.0
Unweighted n of cases	170	335

Source: Puerto Rican Maternal and Infant Health Study.

ing. Women in cohabiting unions were more likely than married women to report that their partners paid for all expenses without their involvement (27% vs. 22%), gave them an allowance to pay for expenses (28% vs. 15%), or gave them money or made purchases on an irregular schedule (15% vs. 7%). It is not clear from the data whether the amount of money available to women and their children varied by union type. However, it is clear that in this population it is unreasonable to assume that cohabiting women have access to their partners' resources that is equivalent to that of married women.[1]

This example illustrates the importance of knowing more about how unions of various types function. It is commonly assumed that as couples begin to bear children in cohabiting unions, the distinction between such unions and marriage is breaking down. Although to some extent this may be true—at least in some settings—our data from Puerto Rico show that even among unions that have produced children, important differences between cohabitation and marriage remain. We need to know more about how multiple dimensions of behavior and sentiment differ for cohabitors and married couples across various settings, and whether those differences change as unions evolve over time. Kiernan's chapter provides an excellent start by presenting highly detailed information on demographic fea-

---

[1] Women who were still living with the baby's father at interview were asked several additional questions about their household finances. Those whose partners provided support were asked who had the final say in the amount of money their partner kept for himself. Cohabiting women were more likely than married women to indicate that their partner had the final say (35% vs. 22%) and less likely to indicate that they had the final say (5% vs. 8%) or that the decision was made jointly (60% vs. 69%). We also asked the women whose partners contributed to a common fund whether their partner usually put all or only part of his earnings into the fund. A lower percentage of women in cohabiting unions (67%) than women in marriages (77%) indicated that their partner put all of his earnings into the common fund.

tures of cohabitation in western European countries. At the same time, much remains to be learned. In closing, I suggest two potentially fruitful directions for future studies of cohabitation. The first is comparative work emphasizing similarities and differences in the conditions under which cohabitation has arisen in different world regions and periods of time. Is contemporary cohabitation in Europe and the United States a new and unique phenomenon—or does it have similar antecedents and characteristics as cohabitation at other times and in other places? A second important direction for future research involves careful consideration of similarities and differences in the ways in which cohabiting unions and marriages function. The fact that cohabitation is less stable than marriage across numerous settings is well documented, but there is much to learn about what goes on in each type of union and how that changes over time and with the addition of children. In short, I encourage researchers to think broadly about the nature of cohabitation and its significance in contemporary societies.

REFERENCES

Blake, J. (1961). *Family structure in Jamaica: The social context of reproduction.* New York: The Free Press of Glencoe.

Blumberg, R. L. (1975). The political economy of the mother-child family revisited. In A. F. Marks & R. A. Romer (Eds.), *Family and kinship in middle America and the Caribbean* (pp. 526–575). Curacao, Netherlands Antilles: Institute of Higher Studies and Leiden, Netherlands: Royal Institute of Linguistics and Anthropology.

Davis, K. (1985). The meaning and significance of marriage in contemporary society. In K. Davis (Ed.), *Contemporary marriage: Comparative perspectives on a changing institution* (pp. 1–90). New York: Russell Sage.

De Vos, S. (2000). Nuptiality in Latin America: The view of a sociologist and family demographer. In R. R. Miller (Ed.), *With this ring: Divorce, intimacy and cohabitation from a multicultural perspective* (pp. 219–244). Stamford, CT: JAI Press.

Fitzpatrick, J. P. (1981). The Puerto Rican family. In C. H. Mendel & R.W. Haberstein (Eds.), *Ethnic families in America: Patterns and variations* (pp. 192–217). New York: Elsevier and North-Holland.

Goody, J. (1996). Comparing family systems in Europe and Asia: Are there different systems of rules? *Population and Development Review, 22,* 1–20.

Greene, M. E., & Rao. V. (1995). The marriage squeeze and the rise in informal marriage in Brazil. *Social Biology, 42,* 65–82.

Hajnal, J. (1965). European marriage patterns in perspective. In D. V. Glass & D. E. C. Eversley (Eds.), *Population in history* (pp. 101-143). London: Edward Arnold.

Hajnal, J. (1982). Two kinds of preindustrial household formation system. *Population and Development Review, 8*, 449–494.

Landale, N. S., Oropesa, R. S., & Gorman, B. K. (2000). Migration and infant death: Assimilation or selective migration among Puerto Ricans? *American Sociological Review, 65*, 888–909.

Parrado, E. A., & Tienda, M. (1997). Women's roles and family formation in Venezuela: New forms of consensual unions? *Social Biology, 44*, 1–24.

Pilon, M. (1994). Types of marriage and marital stability: The case of the Moba-Gurma of North Togo. In C. Bledsoe & G. Pison (Eds.), *Nuptiality in Sub-Saharan Africa: Contemporary anthropological and demographic perspectives* (pp. 130–147). Oxford: Oxford University Press.

Quilodran, J. (1985). Nuptiality patterns and changes in Latin America. In *International Population Conference* (Vol. 3, pp. 269–283). Liege: International Union for the Scientific Study of Population.

Quilodran, J. (1991). *Levels of fertility and patterns of marriage in Mexico*. Mexico: El Colegio de Mexico.

Siman de Bentancourt, A. V. (1988). *Consensual unions in Puerto Rico: Its determinants and consequences*. Unpublished doctoral dissertation, Department of Sociology, University of North Carolina, Chapel Hill.

Steward, J. H., Manners, R. A., Wolf, E. R., Seda, E. P., Mintz, S. W., & Schelle, R. L. (1956). *The people of Puerto Rico*. Chicago: University of Illinois Press.

Vazquez Calzada, J. L. (1988). *The population of Puerto Rico and its historical trajectory*. San Juan, P.R.: University of Puerto Rico.

3

(Re)Envisioning Cohabitation: A Commentary on Race, History, and Culture

Andrea G. Hunter
University of North Carolina at Greensboro

To some listening to such a conversation, *gumbo ya ya* may sound like chaos. We may be better able to understand it as something other than confusion if we overlay it with jazz, for *gumbo ya ya* is the essence of a musical tradition where 'the various voices in a piece of music may go their own ways but still be held together by their relationship to each other.' (Brown, 1991, p. 85)

The rate of cohabitation in the United States, like western Europe, has been another component of the noteworthy transformations in marriage and childbearing that have taken place over the last several decades (Smock & Gupta, chap. 4, this volume). Although the increase in cohabitation cuts across the U. S. population, there are significant variations across racial and ethnic groups that parallel the differences described by Kiernan (chap. 1, this volume) in her cross-national comparisons of western Europe. African Americans spend more of their adult lives loving and raising children in nonmarital cohabiting unions or in other nonmarital partnerships than do non-Blacks (Hunter, 1997; Tucker & Mitchell-Kernan, 1995a). Although the rate of cohabitation among African Americans is only modestly higher than the rate of cohabitation among Whites, Blacks are less likely to convert cohabiting unions to marriage (Bumpass & Sweet, 1989; London, 1991; Manning & Smock, 1995). African Americans are also more likely to have children in cohabiting unions but are less likely to marry to "legitimize" these births than are Whites (Loomis & Landale, 1994; Manning, 1993). These patterns have spawned a lively investigation of the sources of racial differences in cohabitation and its relationship to "traditional" patterns in marriage and childbearing.

Recent studies of cohabitation among African Americans have been framed by the dramatic transformations in marriage and childbearing that have taken place in this population since 1960 (Ellwood & Crane, 1990; Heaton & Jacobsen, 1994; Walker, 1988). Much of this work has focused on the role of economic and demographic factors (e.g., male unemployment and wages, public aid, and sex ratio) in the declining rates of marriages and subsequent rise in nonmarital births (for review, see Tucker & Mitchell-Kernan, 1995b). Although studies do find that a variety of economic and demographic factors are critical for understanding this shift, Raley (1996) noted these factors account for only about 20% of the differences in Black-White marriage rates. To explain the source of remaining differences, researchers have suggested a closer look at African-American attitudes and expectations about marriage and family formation. Although more ambivalent about marriage than members of other racial groups, African Americans value marriage and would like to get married (Bulcroft & Bulcroft, 1993; King, 1999; South, 1993). Indeed, there is no widespread ideological retreat from marriage among African Americans (King, 1999; Tucker & Mitchell-Kernan, 1995a). However, despite an endorsement of mainstream American values about marriage and the family, African Americans have long drawn on a diverse repertoire of union formation, childbearing, and parenting (Frazier, 1939; Gutman, 1976; Hunter & Ensminger, 1992; Stevenson, 1995). In this commentary, to inform the current examination of cohabitation in the United States, I offer a mediation on African-American families, history, and culture that highlights the diverse repertoire of partnering and parenting that has emerged out of the Black experience.

MEDITATIONS ON FAMILIES, HISTORY, AND CULTURE: MINING THE BLACK EXPERIENCE

The explosion of literature on cohabitation in the United States, in my view, is not only an attempt to understand a significant social and demographic transition, it is also a search for a new cultural narrative about courtship, marriage, and child-bearing. Indeed, much of the change in western family life is seen as disordering, not fitting with either how the world once was or how it should be. We theorize and create new narratives about where cohabitation fits as an alternative to marriage, part of courtship and the transition to marriage, an alternative to or another type of singlehood, or a unique postmarital transition. Kiernan's (chap. 1, this volume) suggestion that cohabitation is more of a process than an event is an example of (re) envisioning the ways we interpret cohabitation. If one is to use the stages of partnership transition reviewed by Kiernan as a guide to categorize patterns of union formation among African Americans, it could be argued that they are leading the edge of this transition in the United States (Kiernan, chap. 1, this volume). Hence, it is not surprising that the revisionist narratives that have emerged in the cohabitation literature tend to fit uneasily onto the patterns seen among African Americans.

With few racial differences in attitudes about marriage, researchers have suggested that we need to understand more about the unique history and culture of African Americans. Among family scholars in the United States, it has been difficult to address issues of history, race and culture, and difference without engaging a discourse of social pathology and cultural dysfunction (Hunter, 1992; Miller, 1993). However, interrogating racial differences, like the exploration of cross-national patterns, challenges us to unhinge ourselves from common understandings that are tied to an unspoken history and culture and often to our own unexamined biography. Elsa Barkley Brown (1991), in a wonderful essay on women's history, suggests jazz and *gumbo ya ya* (a Creole term meaning everyone talking at once) as metaphors to explore the intersections and divergences of American women's histories across race and ethnicity, class, and sexuality. *Gumbo ya ya* and jazz may also be useful metaphors for exploring racial and ethnic variations in family life within a society as well as across national boundaries. As Brown suggests, they direct our attention to the multiple rhythms that are being played simultaneously and the ways in which diverse rhythms are in dialogue with or in opposition to each other.

Improvisations

Let us take a step backward to E. Franklin Frazier's (1939) classic monograph *The Negro family in the United States* (1939), which is the single most influential work on the Black family. This work was a sweeping epic and analysis of the social history and the cultural transformations of African Americans from slavery to the early twentieth century urban migration. Revisionist historians have well critiqued Frazier's conclusions about the cultural death of African slaves and the evolution of weak marital and matriarchal family systems under slavery (see, for example, Blassingame, 1972; Genovese, 1974; Gutman, 1976). However, his deeply textured analysis reveals the duality, improvisational character, and diversity of African Americans' approach to sexuality, reproduction, and the family. Frazier described a variety of heterosexual unions including legal marriage, quasi-marital forms (e.g., cohabitation, common-law unions), and nonmarital unions (e.g., quasi-cohabitation, extra-legal relationships) noting that across these contexts children were born and reared (see Stevenson, 1995, for post-revisionist discussion). These pairings occurred within the context of an extended kinship system that bound slaves across time and space and was a source of family survival well into the twentieth century (Frazier, 1939; Gutman, 1976; Hunter, 1993; Ruggles, 1994; Stack, 1974). *The Negro family* (1939) illustrates the diverse repertoire of partnering, childbearing, and parenting among African Americans that was borne out of necessity and grounded in the rich cultural past of African slaves. Although emerging out of shared history and common culture, African-American families are perhaps most distinctive for their variety. Multiple rhythms in the timing and sequencing of family events both support and subvert dominant cultural morays and social conventions. It is a kind of *gumbo ya ya*, that is, everybody talking and doing everything at once. The rich diversity with which African Americans and others can organize their family lives challenges family scholars to find ways to understand the meaning(s) of various arrangements as well as under what conditions individuals engage in alternatives to marriage or other forms of union formation.

Subversions

African Americans, located at the social, economic, and political margins of American life, have created ways of living that support survival and challenge dominant cultural narratives about marriage, childbearing, and the ideal social organization of families. African Americans have also created forms of family organization denied them by locating themselves between and beyond what was legally sanctioned in the larger society. The historical record, for example, indicates that slaves had marriages even while they were not legally sanctioned or morally required by the larger society (Gutman 1976; Will, 1999). The slave community recognized these unions as committed pairings within which couples shared their limited resources and children were born and raised. The existence of slave marriage as an subversive act challenges us to suspend our notions about what is formal and informal or institutionalized or not, and to ask what is created in the spaces that are not governed by law, but nevertheless have a cultural presence. Today, in the face of formidable economic and demographic barriers to legal marriage, Black couples enter into cohabiting relationships where they share their lives and love, have and raise children, share resources, and help and support each other. They also fight and argue, sometimes they stay together and perhaps more often they do not. As suggested by Smock and Gupta (chap. 4, this volume), cohabitation may be different than marriage but these two forms of pairing have much in common; perhaps, this is most strikingly the case for African Americans. It is with a sense of irony that I suggest slave marriages and the late twentieth century decline in Black marriages have something in common. However, they both illustrate a people's ability to navigate, tolerate, and create spaces within the context of formidable barriers (be it the institution of slavery or too few marriageable men) and to exist within and outside (often simultaneously) the social and legal conventions of one's time.

(En)Gendering Counter Narratives

In slavery and in freedom, African-American women would take on economic roles and transform gender relations in ways that were not equaled by White women until the latter half of the twentieth century (Hunter, 1993, 2001; Hunter, 1997; Jones, 1994). In his discussion of the roots of Black matriarchy, E. Franklin Frazier (1939) laments "neither economic necessity nor tradition had instilled in her (the Black woman) the spirit of subordination to masculine authority. Emancipation only tended to confirm the self-sufficiency slavery had taught " (p. 102). In Frazier's view, contested patriarchy and uncontrolled female sexuality and reproduction were the hallmarks of the trouble in Black families. Ideological tensions around patriarchy, sexuality, and reproduction remain an integral part of the research being done on the emergence (and acceptance of) alternative forms of union formation and out-of-wedlock parenting. Exposing these tensions, African-American women's lives, their choices, and their bodies have often been discursive sites of family pathology as well as a cautionary tale for other women (Blum & Duessen, 1996; Collins, 1991).

African-American women's accounts of alternative marital and childbearing patterns have been explored in a number of early Black community studies (Drake & Cayton, 1945; Frazier, 1939), ethnographies of urban communities (Aschenbrenner, 1975; Rainwater, 1970; Stack, 1974), and recent qualitative studies on marriage and motherhood (e.g., Blum & Duessen, 1996; Jarrett, 1994). These texts reveal women's counter narratives with which they envisioned themselves and their lives within and beyond social conventions. Women (often simultaneously) expressed a value of and healthy cynicism about marriage. They spoke about a woman's independence, the ability and strength to "go it alone" without a partner, and a desire for autonomy from men's authority. The role of mother emerged as a prominent part of women's identities, sometimes eclipsing that of wife or partner. Women also spoke of their connections to other women and kin-based networks that supported them as mothers. Women, whose lives had taken many turns outside the conventional script of courtship, marriage, and childbearing, suggested that different types of relationships (e.g., legal marriage, cohabitation, causal liaison, and being alone) are best at different times in a woman's life. Furthermore, women tended to evaluate their lives and actions based on the circumstances and choices available rather than an unyielding abstract moral code. In doing so, they created narratives about their lives that were not only in opposition to culturally dominate (read White) American scripts, but also contested the values and ideology of the Black elite who saw the adherence to patriarchy and "intact" families as necessary for Black social mobility and integration into the mainstream of American life (see, for example, Drake & Cayton, 1945; Frazier, 1939; Wilson, 1987).

Carol Stack's (1974) *All our kin* and Joyce Aschenbrenner's (1975) *Lifelines*, classic ethnographic studies of urban African-American families and kin networks, illustrate the diverse trajectories of union formation (or not), childbearing (martial and nonmarital), and parenting (own child or someone else's) that occur across Black women's life course. They found that women simultaneously drew on conventional and counter narratives and this was no less true of the way they lived their lives. Women made their choices based on what was dealt them and the knowledge that life is not always what you want it to be, but it is what you make of it. The result is that the women studied had life course trajectories as different from each other as they were from the conventional patterns of White women. Both Stack and Aschenbrenner eschewed the discourse of family pathology and sexual promiscuity that had defined the academic literature at the time their works were published. It meant, as scholars, they had to find new ways to narrate African-American women's lives that provided not only an interpretive coherence to their life choices but also took seriously how they made sense of their own lives. To do so was not simply an exercise in cultural relativism, but an attempt to respect people's lives and to treat them with dignity. It is a challenge that social researchers continue to face as they work to understand the lives of African Americans as well as the growing diversity in American family life in general.

CONCLUSIONS

Racial Differences in a Post World

African Americans, because their lives and families have diverged from that of White Americans, have historically been viewed as situated at the intersection of order and disorder. In the first hundred years after Emancipation, a substantial minority of African Americans lived in alternative family living arrangements and racial differences in family structure, marriage, and nonmarital childbearing were evident (Frazier, 1939; Gordon & McLanahan, 1991; Gutman, 1976; Miller, 1993; Ruggles, 1994). However, up to more than 70% of Black children lived with two parents in either nuclear or extended family households (Billingsley, 1992; Walker, 1988). As we look across the twentieth century, there is little in the Black historical experience of disenfranchisement, racial discrimination, segregation, and economic and social inequality to decrease the patterns that most disturb family scholars and policy makers. Today, most African American children live in alternative family living arrangements and racial differences in several areas of family life have widened (Ellwood & Crane, 1990; Heaton & Jacobson, 1994; Manning & Smock, 1997). It is with a sense of confusion among some scholars (and irony among others) that it is in the post world (i.e., postmodern, post-industrial, and post-civil rights) that one sees the most dramatic declines in "traditional" family arrangements among African Americans. In an era where the legal, social, and economic divide between Blacks and Whites has narrowed, social researchers continue to look to the past to understand the source of racial differences in contemporary family patterns and often in exasperation they concede that something cultural must be at work.

Perhaps family scholars have so often looked to the past because the examination of proximal factors leaves explanatory gaps, and to culture because so much of our political rhetoric points to values as the source of racial differences. Furthermore, Collins (1998) suggests that the vestiges of scientific racism and social researchers' emphasis on social class as an outcome rather than a cause of family organization have created a particular lens for the study of African-American families. She argues "cultural and psychological values have long been emphasized as central to understanding Black family organization instead of economic and political phenomena, such as industrial and labor markets, employment patterns, migration histories, residential patterns, and governmental policies" (Collins, 1998, p. 2). African-American family patterns, past and present, do illustrate the capacity of Black cultural traditions to accommodate complex and diverse patterns in union formation and family life that reflect both choice and circumstance

(Billingsley, 1992). However, if social researchers are to understand the rather dramatic transformations in Black marital and family patterns that have taken place over the last forty years, it is important to view the cultural tools and adaptive strategies relied on by African Americans within the broader context of shifts in the economy, demography, and the body politic as well as the enduring influence of social stratification (race, class, and gender).

In conclusion, in this commentary, I have drawn on the African-American experience to highlight ways family scholars may (re) envision narratives of cohabitation that unhinge them from notions of how things ought to be, so they may better understand how things are. Improvisations in family organization, subversions of social and legal conventions, and the creation of counter narratives that both support and subvert "traditional" family values are not confined to Black life. Indeed, the diversity of contemporary American family life is a kind of *gumba ya ya*, everybody talking and doing everything at once. Brown (1991) reminds women's historians that when interrogating differences, be it race, class, ethnicity, or sexuality, that the aim is not only to isolate one conversation but also the "trick is then how to put that conversation in a context that makes evident its dialogue with so many others" (p. 85). This is a formidable challenge for family scholars. However, if one is to interrogate racial differences and to make sense of the variety that is seen within and across race and ethnicity in the United States, it is a challenge that must be taken up.

REFERENCES

Aschenbrenner, J. (1975). *Lifelines: Black families in Chicago*. New York: Holt, Rinehart and Winston.

Billingsley, A. (1992). *Climbing Jacob's ladder*. New York: Simon & Schuster.

Blassingame, J. W. (1972). *The slave community: Plantation life in the antebellum South*. New York: Oxford University Press.

Blum, L. M., & Duessen, T. (1996). Negotiating independent motherhood: Working-class African American women talk about marriage and motherhood. *Gender & Society, 10*, 199–211.

Brown, E. B. (1991). Polyrhythms and improvisation: Lessons for women's history. *History Workshop Journal, 31–32*, 84–89.

Bulcroft, R. A., & Bulcroft, K. A. (1993). Race differences in attitudinal motivational factors in the decision and to marry. *Journal of Marriage and the Family, 55*, 338–365.

Bumpass, L. L., & Sweet, J. A. (1989). National estimates of cohabitation. *Demography, 26*, 615–625.

Collins, P. H. (1991). *Black feminist thought*. New York: Routledge, Chapman, and Hall.

Collins, P. H. (1998). Intersections of race, class, gender, and nation: Some implications for Black family studies. *Journal of Comparative Family Studies, 29*, 27–37

Drake, S. C., & Cayton, H. R. (1945). *Black metropolis. Vol. 2: A study of Negro life in a northern city*. New York: Harcourt, Brace, & World, Inc.

Ellwood, D. T., & Crane, J. (1990). Family change among Black Americans: What do we know? *Journal of Economic Perspectives, 4*, 65–84.

Frazier, F. E. (1939). *The Negro family in the United States*. Chicago, IL: University of Chicago Press.

Genovese, E. (1974). *Roll, Jordan, roll: The world the slaves made*. New York: Vintage.

Gordon, L., & McLanahan, S. (1991). Single parenthood in 1900. *Journal of Family History, 16*, 97–116.

Gutman, H. G. (1976). *The Black family in slavery and freedom: 1750-1925*. New York: Vintage Press, Random House.

Heaton, T. B., & Jacobson, C. K. (1994). Race differences in changing family demographics in the 1980's. *Journal of Family Issues, 12*, 290–307.

Hunter, A. G., (1992, March). *African American families reconsidered: Old dilemmas, new directions*. Paper presented at invited panel at the Biennial Meetings of the Society for Research on Child Development Pre-Conference of the Black Caucus of the Society for Research in Child Development, New Orleans, LA.

Hunter, A. G. (1993). Making a way: Strategies of southern urban Afro-American families, 1900 and 1936. *Journal of Family History, 18*, 231–248.

Hunter, A. G. (1997). Living arrangements of African American adults: Variations across age, gender, and family status. In R. Taylor, J. Jackson, & L. Chatters (Eds.), *Family life in Black America* (pp. 262–276). Thousand Oaks, CA: Sage Publications.

Hunter, A. G. (2001). The other breadwinners: The mobilization of secondary wage earners in early twentieth-century Black families. *The history of the family: An International Quarterly, 6*, 69–94.

Hunter, A. G. & Ensminger, M. E. (1992). Diversity and fluidity in children's living arrangements: Family transitions in an urban Afro-American community. *Journal of Marriage and the Family, 54*, 418–427.

Hunter, T. W. (1997). *To 'joy my freedom: Southern Black women's lives and labors after the civil war*. Cambridge, MA: Harvard University Press.

Jarrett, R. L. (1994). Living poor: Family life among single parent, African-American women. *Social Problems, 41*, 30–49.

Jones, J. (1985). *Labor of love, labor of sorrow*. New York: Basic Books.

King, A. E. O. (1999). African American females' attitudes toward marriage: An exploratory study. *Journal of Black Studies, 29*, 416–437.

Manning, W. D. (1993). Marriage and cohabitation following premarital conception. *Journal of Marriage and the Family, 55,* 839–850.

Manning, W. D., & Smock, P. J. (1995). Why marry? Race and the transition to marriage among cohabitors. *Demography, 32,* 509–520.

Manning, W. D., & Smock, P. J. (1997). Children's living arrangements in unmarried-mother families. *Journal of Family Issues, 18,* 526–545.

Miller, A. T. (1993). Social science, social policy, and the heritage of African American families. In M. B. Katz (Ed.), *The underclass debate* (pp. 254–292). Princeton, NJ: Princeton University Press.

London, K. (1991). Cohabitation, marriage, and martial dissolution: United States. (Advance Data No. 194). Hyattsville, MD: National Center for Health Statistics.

Loomis, L. S., & Landale, N. S. (1994). Nonmarital cohabitation and childbearing among Black and White American women. *Journal of Marriage and the Family, 56*(4), 949–963.

Rainwater, L. (1970). *Behind ghetto walls: Black families in a federal slum.* Chicago, IL: Aldine Publishing Company.

Raley, K. (1996). A shortage of marriageable men? A note on the role of cohabitation in Black-White differences in marriage rates. *American Sociological Review, 61,* 973–984.

Ruggles, S. (1994). The origins of African-American family structure. *American Sociological Review, 59,* 136–151.

Stack, C. (1974). *All our kin.* New York: Harper & Row Company.

Stevenson, B. E. (1995). Black family structure in colonial antebellum Virginia: Amending the revisionist perspective. In M. B. Tucker & C. Mitchell-Kernan (Eds.), *The decline of marriage among African Americans: Causes, consequences, and policy implications* (pp. 27–56). New York: Russell Sage Foundation.

South, S. J. (1993). Racial and ethnic differences in the desire to marry. *Journal of Marriage and the Family, 55,* 357–370.

Tucker, M. B., & Mitchell-Kernan, C. (1995a). Marital behavior and expectations: Ethnic comparisons of attitudinal and structural correlates. In M. B. Tucker & C. Mitchell-Kernan (Eds.), *The decline of marriage among African Americans: Causes, consequences, and policy implications* (pp. 145–171). New York: Russell Sage Foundation.

Tucker, M. B., & Mitchell-Kernan, C. (1995b). Trends in African American family formation: A theoretical and statistical overview. In M. B. Tucker & C. Mitchell-Kernan (Eds.), *The decline of marriage among African Americans: Causes, consequences, and policy implications* (pp. 3–26). New York: Russell Sage Foundation.

Walker, H. (1988). Black and White differences in marriage and family patterns. In S. M. Dombusch & M. H. Strober (Eds.), *Feminism, children and the new families* (pp. 87–112). New York: The Guilford Press.

Wills, T. E. (1999). Weddings on contested grounds: Slave marriage in the antebellum South. *The Historian, 62*, 99–118.

Wilson, W. H. (1987). *The truly disadvantaged*. Chicago, IL: University of Chicago Press.

II

What Is the Role of Cohabitation in Contemporary North American Family Structure?

4

Cohabitation in Contemporary North America

Pamela J. Smock
The University of Michigan

Sanjiv Gupta
The University of Massachusetts-Amherst

> Of all the institutions of society, marriage is the most fundamental, most far-reaching and most vital. It preceded society; it made society possible; it binds society together. It is the basis of social order and improvement, and the chief support of morality, religion, and law. (Cook, 1888, p. 680)

Over the past few decades, unmarried, heterosexual cohabitation has transformed family patterns in the United States, Canada, and other industrialized nations.[1] Commentators and social scientists alike have been grappling with the implications of the dramatic rise in cohabitation. Most broadly, some interpret cohabitation as a manifestation of a serious retreat in marriage—that is, that cohabitation is symptomatic of, and reinforces, a decline in the centrality of marriage as the foundation of family life.

This chapter describes, assesses, and reflects on the role of unmarried cohabitation in contemporary family structure, and its attendant implications, in Canada and the United States.[2] A major theme of this chapter is that cohabitation challenges static conceptions of family structure as well as its legal and social bases, which have hitherto been defined largely by marriage. Although cohabitation is certainly not the only recent challenge to marriage, as the most "marriage-like" family form, we argue, it is the most proximate challenge.

The organization of the chapter is as follows. First, we briefly review the trends and basic features of cohabitation in Canada and the United States. Second, we evaluate the role of cohabitation in family structure, concluding that cohabitation increases and reinforces the dynamism of the life course in terms of family events. The third section discusses how the role of cohabitation varies across population subgroups; we focus on cultural and social class variation. Fourth, we present evidence that cohabitation itself has been changing substantially over time, and

---

[1] We use the term *cohabitation* throughout this chapter to refer to romantic partners who are living together but not married. In Canada, this situation is often referred to as *common-law marriage*. We mainly use the term *cohabitation*, however, because common-law marriage in the United States has a legal standing distinction from cohabitation in several states.

[2] See Casper and Bianchi (in press), Popenoe and Whitehead (1999), Seltzer (2000), and Smock (2000) for other recent reviews of social science research about cohabitation.

outline the implications of these changes for gauging cohabitation's role in family structure. Fifth, we consider the question of whether, and in what ways, cohabitation is similar to marriage, arguing that the boundaries between the two may be becoming more blurred than assumed. Finally, we consider the extent to which cohabitation has become "institutionalized" in the United States and Canada, an area in which the two countries now depart substantially.

COHABITATION IN NORTH AMERICA

Recent decades have ushered in far-reaching changes in family patterns in Canada and the United States. Following World War II, both countries experienced a brief "pro-family" period characterized by earlier ages at marriage, a rapid pace of childbearing, low levels of divorce, and low levels of nonmarital childbearing. Subsequently, the last two or three decades have been marked by lower levels of childbearing, higher divorce rates, increases in the average age at marriage, rising nonmarital childbearing, and rising levels of cohabitation (Milan, 2000).

In general, the same explanations that have been posed to understand changes in family patterns overall are also used to explain the trend in cohabitation; cohabitation is taken to be just one component of a constellation of longer term changes occurring in the United States, Canada, and in Europe (Cherlin & Furstenberg, 1988; Kiernan, 1988, 1999). Although some trends, including cohabitation in Canada and the United States, began in earnest in the 1960s or 1970s, divorce has been gradually rising for more than a century and there is wide consensus that even the most recent trends have quite long-term historical roots (Bumpass, 1990; Popenoe, 1993).

Scholars emphasize two major aspects of long-term social change to explain the rise of cohabitation. The first may be labeled *cultural*. Rising individualism and secularism figure prominently in this category (Lesthaeghe, 1983; Lesthaeghe & Surkyn, 1988; Rindfuss & VandenHeuvel, 1990; Thornton, 1989). The former refers to the increasing importance of individual goal attainment over the past few centuries and the latter to the decline in religious adherence and involvement. A more proximate and direct cultural source of cohabitation's rise is the "sexual revolution." As Bumpass (1990) noted, this revolution eroded the main grounds for earlier disapproval of cohabitation (i.e., that unmarried persons were having sexual relations). Once this stigma was removed, cohabitation was free to escalate.

The second set of factors is generally labeled *economic*. This set ranges from broad conceptualizations of the massive social changes wrought by industrialization (Goode, 1963) to narrower ones focusing on women's changing roles in the labor market and concomitant shifts in values and attitudes about gender roles (Cherlin & Furstenberg, 1988).

Trends

Unmarried cohabitation has become a quite prominent feature of family life in both Canada and the United States. Figs. 4.1a and 4.1b show the absolute number of cohabiting couple households to illustrate the upward trend over time. In both countries, the trend has been fairly steep (see Casper & Cohen, 2000, for a discussion of measurement issues associated with the study of cohabitation in the United States and Dumas & Bélanger, 1997, for Canada. See the appendix for a description of the data sources used to study cohabitation in both countries). These absolute levels (which imply that cohabiting couple households account for roughly 14% of all couple households in Canada and less than this for the United States) are misleading for gauging the prominence of cohabitation. This is because co-

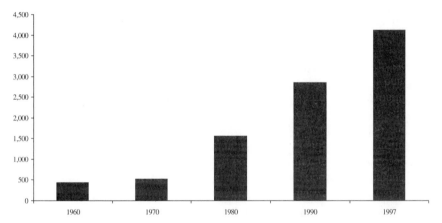

FIG. 4.1a   Number of cohabiting couple households in the United States, 1960–1997 (in 1,000s; *Source:* Casper & Cohen, 2000).

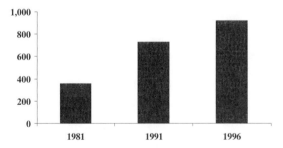

FIG. 4.1b   Number of cohabiting couple families in Canada, 1981–1996 (in 1,000s; *Source:* Statistics Canada, 1981, 1991, and 1996 census).

habitation tends to be a transitory phenomenon. For most couples, cohabitations are relatively brief, with the majority ending them either by terminating the relationship or by marrying within a few years. Recent estimates from the United States suggest that only about one sixth of couples remain cohabiting for 3 years, and only about one tenth cohabit for 5 years or more (Bumpass & Lu, 2000). Better indicators of its popularity thus take into account the experiences of those who have cohabited in the past but are not cohabiting at the time of a survey or a census.

Figure 4.2, for example, shows the proportion of first coresidential unions (including both cohabitations and marriages) that are cohabitations. In the United States, this proportion rose from 43% for unions formed between 1980 and 1984 to 54% for those formed between 1990 and 1994 (Bumpass & Lu, 2000, Table 3). Patterns are similar for Canada, with cohabitation becoming the predominant first union over time. Among first unions formed between 1970 and 1974, approximately 17% were cohabitations compared to almost 60% for unions formed between 1990 and 1995 (Dumas & Bélanger, 1997; Turcotte & Bélanger, 1997).

Similarly, as Fig. 4.3 illustrates, the percentage of first marriages in the United States preceded by cohabitation, either with the future spouse or another partner, rose from about 10% for those marrying between 1965 and 1974 to 56% for those marrying between 1990 and 1994 (Bumpass & Lu, 2000; Bumpass & Sweet, 1989). Cohabitation is even more common before a second marriage (Bumpass & Sweet, 1989), thus playing an important role both before and after marriage (Brown, 2000a; Bumpass & Sweet, 1989; Casper & Bianchi, in press; Chevan, 1996, Morrison & Ritualo, 2000; Péron, 1999; Z. Wu & Balakrishnan, 1994). In the United States, for example, the majority of cohabiting-couple households contain at least one partner who had previously been married (U.S. Bureau of the Census, 1998a).

As implied by these numbers, nearly a majority of younger adults in both countries have experienced cohabitation at some point. Nearly 50% of 30- to 39-year-old U.S. women in 1995 reported having cohabited at least once (Bumpass & Lu, 2000). The percentage is nearly identical for Canada, and a substantially higher 60% among 20- to 29-year-olds in Canada (Le Bourdais, Neill, & Turcotte, 2000). Turcotte and Goldscheider (1998), in fact, estimate that the likelihood of cohabiting is 8 and 10 times higher for Canadian men and women, respectively, who were born between 1961 and 1970 than for those born in 1950 or before, even taking account of an array of other factors that are associated with the propensity to cohabit.

Attitudinal data underscore just how normative cohabitation has become. The 1995 Monitoring the Future (MTF), a survey of U.S. high school seniors, presented respondents with the following statement: "It is usually a good idea for a couple to live together before marriage." Sixty-two and 55% of young men and women, respectively, agreed with this statement (Johnston, Bachman, & O'Malley, 1995).

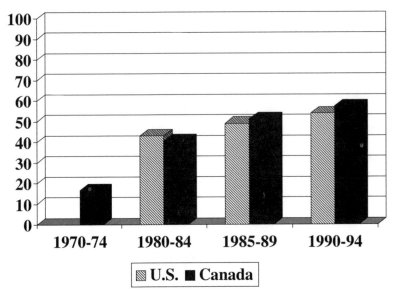

FIG. 4.2   Percent of first unions beginning as cohabitations by union cohort (*Source*: Bumpass & Lu, 2000, Table 3; Turcotte & Bélanger, 1997,Table 2).

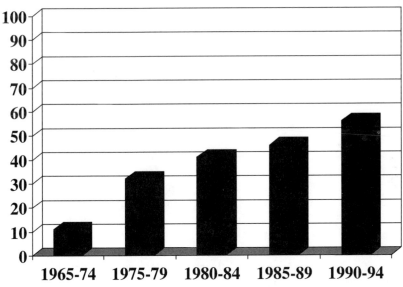

FIG. 4.3   Percent of first marriages preceded by cohabitation by marriage cohort, U.S. (*Source*: Bumpass & Lu, 2000, Table 3; Bumpass & Sweet, 1989, Table 2).

The Presence of Children

Cohabitations often include children. Here, again, is a case in which cross-sectional statistics tell one story and measures of experience tell another. Estimates drawn from the former indicate that only a small proportion of children live in cohabiting households at any one point in time. In Canada, for example, roughly 7% to 8% of all children under age 15 in 1991 lived in a cohabiting couple household (LaPierre-Adamcyk & Marcil-Gratton, 1999); U.S. data suggest that just under 4% of all children lived in a cohabiting couple household in 1990 (Manning & Lichter, 1996).

However, the proportion of children who will ever live in a cohabiting household during childhood is estimated to be far higher—a substantial 40% for the United States (Bumpass & Lu, 2000). Moreover, the percentage of children now born into cohabitations is not trivial; among Canadian children born in 1993 and 1994, about 20% were born into cohabiting couple households (Marcil-Gratton, 1998).

Who Cohabits?

Other than the dramatic increase over time, with younger cohorts of men and women increasingly likely to cohabit, some factors do emerge about the "type" of individual most prone to cohabitation, or instead, to marriage without cohabitation beforehand.

First, cohabitation tends to be selective of people who are slightly more liberal, less religious, and more supportive of egalitarian gender roles and nontraditional family roles (Clarkberg, Stolzenberg, & Waite, 1995; Lye & Waldron, 1997; Thornton, Axinn, & Hill, 1992; Z. Wu & Balakrishnan, 1992). For example, one study found that Canadian women who reported that they did not attend any religious services in the past year were almost three times more likely to select cohabitation rather than marriage as a first union. This study also found that women who attend church daily have a much greater tendency to legalize their cohabitation (Turcotte & Bélanger, 1997). Notably, similar patterns exist in many European nations. Among 20- to 39-year-old women who had been in a union, church attenders were somewhat more likely to marry without cohabiting than women who had never attended church (Kiernan, chap. 1, this volume).

Second, there are apparently some intergenerational effects connecting cohabitation to family background. Turcotte and Bélanger (1997) found that controlling for other factors that are associated with cohabitation, the dissolution of parents' marriages before age 15 substantially increases the likelihood of cohabitating. Additionally, based on a U.S. data set that follows a cohort of children and their mothers over time, a series of studies finds that children whose parents divorced and whose mothers expressed more approval of cohabitation were more likely to cohabit as young adults than other children (Axinn & Thornton, 1993; Thornton, 1991; Thornton et al., 1992, see also Wolfinger, in press).

A third dimension of differentiation appears to be social class (i.e., economic standing, educational attainment). For example, recent data show that among 19- to 44-year-old women, nearly 60% of high school drop-outs have cohabited compared to under 37% for college-educated women (Bumpass & Lu, 2000). We return to the issue of cohabitation and social class in a later section.

THE IMPLICATIONS OF COHABITATION FOR THE LIFE COURSE

Cohabitation reinforces the dynamism of the life course, with the evidence largely suggesting that cohabitation promotes greater instability in family life. The source of this effect lies in the greater fragility of cohabitation compared to marriage, resulting in increasing numbers of adults and children who will experience union separation and enter subsequent unions. Although the family has generally been "unstable" in the past as well—characterized by disruptions due to mortality of parents, spouses, and siblings, and due to the home-leaving and returning of children as they were sent out to work (Coontz, 1992, 2000; Hareven, 1991, 1994; Watkins, Menken, & Bongaarts, 1987)—cohabitation represents a relatively new source of such instability.

The mechanism is twofold. First, cohabiting unions are themselves less stable than marriage. More than 50% of cohabiting unions in the United States, whether or not they are legalized by marriage, end by separation within 5 years compared to roughly 20% for marriages (Bumpass & Lu, 2000; Bumpass & Sweet, 1989). Similar differentials exist in Canada, although absolute levels differ somewhat (e.g., Le Bourdais & Marcil-Gratton, 1996; Z. Wu & Balakrishnan, 1995). Of women who were 30 to 39 years old at the time of the survey, almost two thirds of those whose first union was a cohabitation had experienced separation compared to one third of those who had married first (Le Bourdais et al., 2000).

The second mechanism is that marriages preceded by cohabitation—a growing proportion of marriages—are more likely to end than marriages not prefaced by cohabitation. This is the case in the United States, Canada, and other countries as well (Axinn & Thornton, 1992; Bennett, Blanc, & Bloom, 1988; Booth & Johnson, 1988; DeMaris & MacDonald, 1993; DeMaris & Rao, 1992; Hall & Zhao, 1995; Lillard, Brien, & Waite, 1995; Rao & Trussell, 1989; Schoen, 1992; Teachman & Polonko, 1990; Teachman, Thomas, & Paasch, 1991; Thomson & Colella, 1992). Given the wide variation in data, samples, measures of marital instability, and independent variables, the degree of consensus about this central finding is impressive.

There are two main explanations for this relationship and both have received some empirical support. One explanation for this relationship is what is termed the *selection hypothesis.* This refers to the idea that people who cohabit before marriage differ in important ways from those who do not, and these ways increase the likelihood of marital instability. That is, the characteristics that select people into cohabitation in the first place, such as nontraditional values and attitudes, are also those that increase the risk of marital instability. The second explanation is that there is something about cohabitation itself (i.e., the experience of cohabitation) that increases the likelihood of marital disruption above and beyond one's characteristics at the start of the cohabitation. For example, through cohabitation people may learn about and come to accept the temporary nature of relationships, and that there are alternatives to marriage. Note that the two explanations are not mutually exclusive, with the first focusing on the characteristics that select people initially into cohabitation and the second positing that the experience of cohabitation alters these characteristics to make people even more divorce-prone.

The upshot of these sorts of patterns is illustrated in Fig. 4.4, which shows the percent of Canadian women who report having experienced at least two unions and at least one union separation by birth cohort (Le Bourdais et al., 2000). The proportion of women who experienced at least two unions tripled over time, rising from 14% among those born between 1926 and 1935 to nearly 40% for the 1956-1965 birth cohort.

Not surprisingly, similar findings emerge for children. Children who experience parental cohabitation are more likely to undergo further transitions in family structure. Graefe and Lichter (1999), for example, estimate that most children in

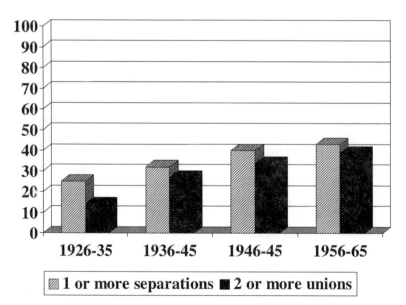

FIG. 4.4   Percent of women experiencing events by birth cohort, Canada, 1995 (*Source*: Le Bourdais, Neill, & Turcotte, 2000).

the United States who are born into, or ever live in, a cohabiting family will experience a change in family structure within a few years. Similarly, Marcil-Gratton (1998), drawing on a Canadian survey of children and youth, found that children who were born to married parents face far lower risks of parental separation than either children born to cohabiting parents or even children born to married parents who had previously cohabited. Focusing on children born in 1983 and 1984, Marcil-Gratton found that about 20% of children overall experienced their parents' separation before the age of 10. But this varies considerably by the child's family status at birth. For children born to married parents who had not cohabited, the percentage is 13.6, yet 60% of those born to cohabiting parents had experienced family disruption by age 10 (Marcil-Gratton, 1998, Table 4.1; see also Marcil-Gratton & Le Bourdais, 1999). These patterns are of concern to researchers and policymakers because there is evidence that the number of changes in family structure is important for children's well-being—the fewer the changes, the better for children (Wu, 1996; Wu & Martinson, 1993).

VARIATIONS IN THE ROLE OF COHABITATION

Aggregate statistics and generalizations conceal important variation in the role of cohabitation among different population subgroups. This is certainly the case in North America. The extant evidence overall suggests that the meaning of cohabitation varies along social class and cultural lines. We discuss each in turn. Additionally, we interweave a discussion of race/ethnic diversity in the meaning of cohabitation in the United States, an issue that is intricately related to both culture and social class; and we focus especially on Quebec in our discussion of culture because it departs substantially from the rest of Canada in terms of the role of cohabitation in family life.

Social Class

Social class—or one's economic circumstances and prospects—is correlated with family patterns. Numerous studies suggest that both becoming married and remaining married are associated with socioeconomic status (SES); those with the best economic prospects are more likely to marry and subsequently to enjoy more stable unions. For example, separation and divorce tend to be more common among those who are less economically advantaged in the first place. Its likelihood is inversely related to indicators of SES such as family income and educational attainment and positively related to economic hardship (e.g., Dechter, 1992; Espenshade, 1979; Hoffman & Holmes, 1976; Holden & Smock, 1991; Martin & Bumpass, 1989; Morgan, 1991; Ono, 1998; Smock, Manning, & Gupta, 1999; Z. Wu & Pollard, 2000). Similarly, if a male's economic situation is good, he is more likely to marry than a man with a poor economic situation (Lichter, LeClere, &

McLaughlin, 1991; Lichter, McLaughlin, Kephart, & Landry, 1992; Lloyd & South, 1996; Mare & Winship, 1991; Oppenheimer, Kalmijn, & Lim, 1997; Smock & Manning, 1997; Testa, Astone, Krogh, & Neckerman, 1989; Wilson, 1987). Although most social scientists argue that causality runs primarily from economic well-being to family patterns, many acknowledge effects in the other direction as well (e.g., Waite, 1995).

Correspondingly, cohabitation tends to be more selective of people of slightly lower levels of educational attainment and income than is marriage (Bumpass & Lu, 2000; Cohen, 1999; Hao, 1996; Manning & Lichter, 1996; Morrison & Ritualo, 2000; Nock, 1995; Thornton, Axinn, & Teachman, 1995; Waite, 1995). Median household income for cohabiting young adults was roughly 85% that of their married counterparts in the United States in 1998 (authors' calculations from Casper & Bianchi, in press, Table 2.3). Although an educational gradient does not appear to exist in Canada overall (e.g., Turcotte & Bélanger, 1997), Canadian cohabitors experience a similar income shortfall compared to married couples (Mongeau, 1999, Table 2). Correspondingly, studies indicate that children already disadvantaged in terms of parental income and education are relatively more likely to experience a parent's cohabitation (Bumpass & Lu, 2000; Graefe & Lichter, 1999). It also appears that children born in cohabiting unions whose parents subsequently separated are significantly less likely to receive regular child support payments than are children born into married couple families (Marcil-Gratton & Le Bourdais, 1999).

Furthermore, studies that either examine marriage among cohabitors or the choice between cohabitation and marriage as one's first union find that positive economic situations accelerate marriage and decrease the chance of separation (e.g., Clarkberg, 1999; Manning & Smock, 1995; Smock & Manning, 1997; Z. Wu & Pollard, 2000). For example, analyzing young adults' transitions into their first coresidential unions with United States data, Clarkberg (1999) found that relative income—how well an individual is doing relative to others in similar circumstances—has substantially stronger positive effects on marriage than on cohabitation.

These social class differentials have important implications for understanding race and ethnic differences in family patterns in the United States. For several reasons, including residential segregation, inequality in access to quality public schooling, and job segregation, race and ethnicity tend to be correlated with income and wealth. Whites, on average, enjoy substantially higher income and wealth. There are thus also fairly marked race and ethnic differences in family patterns (i.e., marriage rates, nonmarital childbearing) and a large research literature exists attempting to explain these (Bennett, Bloom, & Craig, 1989; Bulcroft & Bulcroft, 1993; Lichter et al., 1991, 1992; Mare & Winship, 1991; McLanahan & Casper, 1995; Raley, 1996; South, 1991, 1993; Wilson, 1987). In 1998, for example, 17% of 30- to 34-year-old White women had never been married compared to 47% among Black women (U.S. Bureau of the Census, 1998a).

The prominence, or role, of cohabitation also seems to vary by race and ethnicity. Consider these examples. First, Hispanics and Blacks are more likely than Whites to give birth to children while cohabiting (Loomis & Landale, 1994; Manning, 1999). Second, Bumpass, Sweet, and Cherlin (1991) reported that cohabitation compensated for a full 83% of the decline in marriage by age 25 over recent cohorts for Blacks compared to 61% for Whites. Third, greater proportions of Hispanics and Blacks than Whites select cohabitation as their first union (Clarkberg, 1999; Loomis & Landale, 1994; Willis & Michael, 1994). Fourth, Blacks more commonly separate from, rather than marry, their cohabiting partners, and cohabiting Whites marry more quickly than Hispanics (Brown, 2000b; Manning 1999; Manning & Smock, 1995). Finally, Hispanics express more approval of cohabitation than Whites and experience a cultural context that is relatively supportive of cohabitation (e.g., Fennelly, Kadiah, & Ortiz, 1989; Oropesa, 1996).

Not surprisingly, and discussed by Manning (chap. 8, this volume), there are race/ethnic differences in the likelihood of children experiencing parental cohabitation. Bumpass and Lu (2000) estimated that more than one half (57%) of Black, two fifths (42%) of Hispanic, and one third (35%) of White children born in the early 1990s are expected to spend some of their childhood in a cohabiting parent family. These findings are consistent with Astone, Schoen, Ensminger, and Rothert's (1999) recent study of a cohort of Black men in Baltimore, which finds that a good deal of fatherhood among Blacks is occurring in the context of cohabitation.

Culture

Researchers have increasingly recognized the necessity of looking beyond economics and considering cultural differences as explanations for family patterns (Cherlin, 1992; Manning & Landale, 1996; Morgan, McDaniel, Miller, & Preston, 1993; Seltzer, 2000). The term *culture* generally refers to a set of beliefs, values, and behavior patterns that characterize a group. These groups may range in size from a small community to western societies as a whole; they may be defined by religion, by race or ethnicity, by region or other dimensions.

There is evidence of cultural variation in the role and meaning of cohabitation. For the United States, race and ethnic variation in cohabitation's role, as well as other family patterns, is not entirely reducible to economics. For example, Manning and Smock (2000) examined the marriage intentions of White, Black, and Hispanic cohabiting women. They find that Black cohabiting women have significantly lower odds of expecting to marry their partners than White or Hispanic women, even after taking account of the education of both the women and their partners, and their partners' income (see, also, Clarkberg, 1999; Landale & Fennelly, 1992; Landale & Forste, 1991; Manning & Smock, 1995; Oropesa, 1996; Oropesa, Lichter, & Anderson, 1994; Raley, 1996).

For Canada, the starkest differential in the role of cohabitation is between Quebec and the rest of Canada, with cohabitation a much more prominent feature of family life in the former (Belliveau, Oderkirk, & Silver, 1994). Social scientists and commentators have thus reached the conclusion that Quebec has "retreated" from marriage, and embraced cohabitation, more than the rest of Canada.

As illustrated in Fig. 4.5, of all unions formed between 1990 and 1994, a striking 80% were cohabitations in Quebec, compared to 50% for the rest of Canada. Similarly, 66% of recent marriages in Quebec were preceded by cohabitation compared to approximately 40% for rest of Canada (Dumas & Bélanger, 1997). And, as shown in Fig. 4.6, cohabitation accounts for about 25% of couple households in Quebec compared to under 11% for the rest of Canada (Dumas & Bélanger, 1997; Le Bourdais & Marcil-Gratton, 1996).

These differentials appear to have cultural origins (Le Bourdais & Marcil-Gratton, 1996; Pollard & Wu, 1998). Containing approximately 25% of the Canadian population, it is argued that Quebec is a separate culture, and not just a region (Pollard & Z. Wu, 1998). Le Bourdais and Marcil-Gratton (1996) wrote the following:

Quebeckers remain French, by their origin as well as their culture, and most of all in their day-to-day way of life. In Quebec people are born French, grow up, go to school, marry, attend church, go to movies, the theater, buy books, work read maps and get around in cars, buses trains and planes. . . in French. . . This

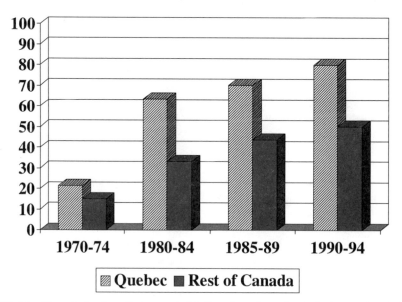

FIG. 4.5   Percent of unions that are cohabitations by union cohort, Quebec and rest of Canada (*Source*: Le Bourdais et al., 2000).

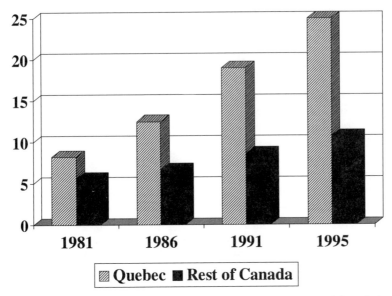

FIG. 4.6   Proportion of couples that are cohabiting in Quebec and rest of Canada by year (*Source*: Turcotte & Bélanger, 1997, Table 2).

rather tedious list is only meant to reinforce the point that Quebec is a different society than those of its neighbors, both outside and inside of Canada (pp. 416–417).

Empirical studies underscore the importance of a common language. One study found that being French-speaking (about 90% of those in Quebec) is a more influential factor than living in Quebec when predicting whether a first union is a cohabitation. Non-Francophone residents of Quebec are significantly less likely to enter a cohabitation, and actually have a lower propensity to do so than Canadians residing in other provinces (Turcotte & Bélanger, 1997).

Other aspects of cohabitation differ in Quebec, and these are important because they suggest that cohabitation is more marriage-like in Quebec than elsewhere. First, cohabitation is of somewhat longer duration in Quebec (Le Bourdais & Marcil-Gratton, 1996; see also Dumas & Bélanger, 1997; Turcotte & Bélanger, 1997). Quebec women are also less likely to transform cohabitations into marriage and they do so more slowly (Turcotte & Bélanger, 1997). Perhaps most significant, among children born in 1993 and 1994, about 20% in Canada overall were born to cohabiting couples compared to a striking 43% in Quebec (Marcil-Gratton, 1998). In fact, only about 25% of children in Quebec were born to a "traditional" family consisting of married parents who did not live together before marriage compared to almost 50% in Ontario (Marcil-Gratton, 1998).

THE SHIFTING NATURE OF COHABITATION

Consideration of the Quebec case leads to perhaps the central debate about the significance of cohabitation: whether it is a threat to legal marriage. A decade or so ago, by most accounts, cohabitation was generally not deemed to be so. As part of the process leading to marriage or remarriage, it was thought, cohabitation plays much the same role as engagement. The large proportions of cohabitors that subsequently married or had plans to marry generally supported this notion (Brown & Booth, 1996; Bumpass, 1990).

Yet, evidence has recently begun to emerge from both Canada and the United States that cohabitation's central features have been changing fairly substantially over very short periods of time. The most important implication of these changes is that cohabitation has lost much ground as a precursor to marriage. The matter is complex, however. Although cohabitations appear to be increasingly unstable and less likely to lead to marriage, there may be a growing segment of cohabiting unions that do endure, with or without childbearing. Taken together, we interpret available research as suggestive of a continued decrease in legal marriage as the basis for family life.

The first relevant observation is that the relationship between cohabitation and marriage is clearly altering: Cohabitations are decreasingly being converted into marriages. In the 1990s, in the United States, estimates indicate that about 33% of them resulted in marriage within 3 years of the start of the cohabitation, sharply lower than the 60% estimated for the 1970s (Bumpass, 1995, 1998). This is also the case in Canada. Between 1990 and 1995, about 30% of cohabiting unions were legalized by marriage within 5 years compared to 50% for unions begun before 1980 (Turcotte & Bélanger, 1997; see also Dumas & Bélanger, 1997). Notably, this trend is also evident in other countries (e.g., Murphy, 2000; Touleman, 1997).

Dumas and Bélanger (1997) provided a useful description of the changing nature of cohabitation. Using retrospective data from a 1995 Canadian survey, they examined changes over time in various types of cohabitation. The types were constructed on the basis of duration, whether and when the cohabitation was legalized by marriage, and whether children were born in the union (see Casper & Sayer, 2000, for an analysis of cohabitation types in the United States and Villeneuve-Gokalp, 1991, for France). Two of the categories represent cohabitations leading to marriage ("prelude to marriage" and "trial marriage"). Consistent with the figures just presented, the percentage of cohabitations in these two categories decreased from 38% for unions begun in 1977-1979 to 18% for those begun in 1989-1991.

There are two other trends in the data that are noteworthy. One concerns the proportion of unions that Dumas and Bélanger categorized as "unstable" (i.e., ending within 3 years without marriage). These increased from 14% to 23%. Other studies confirm the increasing instability of cohabitation (e.g., Bumpass & Lu, 2000). Turcotte and Bélanger (1997), for example, estimated that the proportion of women who had separated from their partner within 5 years of the start of the cohabitation was 45% for unions beginning between 1990 and 1995 compared to half that (23%) for those who formed a union before 1980. This trend is not limited to North America (e.g., Touleman, 1997).

The second, and partially countervailing, trend is that an increasing proportion of unions fall into categories suggestive of more permanent cohabitation. Termed *stable* and *substitute for marriage*, Dumas and Bélanger defined these as unions that endured longer than 3 years without marriage, the latter category also including a child being born. The proportion of cohabiting unions in these two categories increased from 44% to 57% over the roughly 10-year period.

A related trend is that children are increasingly involved in cohabitation. In Canada, for example, the proportion of all children born into cohabiting-couple families rose from 10% for children born in the early 1980s to more than 20% for those born in the early 1990s (Marcil-Gratton, 1998). Bumpass and Lu (2000) reported that the share of births to unmarried mothers who were cohabiting increased substantially more between the early 1980s and early 1990s than the share to noncohabiting, single mothers. Now, in the United States, about 40% of children born to purportedly single mothers are actually being born to cohabiting parents.

Here, too, there are some complexities. The trends involving children would suggest that cohabitation is becoming more a substitute or alternative to marriage, given the traditional linkage between childbearing and the socialization of children and legal marriage. Raley (2001), who examined the fertility behavior of young women (aged 15-29) since the 1970s in the United States, presented evidence consistent with this interpretation (see also LaPierre-Adamcyk, Neill, & Le Bourdais, 2000). Specifically, Raley found that pregnant, single women are decreasingly likely to marry before childbirth and increasingly likely to cohabit instead. Thus, single women are now almost as likely to cohabit as marry if pregnant. Among women who became pregnant while cohabiting, there is no significant trend; the vast majority remain cohabiting at childbirth (roughly two thirds).

Yet, Raley also found that the most common pattern, at least during the 30-year period examined here, has been for single, pregnant women to stay single, neither marrying nor cohabiting by the time of childbirth. And this tendency has increased over time. In other words, an important conclusion is simply that fertility, or at least pregnancy among single women, is increasingly decoupled from union formation (see also Pagnini & Rindfuss, 1993; Turcotte & Goldscheider, 1998). Similar patterns appear to exist in Canada (LaPierre-Adamcyk et al., 2000).

MARRIAGE VERSUS COHABITATION

This section reflects on both marriage and cohabitation. Marriage, understandably so, is typically used as the contrast category with which to understand and interpret cohabitation. This characterizes much of the research, including studies that examine the factors that predict cohabitation versus marriage as one's first union or the differences between cohabiting and married individuals or cohabiting and marital relationships. The upshot, however, is twofold: similarities between cohabitation and marriage are de-emphasized; and attention has been deflected away from dramatic changes in marriage over recent decades and the diversity of marriage.

Similarities Between Marriage and Cohabitation

Certainly, there is evidence that cohabitation and marriage differ from one another (e.g., Brines & Joyner, 1999; Brown & Booth, 1996; Nock, 1995, 1998; Rindfuss & VandenHeuvel, 1990; Seltzer, 2000). Cohabitation tends to be short term, marriage is longer term. Cohabitation less often includes childbearing and rearing than marriage. Marriages, on average, tend to be characterized by a higher degree of commitment. Cohabiting couples tend to have less income and wealth than married couples.

At the most fundamental level, however, both marriage and cohabitation are romantic, coresidential unions that allow individuals to pool income, to bear and/or raise children as a couple, and to generally benefit in emotional, social, and economic ways from living with a partner. There is some specific empirical evidence of basic similarity as well. The first kind of evidence comes from mate-selection studies, often called *assortative mating* studies. This type of research analyzes the extent of similarity (i.e., homogamy) between marital and cohabiting partners on basic characteristics (e.g., race, religion, age). Overall, the research suggests substantial similarities in mating patterns between cohabitation and marriage. Although married couples appear to be somewhat more homogamous, homogamy overwhelmingly characterizes both types of couples (Blackwell & Lichter, 2000; Qian, 1998; Qian & Preston, 1993; Schoen & Weinick, 1993). As Blackwell and Lichter (2000) emphasized, any differences are mainly a matter of degree. It is illustrative in this regard to consider the implications of a study by Qian (1998). He examined trends over time in mate selection patterns in the two types of relationships. Focusing on the period between 1970 and 1990, Qian's findings indicate that, by 1990, partner choice patterns were quite similar in cohabiting and marital unions.

Second, and this becomes a matter of interpreting degrees, cohabitors do not appear to differ all that much from married couples in terms of their division of household labor. This is despite evidence that cohabitors tend to have more egalitarian gender-role attitudes than others and that egalitarian gender roles enhance union stability among cohabiting couples but not married couples (Brines & Joyner, 1999; Clarkberg et al., 1995). Using cross-sectional data from the United States, South and Spitze (1994), for example, reported that cohabiting men do the same amount of housework as married men (on average, 19 and 18 hours per week for cohabiting and married men, respectively), whereas cohabiting women do 31 hours of housework per week compared to 37 for married women. Although the numbers for women suggest a difference between cohabitation and marriage, women still perform the vast majority of housework in both contexts (see also Blair & Lichter, 1991; Shelton & John, 1993).

That cohabiting women do so many hours of housework, and cohabiting men much fewer, may be surprising given the expectation that cohabitors would function in a more egalitarian fashion than married people. Stronger evidence for basic similarity between marriage and cohabitation in terms of the division of domestic labor comes from Gupta's (1999) analysis of longitudinal United States data. He tracked changes in men's and women's housework hours over roughly a 5-year period, focusing on the impact of entering and exiting unions (either marriage or cohabitation). Gupta's key finding is that men substantially reduce their housework time both overall and time doing "female-type" tasks specifically (i.e., preparing meals, house cleaning, washing dishes) when they enter either marriage or cohabitation. Women increase theirs under the same circumstances. Moreover, the magnitude of these gender-specific effects is about the same for the two unions. As Gupta stated, "the results show that entry into cohabitation induces changes in housework behavior that are no less gender-typical than does entry into marriage. . . the fact of entry into a coresidential union is of greater consequence for housework time than the form of that union" (p. 710).

Research on psychological well-being is also suggestive of similarity between marriage and cohabitation. Ross (1995) analyzed differences in psychological distress among men and women living in four different circumstances: having no partner, having a partner outside the household, living with a partner in the household, married to and living with partner in household. Essentially, she found that even taking account of an array of other variables, living with a partner and being married to him or her do not have significantly different effects on well-being. As Ross concluded, "it is the underlying social attachment, not the status of being married, that is important to well-being. Even without adjustment for social and economic support, unmarried persons living with their partners have distress levels that are as low as those of married persons" (p. 9). In the same spirit, Bumpass and Sweet (1997), when reflecting on data needs to study today's families, stated, "We must recognize the great variability among cohabiting couples, among married couples, and among non-coresidential relationships, and seek to examine the extent to which these relationship types overlap and differ along a number of key dimensions" (p. 4).

Finally, the boundaries between marriage and cohabitation may be much more blurred than we have assumed and even lead to difficulties in identifying who is married and who is cohabiting. A qualitative study of cohabitors in New Zealand indicates that it is not unusual for cohabiting partners to "pass as married," essentially holding themselves out as married in public settings (Elizabeth, 2000). In some cases, this may even include wearing a wedding ring. One can certainly imagine that "passing as married" extends to responses on surveys or Census forms.

Changes in Marriage

Marriage, too, is dynamic and undergoing great change. Since the 1960s there has been erosion of traditional gender roles specifying husbands as breadwinners and wives as homemakers. This represents a very dramatic shift in marital roles, suggestive of a reorganization and redefinition of marriage itself.

Social commentators and scientists often characterize the past two or three decades as a time of women's increasing "economic independence." The primary basis for this characterization has been the marked increase in women's labor market involvement in recent decades occurring in Canada, the United States, and other countries as well. Although women's labor force participation has been increasing for at least a century, the trend accelerated as of the 1960s. In the 1970s, for example, almost 60% of Canadian wives were not employed outside the home; this figure dropped to 34% in 1990. Conversely, the percentage of wives working full time in the labor market rose from under 30% in 1970 to nearly 50% in 1990 (Mongeau, 1999). Similar changes occurred in the United States. The proportion of married women with children under age 6 who worked in the labor market (either full time or part time) increased from 44% in 1970 to almost 70% in 1996 (Bianchi & Spain, 1996).

An important result of these changes is a substantial decline in the economic dependency of women within marriage (Bianchi, 1995; Cancian, Danziger, & Gottschalk, 1993; Dechter & Smock, 1994; Sørensen & McLanahan, 1987). Using U.S. data, Dechter and Smock (1994) showed that the percent of marriages in which the husband provides 70% or more of the couple's income declined from 78% to 46% among Whites and from 71% to 33% among Blacks between 1963 and 1992.

Moreover, these shifts are not just behavioral ones (e.g., Brewster & Padavic, 2000; Cherlin & Walters, 1981; Mason Czajka, & Arber, 1976; Thornton, 1989; Wilkie, 1993). Consider changes in the response to an item frequently repeated on a United States survey. The item reads: "It is much better for everyone involved if the man is the achiever outside the home and the woman takes care of the home and family." In 1970, 80% of married women in the United States agreed; just 27% agreed in 1991 (Rindfuss, Brewster, & Kavee, 1996). Dramatic attitudinal changes have also occurred among men (Wilkie, 1993).

COHABITATION: AN INCOMPLETE INSTITUTION?

More than two decades ago, family demographer Andrew Cherlin coined the term *incomplete institutionalization* when writing about remarriage (Cherlin,1978). Cherlin argued that many of the problems confronting remarried adults and their children stemmed from a lack of standardized solutions to problems (i.e., from incomplete institutionalization). Examples included, at least at the time of his writing, the lack of clearly defined rights and obligations for stepparents and the absence of kinship terms for all of the relationships formed through second marriages. More recently, Nock (1995) extended this idea to conceptualize the distinctions between cohabitation and marriage. Nock argued that cohabitation and marriage are qualitatively different relationships, with this difference stemming from the degree of institutionalization. As Nock stated, "Cohabitation is an incomplete institution. No matter how widespread the practice, nonmarital unions are not yet governed by strong consensual norms or formal laws" (p. 74).

Nock thus implied that the extent of institutionalization of cohabitation can be assessed along at least two dimensions: (a) social or cultural, and (b) statutory. Although it is fair to say that the social norms governing cohabitation are weaker than those concerning marriage, it is difficult to compare them because these norms are not easily documented. However, because changes in social norms are often reflected and codified in the law, we can achieve substantial insight into the issue of the institutionalization of cohabitation by assessing its legal status.

Canada and the United States differ substantially in the legal status of cohabitation. Catalyzed by a 1999 Supreme Court decision that Ontario's family law was discriminatory against same-gender couples, Canada recently made sweeping changes with the passage of Bill C-23 (see Holland, 2000, for legal background information and analysis). This bill, termed the Modernization of Benefits and Obligations Act, eliminates federal legal distinctions between married and unmarried same-gender and opposite-gender couples, so long as the latter live together for at least 1 year. The upshot is that all conjugal unions are now almost fully equivalent under Canadian federal law, the main remaining distinction being that married people do not have to live together for a year for the benefits and obligations to apply to them. Married and opposite-gender cohabiting couples had already been legally indistinguishable in some areas of federal law for years, such as taxes and social security. For example, members of opposite-gender cohabiting unions have been able to claim federal tax credit for their dependent partners since 1993. Bill C-23 generalizes this to include same-gender couples and extends this symmetry to other areas like bankruptcy and certain aspects of the criminal code by replacing "spouse" with "spouse/common-law partner." At the same time, important areas of family law, such as laws governing union dissolution and child custody, remain under provincial jurisdiction. Although the provinces have been working to revise their laws to conform with the Supreme Court decision, the situation remains in flux and there is considerable variation across provinces.

In the United States, cohabitation remains much less institutionalized than marriage. Consider the mechanics of union dissolution, especially in the areas of child custody and property division. Although divorce is hardly free of legal complications in these areas, the rights of ex-spouses are much better defined than those of ex-cohabiting partners. The upshot is that marriage and divorce are safer, legally speaking, than cohabitation in virtually all respects—government benefits, rights of ex-spouses, child custody, and so on. It is therefore possible that many cohabiting couples marry as much for the sake of legal clarity and convenience as out of respect for the institution of marriage. This may be especially the case for couples who have, or intend to have, children.

At the same time, although United States law has yet to catch up fully to the social reality of widespread cohabitation, it has begun to acknowledge it. The 1976 case of *Marvin v. Marvin* in California was a legal watershed in the recent history of cohabitation in the United States. The suit was brought by the female cohabitor—who had legally changed her last name to her partner's—after her partner married another woman and evicted her (his cohabiting partner) from their shared home. The lower courts upheld his claim that he had no obligations towards an unmarried partner, but the California Supreme Court took another view. In its statement it said that "the mores of the society have indeed changed so radically in regard to cohabitation that we cannot impose a standard based on alleged moral considerations that have apparently been so widely abandoned by so many." Furthermore, the court argued that "in the absence of an express contract, the courts should inquire into the conduct of the parties to determine whether that conduct demonstrates an implied contract. . . or some other tacit understanding between the parties" (Duff & Truitt, 1992, pp. 45-46). The final outcome of the case was not favorable to the litigant, who ultimately failed to receive any financial compensation for the dissolution of the union, but the case opened the way for subsequent exploration of the legal status of cohabitation.

The situation is complicated by the fact that states differ in the degree of legal recognition and protections afforded to unmarried couples; some states still have laws forbidding unmarried cohabitation, although these are rarely enforced. A few states allow true "common-law marriage," requiring a formal divorce to end the relationship even though the partners are not legally married.[3] Common-law marriage is defined as a heterosexual conjugal union in which the partners have lived together for a substantial period of time (the exact amount is not defined in

---

[3] These are Alabama, Colorado, Georgia, Iowa, Kansas, Montana, Ohio, Oklahoma, Pennsylvania, Rhode Island, South Carolina, Texas, and the District of Columbia.

any state), routinely present themselves as a married couple by using the same last name, filing joint tax returns, and so on, and intending to marry.

Issues relating to children are substantially more complex in the case of cohabitation than marriage in the United States. On the one hand, unmarried parents are legally recognized as parents if their names are listed on the birth certificates of their children. Such official acknowledgments of paternity make the children eligible for government benefits, like Social Security survivor payments, regardless of the parents' marital status. But unlike married couples, only one cohabiting partner can claim the child as a dependent for tax purposes. Adoption is trickier for cohabiting couples than for married ones; some states do not allow unmarried couples to adopt, and others make it more difficult for unmarried couples than married ones to show that their homes are suitable environments for raising children. The laws applicable to child custody and visitation rights for ex-cohabiting partners are much less clear and uniform than they are for ex-spouses.

Although cohabiting couples can write contracts to create a partnership with protections very similar to those of marriage, this takes a good deal of effort as well as access to legal information (Ihara, Warner, & Hertz, 1999). Thus, this is an unlikely option for couples without considerable economic and educational resources. Touleman (1997), in fact, found that only 3% of cohabitors in a 1994 French survey report that they had drawn up legal contracts.

In the course of the research for this chapter, we happened upon another indicator of Canada's comparative acceptance of nonmarital conjugal unions. Statistics Canada, the country's national statistical agency, generally presents a separate category for cohabiting couples when providing data on families and households. When it does not, cohabiting and married couples are collapsed into one category, and both are referred to as "husband-wife" families. Indeed, the official definition of *family* is "a married or common-law couple living together, with or without never-married sons or daughters; or a lone parent living with at least one never-married son or daughter" (Péron, 1999). The U.S. Bureau of the Census, in contrast, defines a family as a group of two people or more related by birth, marriage, or adoption and residing together. Correspondingly, the Bureau's widely used publications on the sociodemographic and economic characteristics of United States families offer only married couple, female-householder, and male-householder as categories even though a measure of cohabitation is available (U.S. Bureau of the Census, 1998a, 1998b). There are apparently no immediate plans to alter this practice (Lisa Neidert, personal communication, August 12, 2000).

CONCLUSION

This chapter has surveyed cohabitation in the United States and in Canada. Overall, we find that cohabitation is posing an increasingly potent challenge to marriage as a form of coresidential, conjugal union; in both countries it has grown dramatically in prominence and is more than a step in the marriage process. This is not to say that marriage doesn't retain enormous symbolic power. In fact, an amendment to Bill C-23 insists—even as the Bill equalizes marriage and cohabitation—that marriage retains its special character. The amendment reads: "For greater certainty, the amendments made by this Act do not affect the meaning of the word "marriage," that is, the lawful union of one man and one woman to the exclusion of all others."

Drawing on the "partnership transition" model outlined by Kiernan (chap. 1, this volume), it appears that Canada has entered the third stage whereby cohabitation becomes acceptable and parenthood is not restricted to marriage. The United States probably falls somewhere between the second and third stage, the former being when cohabitation functions as a prelude to marriage.[4] In both countries, we speculate, those who marry without cohabiting first are becoming an increasingly select population, just as cohabitors were initially.

In the case of Canada, cohabitation has been institutionalized by way of formal legal changes, thus validating cohabitation as a legitimate family form. Although the United States has not yet done so, the practice of cohabitation is so widespread that it has been institutionalized to an extent at the social level. Credit card companies have replaced "spouse" with "co-applicant" or "spouse/co-applicant," major hotel chains now have official policies against inquiring into the marital status of guests, and thousands of employers offer some form of benefits to cohabiting partners (Ihara et al., 1999). As it has done before in response to other deep and pervasive social change, United States law may eventually accommodate the rise of cohabitation by according it the same status as marriage.

We close with a quote from a prominent sociologist and suggest that it is as apt today as nearly a century ago: "Perhaps the family still shows more fluctuation and uncertainty than other of our great institutions. . . The family has to a great extent lost its position as a conservative institution and become a field for social change" (Sumner, 1909, p. 590).

---

[4] However, what complicates the fit of both Canada and the United States to this model is that the stages obscure a critical factor in understanding changing family patterns: that coresidential partnership is increasingly decoupled from parenthood.

APPENDIX: A NOTE ON DATA SOURCES

Systematic, representative data about cohabitation was scarce until the mid- to late 1980s in the United States and the early 1980s in Canada. The Canadian Census began identifying common-law unions in 1981 and continues to do so. More detailed information about cohabitation became available with the release of the 1990 and 1995 General Social Surveys. These surveys—with a sample of roughly 11,000 individuals age 15 and up in private households—ascertain information on all marital and cohabiting union, separation, divorce, widowhood, and a broad range of background characteristics.

In the United States, for basic information on cohabitation, one can use the decennial Census or the Current Population Surveys; however, these data sources did not directly identify cohabitors until the 1990s. Prior to that time, it was necessary to infer cohabitation based on information on household composition. Representative surveys began to obtain detailed information about respondents' past and current cohabitation experiences around the mid-1980s. These included the National Survey of Families and Households (NSFH; Sweet, Bumpass, & Call, 1988), the Detroit Area Study (Thornton, 1988), and the National Longitudinal Survey of the High School Class of 1972. The National Survey of Family Growth, primarily a fertility survey, ascertained limited information about cohabitation in the 1980s (e.g., Bachrach, 1987) and included complete cohabitation histories in 1995. The NSFH is particularly popular as a source of knowledge about cohabitation. It obtained complete cohabitation histories from a sample of women and men of all ages and thus is often used as a basis for representative estimates of cohabitation as well as estimates of cohort change in cohabitation. Additionally, the first wave of the NSFH (1987-1988) is unique in oversampling currently cohabiting men and women as well as ascertaining a good deal of information about both members of the couple (Sweet et al., 1988).

ACKNOWLEDGMENTS

This work was supported in part by a grant from the National Institute of Child Health and Human Development (R01-34391). We are grateful to Alan Booth, Céline Le Bourdais, Ann C. Crouter, Ruk Jayakody, Wendy Manning, and the other participants at the 2000 Family Issues Symposium for insightful comments and engaging dialogue.

REFERENCES

Astone, N. M., Schoen, R., Ensminger, M., & Rothert, K. (1999, March). *The family life course of African American men*. Paper presented at the annual meeting of the Population Association of America, New York.

Axinn, W. G., & Thornton, A. T. (1992). The relationship Between cohabitation and divorce: Selectivity or causal Influence? *Demography, 29*, 357–374.

Axinn, W. G., & Thornton, A. T. (1993). Mothers, children, and cohabitation: The intergenerational effects of attitudes and behavior. *American Sociological Review, 58*, 233–246.

Bachrach, C. A. (1987). Cohabitation and reproductive behavior in the U.S. *Demography, 24*, 623–637.

Belliveau, J., Oderkirk, J., & Silver, C. (1994, Summer). Common law unions: The Quebec difference. *Canadian Social Trends*, 8–12.

Bennett, N. G., Blanc A. K., & Bloom, D. E. (1988). Commitment and the modern union: Assessing the link between premarital cohabitation and subsequent marital stability. *American Sociological Review, 53*, 127–138.

Bennett, N. G., Bloom, D. E., & Craig, P. (1989). The divergence of black and white marriage patterns. *American Journal of Sociology, 95*, 692–722.

Bianchi, S. (1995). The changing economic roles of women and men. In R. Farley (Ed.), *State of the union: America in the 1990s* (pp. 107–154). New York: Russell Sage.

Bianchi, S., & Spain, D. (1996). Women, work, and family in America. *Population Bulletin, 51*, 1–48.

Blackwell, D. L., & Lichter, D. T. (2000). Mate selection among married and cohabiting couples. *Journal of Family Issues, 21*, 275–302.

Blair, S. L., & Lichter, D. T. (1991). Measuring the division of household labor: Gender segregation of housework among American couples. *Journal of Family Issues, 12*, 91–113.

Booth, A., & Johnson, D. (1988). Premarital cohabitation and marital success. *Journal of Family Issues, 9*, 255–272.

Brewster, K. L., & Padavic, I. (2000). Change in gender-ideology, 1977-1996: The contributions of intracohort change and population turnover. *Journal of Marriage and the Family, 62*, 477–487.

Brines, J., & Joyner, K. (1999). The ties that bind: Commitment and stability in the modern union. *American Sociological Review, 64*, 333–356.

Brown, S. L. (2000a). Fertility following marital dissolution: The role of cohabitation. *Journal of Family Issues, 21*, 501–524.

Brown, S. L. (2000b). Union transitions among cohabitors: The significance of relationship assessments and expectations. *Journal of Marriage and the Family, 62*, 833–846.

Brown, S. L., & Booth, A. (1996). Cohabitation versus marriage: A comparison of relationship quality. *Journal of Marriage and the Family, 58*, 668–678.

Bulcroft, R. A., & Bulcroft, K. A. (1993). Race differences in attitudinal and motivational factors in the decision to marry. *Journal of Marriage and the Family, 55,* 383–355.

Bumpass, L. L. (1990). What's happening to the family? Interaction between demographic and institutional change. *Demography, 27,* 483–498.

Bumpass, L. L. (1995). *The declining significance of marriage: Changing family life in the United States. (National Survey of Families and Households Working Paper #66).* Madison: Center for Demography and Ecology, University of Wisconsin-Madison.

Bumpass, L. L. (1998). The changing significance of marriage in the United States. Pp. 63–70 In K. O. Mason, N. Nilsuya, & M. Choe (Eds.), *The changing family in comparative perspective: Asia and the United States* (pp. 63–70). Honolulu, HI: East-West Center.

Bumpass, L. L., & Lu, H. H. (2000). Trends in cohabitation and implications for children's family contexts in the United States. *Population Studies, 54,* 29–41.

Bumpass, L. L., & Sweet, J. A. (1989). National estimates of cohabitation. *Demography, 26,* 615–625.

Bumpass, L. L., & Sweet, J. A. (1997, October). Marriage, divorce, and intergenerational relationships. *Paper presented at the Workshop on Research Ideas and Data Needs for the Study of the Well-Being of Children and Families,* Washington, DC.

Bumpass, L. L., Sweet, J. A., & Cherlin, A. (1991). The role of cohabitation in declining rates of marriage. *Demography, 53,* 913–927.

Cancian, M., Danziger, S., & Gottschalk, P. (1993). The changing contributions of men and women to the level and distribution of family income, 1968-1988. In D. Papadimitrou & E. Wolff (Eds.), *Poverty and prosperity in the late twentieth century* (pp. 317–353). London: MacMillan.

Casper, L. M., & Bianchi, S. M. (in press). *Trends in the American family.* Thousand Oaks, CA: Sage.

Casper, L. M., & Cohen, P. (2000). How does POSSLQ measure up? Historical estimates of cohabitation. *Demography, 37,* 237–245.

Cherlin, A. J. (1978). Remarriage as an incomplete institution. *American Journal of Sociology, 84,* 634–650.

Cherlin, A. J. (1992). *Marriage, divorce, remarriage.* Cambridge, MA: Harvard University Press.

Cherlin, A. J., & Furstenberg, F. F. (1988). The changing European family: lessons for the American reader. *Journal of Family Issues, 9,* 291–297.

Cherlin, A. J., & Walters P. (1981). Trends in United States men's and women's sex-role attitudes: 1972-1978. *American Sociological Review, 46,* 453–460.

Chevan, A. (1996). As cheaply as one: Cohabitation in the older population. *Journal of Marriage and the Family, 58,* 656–667.

Clarkberg, M. E. (1999). The price of partnering: The role of economic well-being in young adults' first union experiences. *Social Forces, 77*, 945–968.

Clarkberg, M. E., Stolzenberg, R. M., & Waite, L. J. (1995). Attitudes, values, and entrance into cohabitational versus marital unions. *Social Forces, 74*, 609–634.

Cohen, P. N. (1999, March). *Racial-ethnic and gender differences in returns to cohabitation and marriage: Evidence from the Current Population Survey.* Paper presented at the annual meeting of the Population Association of American, Washington, DC.

Cook, F. G. (1888). Reform in the celebration of marriage. *The Atlantic Monthly, 61*, 680–691.

Coontz, S. (1992). *The way we never were: American families and the nostalgia trap.* New York: Basic Books.

Coontz, S. (2000). Historical perspectives on family studies. *Journal of Marriage and the Family, 62*, 283–297.

Dechter, A. R. (1992). *The effect of women's economic independence on union dissolution* (Working Paper no. 92-28), Madison, WI: Center for Demography, and Ecology.

Dechter, A., & Smock, P. J. (1994). *The fading breadwinner role and the economic implications for young couples* (Institute for Research on Poverty Discussion Paper no. 1051-94). Madison, WI: University of Wisconsin-Madison.

DeMaris, A., & MacDonald, W. (1993). Premarital cohabitation and marital Instability: A test of the unconventionality hypothesis. *Journal of Marriage and the Family, 55*, 399–407.

DeMaris, A., & Rao, V. (1992). Premarital cohabitation and subsequent marital stability in the United States: A reassessment. *Journal of Marriage and the Family, 54*, 178–190.

Duff, A., & Truitt, G. C. (1992). *The spousal equivalent handbook.* New York: Plume.

Dumas, J., & Bélanger, A. (1997). *Report on the demographic situation in Canada 1996: Current demographic analysis.* Ottawa, Ontario: Statistics Canada, Demography Division.

Elizabeth, V. (2000). Cohabitation, marriage, and the unruly consequences of difference. *Gender and Society, 14*, 87–110.

Espenshade, T. (1979). The economic consequences of divorce. *Journal of Marriage and the Family, 41*, 615–625.

Fennelly, K., Kadiah, V., & Ortiz, V. (1989). The cross-cultural study of fertility among Hispanic adolescents in the Americas. *Family Planning Perspectives, 20*, 96–101.

Goode, W. J. (1963). *World revolution and family patterns.* Glencoe, IL: The Free Press.

Graefe, D. R., & Lichter, D. T. (1999). Life course transitions of American children: Parental cohabitation, marriage and single motherhood. *Demography, 36,* 205–217.

Gupta, S. (1999). The effects of marital status transitions on men's housework performance. *Journal of Marriage and the Family, 61,* 700–711.

Hall, D. R., & Zhao, J. (1995). Cohabitation and divorce in Canada: Testing the selectivity hypothesis. *Journal of Marriage and the Family, 57,* 421–427.

Hao, L. (1996). Family structure, private transfers, and the economic well-being of families with children. *Social Forces, 75,* 269–292.

Hareven, T. K. (1991). The history of the family and the complexity of social change. *The American Historical Review, 96,* 95–124.

Hareven, T. K. (1994). Aging and generational relations: A historical and life course perspective. *Annual Review of Sociology, 20,* 437–461.

Hoffman, S., & Holmes, J. (1976). Husbands, wives, and divorce. In G. Duncan & J. Morgan (Eds.), *Five thousand American families: Patterns of economic progress* (pp. 23–75). Ann Arbor, MI: Institute for Social Research.

Holden, K. C., & Smock, P. J. (1991). The economic costs of marital dissolution: Why do women bear a disproportionate cost? *Annual Review of Sociology, 17,* 51–78.

Holland, W. (2000). Intimate relationships in the new millennium: The assimilation of marriage and cohabitation? *Canadian Journal of Family Law, 17,* 114–168.

Ihara, T., Warner, R., & Hertz, F. (1999). *The living together kit: A legal guide for unmarried couples* (9th ed.). Berkeley, CA: Nolo Press.

Johnston, L., Bachman, J. G., & O'Malley, P. M. (1995). *Monitoring the future: Questionnaire response from the nation's high school seniors.* Ann Arbor, MI: Institute for Social Research.

Kiernan, K. (1988). The British family: contemporary trends and issues. *Journal of Marriage and the Family, 9,* 298–316.

Kiernan, K. (1999). Cohabitation in western Europe. *Population Trends, 96,* 25–32.

Landale, N. S., & Fennelly, K. (1992). Informal unions among mainland Puerto Ricans: Cohabitation or an alternative to legal marriage? *Journal of Marriage and the Family, 54,* 269–280.

Landale, N. S., & Forste, R. (1991). Patterns of entry into cohabitation and marriage among mainland Puerto Rican women. *Demography, 28,* 587–607.

LaPierre-Adamcyk, É., & Marcil-Gratton, N. (1999). Family status from the children's perspective. In *Canadian families at the approach of the year 2000* (pp. 207–233). Ottawa, Ontario: Statistics Canada.

LaPierre-Adamcyk, É., Neil, G., & Le Bourdais, C. (2000, March). *Nonmarital childbearing in Canada: From different paths to different meanings.* Paper presented at the annual meeting of the Population Association of America, Los Angeles, CA.

Le Bourdais, C., & Marcil-Gratton, N. (1996). Family transformations across the Canadian/American border: When the laggard becomes the leader. *Journal of Comparative Family Studies, 27,* 415–436.

Le Bourdais, C., Neill, G., & Turcotte, P. (2000). The changing face of conjugal relationships. *Canadian Social Trends, Statistics Canada Catalogue No. 11-008,* 14–17.

Lesthaeghe, R. (1983). A century of demographic and cultural change in Western Europe: An exploration of underlying dimensions. *Population and Development Review, 9,* 411–435.

Lesthaeghe, R., & Surkyn, J. (1988). Cultural dynamics and economic theories of fertility change. *Population and Development Review, 14,* 1–45.

Lichter, D. T., LeClere, F., & McLaughlin, D. (1991). Local marriage markets and the market behavior of black and white women. *American Journal of Sociology, 96,* 843–867.

Lichter, D. T., McLaughlin, C., Kephart, G., & Landry, D. (1992). Race and the retreat from marriage: A shortage of marriageable men? *American Sociological Review, 57,* 781–799.

Lillard, L. L., Brien, M. J., & Waite, L. J. (1995). Premarital cohabitation and subsequent marital dissolution: A matter of self-selection? *Demography, 32,* 437–457.

Loomis, L., & Landale, N. S. (1994). Nonmarital cohabitation and childbearing among black and white American women. *Journal of Marriage and the Family, 56,* 949–962.

Lloyd, K., & South, S. (1996). Contextual Influences on young men's transition to first marriage. *Social Forces, 74,* 1097–1119.

Lye, D., & Waldron, I. (1997). Attitudes toward cohabitation, family, and gender roles: Relationships to values and political ideology. *Sociological Perspectives, 40,* 199–225.

Manning, W. D. (1999, March). *Childbearing in cohabiting unions: Racial and ethnic differences.* Paper presented at the Annual Meeting of the Population Association of America, NY.

Manning W. D., & Landale., N. S. (1996). Racial and ethnic differences in the role of cohabitation in premarital childbearing. *Journal of Marriage and the Family, 58,* 63–77.

Manning, W. D., & Lichter, D. T. (1996). Parental cohabitation and children's economic well-being. *Journal of Marriage and the Family, 58,* 998–1010.

Manning, W. D., & Smock, P. J. (1995). Why marry? Race and the transition to marriage among cohabitors. *Demography, 32,* 509–520.

Manning, W. D., & Smock, P. J. (2000, March). *First comes cohabitation and then comes marriage? A research note.* Paper presented at the annual meeting of the Population Association of America, Los Angeles, CA.

Marcil-Gratton, N. (1998). *Growing up with mom and dad? The intricate family life courses of Canadian children*. Canadian Social Trends, Statistics Canada Catalogue No. 89-566-XIE.

Marcil-Gratton, N., & Le Bourdais, C. (1999). *Custody, access, and child support-Findings from the National Longitudinal Survey of Children and Youth*. Ottawa: Department of Justice.

Mare, R. D., & Winship, C. C. (1991). Socioeconomic change and the decline of marriage for blacks and whites. In C. Jencks & P. E. Peterson (Eds.), *The urban underclass* (pp. 175–202). Washington, DC: Urban Institute.

Martin, T. C., & Bumpass, L. L. (1989). Recent trends in marital disruption. *Demography, 17*, 39–56.

Mason, K. O., Czajka, J. L., & Arber, S. (1976). Change in U.S. women's sex-role attitudes, 1964-74. *American Sociological Review, 41*, 573–596.

McLanahan, S. S., & Casper, L. C. (1995). Growing diversity and inequality in the American family. In R. Farley (ed.), *State of the union: America in the 1990s* (pp. 1–45). New York: Russell Sage.

Milan, A. (2000, Spring). One hundred years of families. *Canadian Social Trends*, 2-12.

Mongeau, J. (1999). The living conditions of families: Income and labor force activity. In *Canadian families at the approach of the year 2000* (pp. 235–271, No. 96-321-MPE No. 4). Ottawa: Statistics Canada.

Morgan, L. (1991). *After marriage ends: Economic consequences for midlife women*. New York: Russell Sage.

Morgan, S. P., McDaniel, A., Miller, A. T., & Preston, S. H. (1993). Racial differences in household and family structure at the turn of the century. *American Journal of Sociology, 98*, 798–828.

Morrison, D. R., & Ritualo, A. (2000). Routes to children's economic recovery after divorce: Are maternal cohabitation and remarriage equivalent? *American Sociological Review, 65*, 560–580.

Murphy, M. (2000). The evolution of cohabitation in Britain, 1960-95. *Population Studies, 54*, 43–56.

Nock, S. L. (1995). A comparison of marriages and cohabiting relationships. *Journal of Family Issues, 16*, 53–76.

Nock, S. L. (1998). *Marriage in men's lives*. New York: Oxford University Press.

Ono, H. (1998). Husbands' and wives' resources and marital dissolution. *Journal of Marriage and the Family, 60*, 674–689.

Oppenheimer, V. K., Kalmijn, M., & Lim, N. (1997). Men's career development and marriage timing during a period of rising inequality. *Demography, 34*, 311–330.

Oropesa, R. S. (1996). Normative beliefs about marriage and cohabitation: A comparison of non-Latino whites, Mexican Americans, and Puerto Ricans. *Journal of Marriage and the Family, 58*, 49–62.

Oropesa, R. S., Lichter, D. T., & Anderson, R. (1994). Marriage markets and the paradox of Mexican American nuptiality. *Journal of Marriage and the Family*, 56, 889–907.

Pagnini, D. L., & Rindfuss, R. R. (1993). The divorce of marriage and childbearing: Changing attitudes and behavior in the U.S. *Population and Development Review*, 19, 331–347.

Péron, Y. (1999). The evolution of census families from 1971 to 1991. In *Canadian families at the approach of the year 2000* (pp. 47–100, No. 96-321-MPE No. 4). Ottawa: Statistics Canada.

Pollard, M. S., & Wu, Z. (1998). Divergence of marriage patterns in Quebec and elsewhere in Canada. *Population and Development Review*, 24, 329–356.

Popenoe, D. (1993). American family decline: A review and appraisal. *Journal of Marriage and the Family*, 55, 542–555.

Popenoe, D., & Whitehead, B. D. (1999). *Should we live together? What young adults need to know about cohabitation and marriage* (The National Marriage Project: The Next Generation Series). Piscataway, NJ: Rutgers University.

Qian, Z. (1998). Changes in assortative mating: The impact of age and education, 1970–1990. *Demography*, 35, 279–292.

Qian, Z., & Preston, S. H. (1993). Changes in American marriage, 1972–1987. *American Sociological Review*, 58, 482–495.

Raley, R. K. (1996). A shortage of marriageable men? A note on the role of cohabitation in black-white differences in marriage rates. *American Sociological Review*, 69, 73–83.

Raley, R. K. (2001). Increasing fertility in cohabiting unions: Evidence for the second demographic transition in the United States? *Demography*, 38, 59–66.

Rao, K. V., & Trussell, J. (1989). Premarital cohabitation and marital stability: A reassessment of the Canadian evidence: Feedback. *Journal of Marriage and the Family*, 51, 535–540.

Rindfuss, R. R., Brewster, K. L., & Kavee, A. L. (1996). Women, work, and children: Behavioral and attitudinal change in the United States. *Population and Development Review*, 22, 457–482.

Rindfuss, R. R., & VandenHeuvel, A. (1990). Cohabitation: A precursor to marriage or an alternative to being single? *Population and Development Review*, 16, 703–726.

Ross, C. E. (1995). Reconceptualizing marital status as a continuum of social attachment. *Journal of Marriage and the Family*, 57, 129–140.

Schoen, R. (1992). First unions and the stability of first marriages. *Journal of Marriage and the Family*, 54, 281–284.

Schoen, R., & Weinick, R. M. (1993). Partner choice in marriages and cohabitations. *Journal of Marriage and the Family*, 55, 408–414.

Seltzer, J. A. (2000). Families formed outside of marriage. *Journal of Marriage and the Family*, 62, 1247–1268.

Shelton, B. A., & John, D. (1993). Does marital status make a difference? Housework among married and cohabiting men and women. *Journal of Family Issues, 14,* 401–420.

Smock, P. J. (2000). Cohabitation in the United States: An appraisal of research themes, findings, and implications. *Annual Review of Sociology, 26,* 1–20.

Smock, P. J., & Manning, W. D. (1997). Cohabiting partners' economic circumstances and marriage. *Demography, 34,* 331–341.

Smock, P. J., Manning, W. D., & Gupta, S. (1999). The effect of marriage and divorce on women's economic well-being. *American Sociological Review, 64,* 794–812.

Sørensen, A., & McLanahan, S. S. (1987). Married women's economic dependency. *American Journal of Sociology, 93,* 659–687.

South, S. J. (1991). Sociodemographic differentials in mate selection preferences. *Journal of Marriage and the Family, 53,* 928–940.

South, S. J. (1993). Racial and ethnic differences in the desire to marry. *Journal of Marriage and the Family, 55,* 357–370.

South, S. J., & Spitze, G. (1994). Housework in marital and nonmarital households. *American Sociological Review, 59,* 327–347.

Sweet, J. A., Bumpass, L. L., & Call, V. (1988). *The design and content of the National Survey of Families and Households* (NSFH Working Paper No. 1, Center for Demography and Ecology). Madison: University of Wisconsin-Madison.

Teachman, J. D., & Polonko. K. (1990). Cohabitation and marital stability in the United States. *Social Forces, 69,* 207–220.

Teachman, J. D., Thomas, J., & Paasch, K. (1991). Legal status and stability of coresidential unions. *Demography, 28,* 571–586.

Testa, M., Astone, N., Krogh, M., & Neckerman, K. (1989). Employment and marriage among inner-city fathers. *Annals of the American Academy of Political and Social Science, 501,* 79–91.

Thomson, E., & Colella, U. (1992). Cohabitation and marital stability: Quality or commitment? *Journal of Marriage and the Family, 54,* 259–267.

Thornton, A. T. (1988). Cohabitation and marriage in the 80s. *Demography, 25,* 497–508.

Thornton, A. T. (1989). Changing attitudes toward family issues in the United States. *Journal of Marriage and the Family, 51,* 873–893.

Thornton, A. T. (1991). Influence of the marital history of parents on the marital and cohabitation experiences of children. *American Journal of Sociology, 96,* 868–894.

Thornton, A. T., Axinn, W. G., & Hill, D. (1992). Reciprocal effects of religiosity, cohabitation, and marriage. *American Journal of Sociology, 98,* 628–651.

Thornton, A. T., Axinn, W. G., & Teachman, J. D. (1995). The influence of school enrollment and accumulation on cohabitation and marriage in early adulthood. *American Sociological Review, 60,* 762–774.

Touleman, L. (1997). Cohabitation is here to stay. *Population: An English Selection,* *9,* 11–46.

Turcotte, P., & Bélanger, A. (1997). *The dynamics of formation and dissolution of first common-law unions in Canada.* Ottawa: Statistics Canada.

Turcotte, P., & Goldscheider, F. (1998). Evolution of factors influencing first union formation in Canada. *Canadian Studies in Population, 25,* 145–173.

U.S. Bureau of the Census. (1998a). Unpublished tables B marital status and living arrangements: March 1998 (update). *Current Population Reports, P20-514.* Washington, DC.

U.S. Bureau of the Census. (1998b). Household and family characteristics: March 1998 (update). *Current Population Reports, P20-515.* Washington, DC.

Villeneuve-Gokalp, C. (1991). From marriage to informal union: Recent changes in the behavior of French couples. *Population: An English Selection, 3,* 81–111.

Waite, L. (1995). Does marriage matter? *Demography, 32,* 483–507.

Watkins, S. C., Menken, J. A., & Bongaarts, J. (1987). Demographic foundations of family change. *American Sociological Review, 52,* 346–358.

Wilkie, J. R. (1993). Changes in U.S. men's attitudes toward the family provider role, 1972–1989. *Gender & Society, 7,* 261–279.

Willis, R., & Michael, R. T. (1994). Innovation in family formation: Evidence on cohabitation in the United States. In J. Ermisch & N. Ogawa (Eds.), *The family, the market and the state in ageing societies* (pp. 9–45). New York: Oxford University Press.

Wilson, W. J. (1987). *The truly disadvantaged.* Chicago: University of Chicago Press.

Wolfinger, N. H. (in press). The effects of family structure of origin on offspring cohabitation duration. *Sociological Inquiry.*

Wu, L. L. (1996). Effects of family instability, income, and income instability on the risk of premarital birth. *American Sociological Review, 61,* 386–406.

Wu, L. L., & Martinson B. C. (1993). Family structure and the risk of a premarital birth. *American Sociological Review, 58,* 210–232.

Wu, Z., & Balakrishnan, T. R. (1992). Attitudes towards cohabitation and marriage in Canada. *Journal of Comparative Family Studies, 23,* 1–12.

Wu, Z., & Balakrishnan, T. R. (1994). Cohabitation after marital disruption in Canada. *Journal of Marriage and the Family, 56,* 723–734.

Wu, Z., & Balakrishnan, T. R. (1995). Dissolution of premarital cohabitation in Canada. *Demography, 32,* 521–532.

Wu, Z., & Pollard, M. (2000). Economic circumstances and the stability of nonmarital cohabitation. *Journal of Family Issues, 21,* 303–328.

5

What Are the Choices for Low-Income Families?: Cohabitation, Marriage, and Remaining Single

Rukmalie Jayakody
The Pennsylvania State University

Natasha Cabrera
National Institute for Child Health and Human Development

As cohabitation becomes increasingly prevalent, social scientists are struggling to understand its meaning and role in American family life. Current estimates indicate that there are about 4.9 million cohabiting households and that 56% of first unions are preceded by cohabitation (Bumpass & Lu, 2000; Casper & Cohen, 2000). Smock and Gupta (chap. 4, in this volume) provide an interesting and timely review on the nature, frequency, and implications of cohabitation for family structure and marriage in the United States and Canada. They argue that the central debate about the significance of cohabitation is whether it is a threat to legal marriage. Overall, they conclude that "cohabitation is posing an increasingly potent challenge to marriage as a form of coresidential, conjugal union" (p. 74).

We focus on this issue—whether cohabitation poses a threat to marriage—within the context of economically disadvantaged families. As several researchers have noted, cohabitation and marriage rates vary dramatically by socioeconomic status. Cohabitation appears to be negatively correlated with both education (Bumpass & Lu, 2000; Manning & Lichter, 1996); Thornton, Axinn, & Teachman, 1995) and income (Casper & Bianchi, in press), whereas marriage is more likely for economically advantaged individuals (Lichter, LeClere, & McLaughlin, 1991; Mare & Winship, 1991; Oppenheimer, Kalmijn, & Lim, 1997). In particular, economic circumstances appear a powerful predictor of marriage. For example, marriage rates for young Black men (aged 18 to 29) vary widely by earnings. While over half of Black men in this age group who earn $20,000 or more a year are married, the rates plummet for those earning less—only 7% earning between $1,000 and $5,000 annually are married (Sum & Fogg, 1990).

It has been argued that cohabitation can pose a threat to marriage in one of two ways. First, cohabitation can threaten marriage by reducing the number of individuals who marry. That is, the option to cohabit could funnel some people out of marriage and into cohabitation. We evaluate this argument by focusing on the union formation decisions of poor, single mothers. Second, cohabitation may threaten marriage by decreasing the stability afforded by marriage. Because cohabitation is less stable than marriage, cohabitation can increase the instability in individual's lives, and this instability can be problematic, especially for children. Focusing on the dramatic increase in nonmarital childbearing and the role cohabitation plays in this phenomenon can help us examine this hypothesis. We argue that nonmarital childbearing is central to discussions of cohabitation because the increases in nonmarital childbearing are better explained by changes in marital behavior than by changes in fertility behavior (Garfinkel & McLanahan, 1986).

Our main argument is that marriage and cohabitation are not the only options for low- income women and that the issue of whether cohabitation threatens marriage must be examined within a range of options that include cohabitation, marriage, and remaining single. While marriage is often treated as the default category when discussing cohabitation, an equally valid choice for many families is remaining single and not marrying and not cohabiting. Evaluating whether cohabitation reduces the number of individuals who marry or whether it increases instability in the life course and thereby jeopardizes well-being requires us to examine the range of options available to this population, which include cohabitation, marriage, and remaining single.

DOES COHABITATION REDUCE
THE NUMBER MARRYING?

In absolute terms, cohabitation may pose a risk to marriage among low-income individuals because more people are choosing to cohabit, which means that fewer people are marrying. Without the availability of cohabitation, these individuals would have married. When cohabitation is available, people are choosing to cohabit instead. This view implies that one decision has already been made—the decision to form a union. After deciding to form a union together, couples must now decide on the type of union, either marriage or cohabitation. These union formation decisions are illustrated in Fig. 5.1. If Fig. 5.1 accurately reflects the decision-making strategy of individuals—that they first decide whether or not to

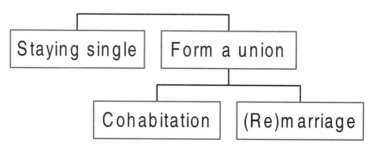

FIG. 5.1   Union formation: Marriage versus cohabitation.

form a union and then decide on what type of union to form—it is clear that co-habitation decreases the number marrying by offering them an alternative union type. If cohabitation was eliminated as an option, through a high tax on cohabiting couples or other penalties, then the number marrying would increase, because those who would have cohabited prior to the tax or penalties would now be left with marriage as the only type of union to form.

For low-income women in the United States, however, the decision-making strategy regarding union formation may be more accurately displayed in Fig. 5.2, where individuals are faced with a three-way decision—do they remain single, marry, or cohabit? It is plausible that for those in improvised economic situations, marriage may be an unrealistic option. Others may find marriage an unattractive option. Rather than deciding between marriage and cohabitation, individuals also consider the alternative to remain single and live without a partner present in the household.

Marriage—An Unrealistic Option

For low-income individuals in particular, marriage may be an unrealistic option. Nonmarriage is particularly common among the poorest segment of the population and this issue has gained increasing policy attention. The recent welfare reform legislation of 1996, for example, includes several references to marriage, arguing that marriage "is the foundation of a successful society" and "is an essential institution that promotes the interests of children" (Personal Responsibility and Work Opportunity and Reconciliation Act of 1996, section 101). In fact, the promotion of marriage has become an important policy goal. Yet, for poor individuals, and particularly for poor women with children, marriage is an increasingly unlikely prospect (Bennett, Bloom, & Craig, 1989; Bumpass & Sweet, 1989).

Economic well-being is an important consideration when contemplating marriage. People across socioeconomic groups consider economic stability as an important prerequisite to marriage. Wilson (1986) argued that the most important factor explaining the decline in marriage and the increase in single-parent families in African-American communities is the declining earnings power of African-American men. Edin (2000) argued that economic factors are a necessary, although not sufficient, factor for marriage among low-income single mothers. Anderson's (1990) ethnographic research also points to the importance of economic considerations in marriage decisions. Anderson reported that young moth-

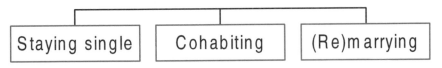

FIG. 5.2 Union formation?

ers hope to marry the fathers of their children, but characterize this as an unrealistic dream of middle-class life because of the economic situations of their partners. Similarly, Sullivan's (1989) ethnographic research suggests that expectations of marriage vary depending on employment status.

In trying to understand why low-income women, and low-income single mothers in particular, do not marry, Edin (2000) conducted in-depth, repeated qualitative interviews with 292 low-income single mothers in three U.S. cities (Edin, 2000). Issues of money emerged as a powerful concept for understanding a woman's likelihood of marrying and staying married. One African-American mother living in Camden, New Jersey told Edin (2000) and her colleagues:

> You can't get married and go on living with your mother. That's just like playing house. She expects your husband to be able to provide for you and if he can't, what he doing marrying you in the first place! (p. 118)

For these women, the father of their child or their boyfriend is likely to have low levels of education, limited skills, and uncertain employment prospects. When faced with the choice of marrying an economically "unstable" man, nearly all the women Edin interviewed told her that rather than marry their child's father, they preferred to live separately or to cohabit. It is not that these women did not want to marry, but that marriage is an unrealistic option for them.

Although conventional wisdom holds that poor parents do not hold marriage in high regard, or that marriage norms in their communities are nonexistent, there is no indication that the value of marriage, or the desire for marriage, if economic conditions permitted, have declined. In talking about marriage, one of Edin's respondents stated, "Am I going to marry him? Of course! If he didn't have a steady job? No, no" (p. 119). Most of the mothers whom Edin interviewed expressed a strong desire to become "respectable." Respectability, as defined by these mothers, meant marriage to an employed partner who earned wages significantly above the minimum wage. Respectability, however, could not be achieved by marrying someone with an unstable work history, someone involved with criminal activity, or someone who had little chance of improving his situation over time.

The economic foundations of marriage are aptly described by one young woman living in Charleston, South Carolina:

> I want to get married. I've always wanted to get married. [My baby's father], he is doing pretty good, but I am not going to marry him until we get some land. [We'll] start off with a trailer, live in that for about 10 years, and then build a dream house. But I am not going to get married and pay rent to someone else. When we save up enough money to [buy] an acre of land and [can finance] a trailer, then we'll marry. (p. 120)

In interview after interview, mothers stressed the seriousness of the marriage commitment and the belief that it should last forever. They expressed strong moral objections to marrying a man whose economic situation would increase their chances of divorce. As one woman stated, "Men simply don't earn enough to support a family. This leads to couples breaking up" (p. 5). Their high esteem for marriage led them to forgo marriage until an economically viable partner came along. For many of these women, marriage is not a realistic option available given their economic situation and the economic situation of the men around them. While sociologists often discuss women's economic independence when examining marriage, these findings indicate that for low-income individuals we should also focus on men's economic dependence. These data raise important issues about the value of marriage and the pragmatic and realistic options available to these women.

Marriage—An Unattractive Option

Although many low-income single mothers viewed marriage as an unrealistic option, others, especially those who had been married in the past, were more reluctant to consider marriage as part of their future (Edin, 2000). The issues of power and trust often came up when women were discussing reasons for not marrying. When single mothers were asked what they liked best about being a single parent, their most frequent response was "I am in charge" or "I am in control." Unions with men, especially marital unions, were increasingly viewed as a threat to their control. Some women also felt that the presence of a man might impede their efforts to spend time with their children.

Other women expressed a reluctance to enter into a marital or cohabiting union because of their distrust of men. Furstenberg (1995, 1988) described this as the "culture of gender distrust" and argued that it is an important factor in men's and women's evaluations of their partners and their marriage and cohabiting prospects. Many women described previous experiences with unfaithful boyfriends and husbands as leading them to believe that men just could not be faithful. As one Black mother said, "I would like to find a nice man to marry, but I know that men cannot be trusted. That's why I treat them the way I do—like the dogs they are. I think that all men will cheat, regardless of how much he loves her" (p. 124).

The distrust between men and women appears to be heightened among couples who experience chronic economic instability and Edin's (2000) findings identify this as an important issue affecting poor mothers' desire to remain unmarried. These women who are looking for a better life often choose not to form a union with a man who might bring them down.

Remaining Single—Not Marrying and Not Cohabiting

Economic considerations are a factor not only in marriage decisions but also in cohabitation decisions. Many mothers choose to remain single when the other alternative is keeping an economically unproductive man around the house. Nearly all the single mothers Edin interviewed said they had a "pay and stay" rule. When a man lost his job, he lost his right to cohabit. As one African-American mother living in Camden, New Jersey said:

> . . . he lost his job at the auto body shop when they went [bankrupt] and closed down. Then he couldn't find another one. . . Finally, I couldn't do it anymore [because] it was just too much pressure on me [even though] he is the love of my life. I told him he had to leave even though I knew it really wasn't his fault that [he wasn't working]. (p. 119)

Some mothers describe the importance of remaining single in order to improve marriage prospects. That is, having an economically unstable man living in the house not only puts a strain on the household budget, but also precluded a woman's ability to form a relationship with an alternative, employed man. As one African-American mother told Edin (2000):

> I've been with the baby's father for almost 10 years, since high school graduation. He's talking marriage, but what I'm trying to do now is get rid of him. He just lost his job. I can do bad by myself, I don't need no one helping me [do bad]. I want somebody better, somebody [who can bring home] a regular paycheck. [So] I'm trying to get rid of him right now. (p. 119)

As long as she is unmarried, she has the flexibility to lower household costs by getting rid of this man and maintain the possibility of replacing him with an economically productive man. These women believe that among the alternatives available to them, remaining single and not cohabiting is the best choice.

In this discussion, we have tried to illustrate that for low-income families, the decisions regarding union formation depicted in Fig. 5.1 may not reflect their range of options or choices. Because of economic conditions and lack of partner trust, marriage may be an unrealistic option. At the same time, the lack of prospective economic security, which makes marriage and cohabitation unattractive, may also increase the benefits to remaining single. Economic and cultural forces may conspire to make union formation, whether marriage or cohabitation, unavailable to them. Because of the unavailability of marriage, the unattractiveness of marriage and cohabitation, and the importance of deciding to remain living alone, it does not appear that cohabitation has posed a serious threat to marriage for this economic group.

DOES COHABITATION RESULT IN POORER OUTCOMES?

The second issue we focus on is whether cohabitation increases instability in an individual's life and thereby results in poorer outcomes for families and children. In examining this issue, we focus on nonmarital childbearing. Nonmarital child-bearing should be included in discussions of marriage and cohabitation because analyses have shown that the dramatic increase in nonmarital births are better explained by changes in marital behavior than by changes in fertility (Garfinkel & McLanahan, 1986). That is, the probability of marrying by the time of the child's birth has decreased for both African Americans and Whites over the past few decades. Rates of nonmarital childbearing have increased dramatically. Nearly one third of all births in the United States today occur outside of marriage and the proportions are even higher among minority populations—69% of African-American births were nonmarital in 1999 (Ventura & Bachrach, 2000). Although these rates are high, it is interesting to note that the rates are even higher in Scandinavian countries (and France). However, while the majority of unmarried parents in Europe are living together at the time of the child's birth, less than half of the unmarried parents in the United States are cohabiting.

Again, focusing on economically disadvantaged families, we argue that rather than posing a threat to marriage, cohabitation plays an important role for some unmarried parents and their children and indicates the hopefulness and optimism held by many individuals toward marriage and family. Additionally, we again argue that the alternative of not marrying and not cohabiting needs to be considered. Although cohabitation may be less stable than marriage and produce poorer outcomes than marriage (Smock & Gupta, chap. 4, this volume), there may be benefits when cohabitation is compared to remaining single (not marrying and not cohabiting). Especially for children, having your parents cohabit may have advantages compared to having them never live together.

In discussing these issues, we rely primarily on data from the Fragile Families and Child Well-being Study, a national, birth cohort study of unmarried parents and their children (Reichman, Garfinkel, McLanahan, & Teitler, in press). To generate a random sample of births, all parents giving birth in city hospitals over a period of time were interviewed. Most parents were interviewed in the hospital immediately after their child's birth, but some fathers were interviewed in the field shortly after the birth. Results indicate that the vast majority of unmarried parents are committed to one another and have high hopes of raising their child together (McLanahan, Garfinkel, Reichman, & Teitler, 1999). Nearly 82% of parents in this sample were romantically involved with each other at the time of their child's birth—46% were cohabiting and 36% were romantically involved but living apart. Not only are most unmarried parents romantically involved at the time of the child's birth, but most fathers contributed financially during the pregnancy and plan to stay involved with the mother and their child after the birth. Results also indicate that unmarried parents have high hopes about their chances of getting married. Fathers, in particular, are optimistic about marriage, with almost three quarters reporting a "pretty good" or "almost certain" chance of marrying the mother (Waller, 1999).

These results indicate that families hold marriage in high esteem and do not appear to consider cohabitation the end but rather the beginning of a more serious relationship. That is, parents who are cohabiting at the time of the child's birth assess their chances of marrying as being much higher than noncohabiting parents. Assessing relationship quality, Carlson and McLanahan (2000) found that cohabitors experienced higher levels of relationship quality than noncohabiting parents. These authors conclude that for all items of supportiveness and companionship,[1] cohabiting couples appear to be somewhat more similar to married couples than to noncohabiting, unmarried parents.

McLanahan and colleagues (1999) stated that "though many of these unmarried couples do not live together, they view themselves as collaborative units" (p. 21). One of the most important findings from this survey is that the vast majority of unwed parents view themselves as families. At the time of the child's birth, 82% of unwed parents are in romantic relationships, nearly 80% believe their chances of marriage are good, and more than 90% of the mothers want the father to be involved in raising the child (McLanahan et al., 1999).

These findings offer much hope for the future of these unmarried families and point to the importance of strengthening families, regardless of their marital status. We believe that these preliminary results from the Fragile Families data suggest that cohabitation is not necessarily a threat to marriage and that many individuals view cohabitation as a step toward it. At the very least, it is clear that cohabitation is an important indicator of expectations to marry (Waller, 1999). Unfortunately, we know that this optimism about marriage and family that follows a child's birth is not long lived. The stress and pressure of daily life alter this rosy picture so that in a few years mothers and fathers are more antagonistic toward each other and fathers are less involved with their children. With additional supports, however, these families may be able to achieve their marital and family expectations.

Cohabitation, when compared to remaining single, may be an important predictor of future father involvement if the parents' marital expectations are not realized. For example, studies have found that the mother and father living together at the time of the birth is an important positive predictor of father involvement. The desire to marry the mother and to stay involved in the child's life shown by cohabiting parents at the time of the birth, may result in more positive mother–

---

[1] Supportiveness in the relationship is measured by mother's reports about the frequency that the father (a) is fair and willing to compromise when they have a disagreement; (b) hits or slaps her when he is angry; (c) expresses affection or love; (d) insults or criticizes her or her ideas; and (e) encourages or helps her to do things that are important to her. Companionship is represented by mothers' reports of whether they have done any of he following four activities with the baby's in the past month: (a) visited with friends; (b) gone out to a movie, sporting event or some other entertainment; (c) ate out at a restaurant; and (d) helped each other solve problems.

father relationships and thereby result in more involved nonresident fathers. Even if cohabitation does not translate into marriage, this positive relationship between a mother and a father may be carried forward.

CONCLUSION

Is cohabitation posing an increasing threat to marriage? We argue that in order to answer this question all the choices available to low-income families need to be considered. Rather than marriage versus cohabitation, three choices are available: marriage, cohabitation, and remaining single. When all three options are considered, we believe there is little evidence supporting the claim that cohabitation increasingly threatens marriage among economically disadvantaged families in the United States. Although the large number of people cohabiting may be seen as decreasing the marriage pool, it seems unlikely that many of these cohabiting couples would marry if cohabitation was eliminated. Many would remain single. Cohabitation, when compared to marriage, does appear to increases instability in the life course and results in poorer outcomes. However, when compared to remaining single, we believe that cohabitation likely holds some benefits for parents and children. Emphasizing the benefits of marriage over cohabitation is an unrealistic focus for many poor families. Instead, all available options, including remaining single, need to be considered. While marriage may be the ideal, cohabitation or living alone appear the most realistic choices available to many poor families.

ACKNOWLEDGMENTS

We thank Marcy Carlson and Ariel Kalil for helpful comments on prior drafts.

REFERENCES

Anderson, E. (1990). *Streetwise: Race, class, and change in an urban community.* Chicago: University of Chicago Press.

Bennett, N. G., Bloom, D. E., & Craig, P. (1989). The divergence of black and white marriage patterns. *American Journal of Sociology, 95,* 692–722.

Bumpass, L. L., & Lu, H. H. (2000). Trends in cohabitation and implications for children's family contexts in the United States. *Population Studies, 54,* 29–41.

Bumpass, L. L., & Sweet, J. A. (1989). National estimates of cohabitation. *Demography, 26,* 615–625.

Carlson, M., & McLanahan, S. (2000). Parent's relationship quality and father involvement in fragile families. Working Paper #00-09-FF. Princeton, NJ: Bendheim-Thoman Center for Research on Child Well-being, Princeton University.

Casper, L. M., & Bianchi, S. M. (Forthcoming). *Trends in the American family.* Thousand Oaks, CA: Sage.

Casper, L. M., & Cohen, P. (2000). How does POSSLQ measure up? Historical estimates of cohabitation. *Demography, 37*, 237–245.

Edin, K. (2000). What do low-income single mothers say about marriage? *Social Problems, 47*, 112–133.

Furstenberg, F. F. (1988). Good dads—bad dads: Two faces of fatherhood? In A. Cherlin (Ed.), *The changing American family and public policy* (pp. 193–218). Washington, DC: The Urban Institute Press.

Furstenberg, F. F. (1995). Fathering in the inner city: Paternal participation and public policy. In W. Marsiglio (Ed.), *Fatherhood: Contemporary theory, research, and social policy* (pp. 119–147). Thousand Oaks: Sage.

Garfinkel, I., & McLanahan, S. S. (1986). *Single mothers and their children: A new American dilemma.* Washington, DC: Urban Institute Press.

Lichter, D. T., LeClere, F., & McLaughlin, D. (1991). Local marriage markets and the market behavior of black and white women. *American Journal of Sociology, 96*, 843–867.

Manning, W. D., & Lichter, D. T. (1996). Parental cohabitation and children's economic well-being. *Journal of Marriage and the Family, 58*, 998–1010.

Mare, R. D., & Winship, C. C. (1991). Socioeconomic change and the decline of marriage for blacks and whites. In C. Jencks & P. E. Peterson (Eds.), *The urban underclass* (pp. 175–202). Washington, DC: Urban Institute.

McLanahan, S., Garfinkel, I., Reichman, N., & Teitler, J. (1999). Unwed parents or fragile families? Implications for welfare and child support policy. Working Paper #00-04. Princeton, NJ: Bendheim-Thoman Center for Research on Child Well-being, Princeton University.

Oppenheimer, V. K., Kalmijn, M., & Lim, N. (1997). Men's career development and marriage timing during a period of rising inequality. *Demography, 34*, 311–330.

Reichman, N., Garfinkel, I., McLanahan, S., & Teitler, J. (in press). The fragile families and child well-being study: Background, research design, and sampling issues. *Children and Youth Services Review.*

Sullivan, M. (1989). *Getting paid: Youth crime and work in the inner city.* Ithaca: Cornell University Press.

Sum, A., & Fogg, N. (1990). The changing economic fortunes of young black men in America. *Black Scholar, 21*, 47–55.

Thornton, A., Axinn, W., & Teachman, J. (1995). The influence of school enrollment and accumulation on cohabitation and marriage in early adulthood. *American Sociological Review, 60*(5), 762–774.

Ventura, S. J., & Bachrach, C. S. (2000). *Nonmarital childbearing in the United States, 1940-1999.* National Vital Statistics Report, *48*(6). Hyattsville, MD: National Center for Health Statistics.

Waller, M. (1999). High hopes: Unmarried parents' expectations about marriage at the time of their child's birth. Working Paper #99-07-FF. Princeton, NJ: Bendheim-Thoman Center for Research on Child Well-being, Princeton University.

Wilson, W. J. (1986). *The truly disadvantaged: The inner city, the underclass, and public policy.* Chicago: University of Chicago Press.

Wilson, W. J. (1996). *When work disappears: The world of the new urban poor.* New York: Alfred A. Knopf.

6

What Mothers Teach, What Daughters Learn: Gender Mistrust and Self-Sufficiency Among Low-Income Women

Rebekah Levine Coley
Boston College

The prevalence of cohabitation has risen dramatically in recent decades, with demographers and other social scientists eager to understand the meaning, precursors, and impacts of this family form. In their comprehensive chapter on demographic trends in cohabitation in North America, Smock and Gupta (chap. 4, this volume) review the changing patterns of family formation, and discuss the primary factors that have been proposed as correlates or predictors of cohabitation, marriage, and nonmarital childbearing, such as social class, religion, egalitarianism, and liberalism. Smock and Gupta also review patterns of cohabitation among various racial/ethnic groups, which indicate substantially higher rates of cohabitation and nonmarital childbearing (both within and outside of cohabiting unions) among African Americans and Hispanics than among non-Hispanic Whites in the United States. Like others, Smock and Gupta attribute these racial/ethnic differences primarily to income and wealth differentials. They also note that "culture," that is the "set of beliefs, values, and behavior patterns that characterize a group" (p. 63) likely impacts both the role and meaning of cohabitation in different subgroups.

However, Smock and Gupta's chapter leaves unanswered numerous questions concerning the propagation and development of beliefs related to cohabitation, marriage, and nonmarital childbearing. Furthermore, they devote little attention to the question of whether gender influences beliefs or behaviors related to cohabitation. These are the topics on which I focus. Given the significantly different patterns of cohabitation and marriage between lower income versus higher income groups and between African Americans and Hispanics versus Whites in the United States, how can we move beyond economic explanations to focus on possible differences in the meaning and role of cohabitation in these groups? How do gender roles and beliefs play a part in explaining changing family patterns? In short, I claim that one must consider individuals' and groups' psychological understanding of the intersections between partnering, childbearing, and marriage in order to gain a greater understanding of the demographic patterns.

THE DICHOTOMIZATION OF FAMILY ROLES

One way in which one can seek to better understand the growing prevalence of cohabitation is to compare it to other patterns of family relationships. For this purpose, I consider fathering behaviors. Smock and Gupta note the increasing dichotomization in cohabitation, whereby in some cases it appears that cohabitation is becoming a substitute for marriage, with long-term stability and childrearing becoming increasingly prevalent. Within North America, this pattern is especially apparent among French speakers in Quebec (see Smock and Gupta's summary of the literature in this area), and among Puerto Ricans residing in the mainland United States (Manning & Lansdale, 1996). In other cases, it appears that cohabitation is becoming more unstable and short term and less linked to marriage, with an increasing proportion of cohabiting unions separating within a few years.

Interestingly, a similar dichotomy is apparent in data on paternal involvement and parenting behaviors, with some fathers becoming more involved and invested in childrearing and parenting than ever before, while at the same time an increasing proportion of fathers are becoming highly disengaged from their children, not living with them, not providing financial support, and not "parenting" their children in a meaningful sense (Cabrera, Tamis-LeMonda, Bradley, Hofferth, & Lamb, 2000; Coley, 2001; Coley & Chase-Lansdale, 1999; Furstenberg, 1988, 1995). This pattern may be seen as indicative of the voluntary nature of fatherhood in today's society, supported by the lack of clear cultural, moral, and even legal guidelines regarding family responsibilities and roles (Coley, 2001).

In short, one could hypothesize that the division in patterns of cohabitation in recent years is part of a broader trend of a dichotomization in the stability of family roles and relationships, exemplified by the split seen in fathers' involvement with their children. As family roles become more diverse and less directed by societal norms, and as women's increased financial independence leads to a wider variety of familial and childrearing options, we see a broader array of behaviors, with a seemingly greater propensity not for "regression to the mean" but rather for movement to the borders of behavior. Further research is needed to more fully compare and contrast these family patterns and to address whether similar economic factors and cultural norms do indeed underlie them both. Additionally, more attention is needed to examining the development of individuals' conceptions of family and parental roles and the ways in which such conceptions predict family behaviors.

BENEFITS AND COSTS OF COHABITATION
AND MARRIAGE

A second manner in which one can consider the meaning and prevalence of cohabitation is by addressing the similarities and the differences in individuals' experiences between cohabitation and marriage. One way of doing this is by address-ing gender differences. On the similarities side, Smock and Gupta (Chap. 4, this volume) state that both cohabitation and marriage are "romantic and coresidential unions that allow individuals to pool income, to bear and/or raise children as a couple, and to generally benefit in emotional, social, and economic ways from living with a partner" (p. 68). While concurring on the similarities between the two residential states (although see Waite, 1999–2000 for an alternative view), I think it is also important to consider differences on these points within both cohabitative and marital states, primarily by looking at gender-based differences. For example, both cohabitation and marriage appear to confer similar positive influences on psy-chological well-being, yet research indicates that these benefits are more pronounced for men than for women (Waite, 2000). Additionally, a similar pattern of division of labor is seen in both cohabiting and married couples, but in both, women per-form the lion's share of the housework and childrearing tasks (Gupta, 1999). In each of these areas, therefore, similar patterns are apparent in marriage and in co-habitation, and in both cases partnerships appear to offer higher benefits for men than for women.

In other arenas, however, women appear to be the primary beneficiaries of legal rights related to parenthood and marital status. For example, presuming that children are born to a couple and that paternity is established, children of previ-ously cohabitating parents theoretically have similar rights to government ben-efits and child support as do children of previously married parents. As women are most likely to be the residential parent following a partner dissolution, they are also the most likely recipients of such financial benefits. Additionally, cohabi-tation confers fewer legal rights regarding tax breaks and less clear child custody and visitation rights than do marriages, thus presumably disadvantaging men more than women in, or following the dissolution of, cohabiting unions versus mar-riages. In summary, a brief consideration of the gender-related patterns of costs and benefits of cohabitation indicate that although men appear to benefit more on personal and psychological levels, when considering issues related to children, women, as the typical custodial parents, appear to have a slight advantage in the rights granted by the legal system.

GENDER MISTRUST AND THE MOVEMENT AWAY FROM MARRIAGE

A third and related issue to consider in delving into the meaning of cohabitation, marriage, and nonmarital childbearing is that of male–female relationships, ex-pectations, and beliefs. In discussing various hypotheses concerning the decreas-ing prevalence of marriage and the increasing prevalence of cohabitation, Smock and Gupta focus primarily on socioeconomic (education, income, and wealth) and philosophical (egalitarianism, liberalism, religiosity) predictors. They also briefly note the importance of cultural beliefs and values and their impact on expectations and behaviors regarding partnering and childbearing. These later constructs deserve further attention and expansion.

Wilson (1987), in his seminal book *The truly disadvantaged*, proposed a theory concerning a lack of "marriageable men" within urban African-American communities. Given the declines in low-skilled men's employment and wages in recent decades, Wilson argued, substantial proportions of urban low-income African-American women have disengaged from marriage due to men's weak presentation as marriageable material.

Edin (2000) expanded on this concept with her provocative qualitative work with low-income mothers from multiple racial/ethnic backgrounds. Edin claimed that low-income women were moving away from marriage because of four factors: affordability, respectability, trust, and control. In short, women saw men's employment and economic stability as a necessary precursor to marriage, and as a defining feature of a respectable match. Women's lack of trust in men was also a pervasive theme in their explanations of the low rate of marriage in their communities. Distrusting men's sexual fidelity, their ability to handle money and provide consistent financial support, and their responsibility with children all lead women to discount men's suitability as marital partners. Finally, women reported a strong desire to be in control of their lives, their households, and their children, and viewed marriage as a relinquishing of such control.

In summary, the women in Edin's study viewed marriage as an extremely difficult state to acquire, and one that necessitated a number of preconditions being met. In contrast, cohabitation afforded women greater control and required a lower level of these preconditions. As cohabitation is more easily disengaged from than marriage, women saw it as a viable alternative until they could find a partner with adequate financial resources and trustworthiness and could themselves be in a strong enough financial position to allow the loss of control that marriage required. The level of gender mistrust displayed by the women in Edin's sample was a striking example of psychological processes that effect the prevalence of cohabitation and partner instability.

Edin's work suggests that much of this gender mistrust comes from women's personal experiences with men. However, women are also likely to learn from the experiences of others close to them such as siblings and peers. Such learning can also happen across generations, and it is possible that the beliefs and behaviors of new cohorts of young people are influenced by the lessons that they learn from their families and parents.

This question will be addressed with data from the Families and Communities (FIC) Study, a survey of 302 low-income African-American families with adolescent daughters (age 15–18 years) in Chicago. This study collected extensive interview information from a representative sample of adolescent girls and their mothers from three high poverty urban neighborhoods concerning a wide variety of demographic, economic, psychological, and attitudinal characteristics.

Most of the families in the sample were headed by single mothers: 16% of the women were married, and 18% were cohabiting with a partner, although 68% had been married at least once, and 60% had cohabited at least once. The families were predominantly poor: 62% had incomes below the poverty line with an additional 29% characterized as near poor, 50% were welfare recipients, and the average education of the mothers was less than high school (see Coley & Chase-Lansdale, 2000b, for a more extensive description of the sampling procedures, sample characteristics, and measures employed in the Families in Communities Study).

During extensive in-person interviews with the mothers in the FIC study, we asked a number of open-ended questions to tap into women's conceptions of men and male–female relationships, the messages that they were relaying to their daughters in this arena, and the lessons that daughters were internalizing. More specifically, we asked mothers to share with us how they described their daughters' biological fathers to them (the daughters); what they had taught their daughters about men; and what lessons or expectations they thought their daughters had learned by watching their own relationships with men. Mothers also reported on their hopes and dreams for their daughters' future success. Consideration of mothers' responses provide insight into both their conceptions of romantic relationships, and how such conceptions might be passed down through generations and in turn influence the future cohabitation and marriage decisions of young women.

As few of the daughters' biological fathers resided in the families' households, we first asked each mother how she described her daughter's biological father to her daughter. This question, like the ones that I discuss following, was open-ended, and the answers were coded categorically. More than one third of the mothers (37%) reported quite positive and supportive messages about their daughter's biological fathers, noting such characteristics as his work effort and his caring for his daughter. Others relayed more general positive messages, such as the woman who replied "She has a good father, the best you can have. You don't find them like him today."

On the other hand, a lesser but still significant proportion of women (20%) relayed strikingly negative messages about their daughters' biological fathers. Some of these responses indicated the prevalence of violent behavior and drug addiction, whereas others discussed fathers' more general lack of responsibility and inability to fulfill their parental responsibilities of being loving and available parents to their children.

Another group of mothers reported either neutral (15%) or conflicting messages with both positive and negative connotations entwined (5%). Although many mothers stated that their daughters knew their fathers, and they wanted their daughters to make up their own minds, some of these responses also appeared to indicate the possibility of veiled negative messages, such as the mother who stated "I let her make her own decisions. I never talk bad about him even though we have been divorced a long time." Others admitted to the complexity of personal relationships, noting that although their daughter's father had been a violent or irresponsible spouse, he nonetheless cared deeply for his children. Other women relayed that their daughters' fathers were loving and caring fathers, but were not able to act on such desires because of drug addiction or irresponsible or illegal behaviors. Finally, a significant proportion of mothers (23%) reported that they did not discuss their daughter's biological father at all or that they let their daughters make up their own minds about him.

In summary, mothers' lessons to their daughters about girls' biological fathers were complex and multidimensional, and although a plurality of mothers relayed very positive descriptions, others vacillated between supportive and disparaging messages, at times seeming to veil notes of caution and negativity even behind seemingly positive words. Given the substantial proportion of mothers in the sample who had weathered a divorce or cohabitational break-up, and the smaller proportion of biological fathers in the sample who were playing active, residential parenting roles (see Coley & Chase-Lansdale, 2000a), it is perhaps not surprising that many mothers sounded cautionary tales concerning their daughters' biological fathers.

However, the picture becomes even more cautionary when one considers the general lessons that mothers reported teaching their daughters about men. When we asked women to describe what they have taught their daughters about men, nearly all of the mothers reported negative or at best neutral messages. Only a handful of mothers (6%) reported passing down positive and hopeful constructions of men and relationships, for example by encouraging their daughters to find a good man, "someone who has similar interests as she does, who trusts in god, who respects her for who she is." In contrast, almost half of the mothers (49%) relayed significantly negative messages about men, whereas nearly as many (44%) reporting relatively neutral messages with a focus on being cautious, looking for a "good" rather than "bad" man, and staying with a man only if he showed respect.

The mothers who reported what we viewed as negative and derogatory lessons about men discussed a range of issues. Some talked in relatively general and sweeping terms about men being irresponsible, untrustworthy, and self-serving, such as the mother who noted that she warns her daughter "Don't let men use you, because men are users. Men aren't capable of taking care of women, they want them [women] to take care of them [men]." Others drove home the importance of avoiding men's violence and sexually predatory behaviors. Finally, a significant proportion of mothers focused more directly on the importance of distrusting and not depending on men and instead on building self-reliance and financial and emotional independence. One mother noted that she teaches her daughter "don't depend on them [men] to do anything for you and don't let them discourage you in what you want to do," whereas another retorted "Don't trust them; don't believe what they have to say. They will tell you anything you want to hear. Use your own judgement, and don't let anyone else make the decisions."

The mothers who relayed what we construed as more neutral or balanced messages to their daughters also often sounded notes of self-reliance, but were more likely to do so in the context of being cautious, being choosy, and demanding respect from men. Mothers warned their daughters to go slowly in initiating relationships, and to focus on other priorities like educational objectives first. They spoke also of caution and prudence in sexual relations, the importance of self-respect for one's body, and the necessity of using birth control to protect against unwanted pregnancies. Many mothers focused on the range of men, reminding their daughters that there were both good and bad men, and that one had to be selective and careful, such as woman who proverbially warned her daughter "You might have to go try a lot of bad apples just to find one good one." Finally, the issue of respect came up frequently in mothers' comments as they relayed the significance that they placed on their daughters' demanding respect from men, and the necessity of respecting oneself so that others (men) would respect one too.

The question about what mothers actively taught their daughters about men was followed by one asking what they believed their daughters had learned from watching their (the mothers') relationships with men. Mothers' replies followed a similar pattern as the previous question, with a small proportion of mothers (13%) reporting positive lessons about men's good qualities and the importance of a strong and loving relationship; a substantial number of neutral lessons concerning the need to demand respect, take things slowly, and expect relationships to include a lot of hard work (30%); and a plurality of families (43%) in which the predominant lessons seemed starkly negative, focused on messages such as distrust of men, fear of violence, and the central importance of independence. Other mothers (15%) reported not having any romantic relationships, or claimed that their daughters did not pay attention or learn from them.

Throughout all of these discussions with mothers concerning their lessons to their daughters about men, romantic relationships, and fathers, one striking commonality was the almost complete lack of mention of marriage. Although mothers talked about women's strength and self-reliance, about the importance of respect, and about both disparaging and hopeful views of relationships, they almost never mentioned marriage. Their constructs of male–female relationships focused primarily on relational matters and often on the centrality of financial, emotional, and general independence. These comments were essentially never placed within the realm of marriage in an outright fashion. Additionally, mothers' comments also very rarely discussed issues of cohabitation or sharing households. One could postulate, however, that in asking very general questions about relationships, we would not necessarily expect to receive substantial specific mention of marriage or cohabitation.

Yet even in response to more direct probing, the importance or centrality of marriage or cohabitation was essentially absent. In a final open-ended question in the Families in Communities Study, we asked mothers "What is the most important thing you hope (daughter) does in her life?" Given the centrality of the marital relationship in the life course of most adults, one could hypothesize that marriage might be a prominent goal that many mothers would focus on for their daughters. Yet within this sample, only 9% of the mothers mentioned marriage or a stable, long-term, or happy relationship among their central goals for their daughters.

SUMMARY

In short, data from the Families in Communities Study reinforces the central finding of other qualitative work with low-income women that reports a significant amount of gender mistrust and prevalent negative views of men and relationships. Both through their explicit words and through their own behaviors and experiences, low-income African-American mothers in the sample reported relaying lessons to their daughters extolling the virtues of self-reliance and self-sufficiency, while providing predominantly cautionary and negative views concerning men and relationships. Moreover, these data imply that mothers may be actively propagating these attitudes in the minds of their daughters through both direct and more subtle lessons. As such, these findings indicate that maternal lessons and examples might be one important mechanism through which patterns away from marriage and toward more unstable forms of relationships, including cohabitation, are growing within low-income and minority populations.

ACKNOWLEDGMENTS

The Families in Communities Study, directed by P. Lindsay Chase-Lansdale, was funded through generous support from the Carnegie Corporation of New York, the Ford Foundation, and the Harrison Steans Foundation. The author greatly appreciates the support and collaboration of Dr. Chase-Lansdale, and also thanks the families involved in the FIC study for contributing their time and insights, and Jodi Morris for her assistance in preparing this manuscript. Address correspondence to Rebekah Levine Coley, Applied Developmental and Educational Psychology, Lynch School of Education, Boston College, 140 Commonwealth Ave., Chestnut Hill, MA 02467 or through electronic mail at coleyre@bc.edu.

REFERENCES

Cabrera, N. J., Tamis-LeMonda, C. S., Bradley, R. H., Hofferth, S., & Lamb, M. E. (2000). Fatherhood in the twenty-first century. *Child Development, 71,* 127–136.

Coley, R. L. (2001). (In)visible men: Emerging research on low-income, unmarried, and minority fathers. *American Psychologist, 56*(9), 743–753.

Coley, R. L., & Chase-Lansdale, P. L. (1999). Stability and change in paternal involvement among urban African American fathers. *Journal of Family Psychology, 13*(3), 1–20.

Coley, R. L., & Chase-Lansdale, P. L. (2000a). *The sting of disappointment: Father-daughter relationships in low-income African American families.* Manuscript under review.

Coley, R. L., & Chase-Lansdale, P. L. (2000b). Welfare receipt, financial strain, and African-American adolescent functioning. *Social Service Review,* 380–404.

Edin, K. (2000). Few good men: Why poor mothers don't marry or remarry. *The American Prospect* (January), 26–31.

Furstenberg, F. F. (1988). Good dads-bad dads: Two faces of fatherhood. In A. J. Cherlin (Ed.), *The changing American family and public policy* (pp. 193–218). Washington, DC: Urban Institute Press.

Furstenberg, F. F. (1995). Fathering in the inner city: Paternal participation and public policy. In W. Marsiglio (Ed.), *Fatherhood: Contemporary theory, research, and social policy* (pp. 119–147). Thousand Oaks, CA: Sage.

Gupta, S. (1999). The effects of marital status transitions on men's housework performance. *Journal of Marriage and the Family, 61,* 700–711.

Manning, W. D., & Lansdale, N. S. (1996). Racial and ethnic differences in the role of cohabitation in premarital childbearing. *Journal of Marriage, 58,* 63–77.

Waite, L. J. (1999-2000). The negative effects of cohabitation. *The Responsive Community, 10,* 31–38.

Waite, L. J. (2000). *The case for marriage: Why married people are happier, healthier, and better off financially.* New York: Doubleday.

Wilson, W. J. (1987). *The truly disadvantaged.* Chicago, IL: The University of Chicago Press.

7

The Impact of Cohabitation on the Family Life Course in Contemporary North America: Insights From Across the Border

Céline Le Bourdais and Heather Juby
Centre interuniversitaire d'études démographiques
Institut national de la recherche scientifique / Université de Montréal

J'ai l'honneur de ne pas te demander ta main, ne gravons pas nos noms au bas d'un parchemin.[1] - Georges Brassens

Smock and Gupta's chapter (chap. 4, this volume), *Cohabitation in Contemporary North America*, compares and contrasts the evolution of cohabitation in the United States and Canada over the last decades of the 20th century. They discuss the role of cohabitation in family structure, cultural and social class variations, changes within cohabitation itself over the last decade, to what extent it resembles marriage, and how far it has become "institutionalized" in the two countries. Interesting and thought provoking, the chapter draws on an impressive body of research from both countries to explore their very different treatment of cohabitation. Particularly striking, from our perspective, is that the analysis of the central theme of this session—the implications of cohabitation for family structure—draws almost entirely on Canadian research. On reflection, it seemed to us that the absence of information on family structure stems from the evolution not so much of cohabitation itself in the United States as from the attitude toward it, both on the part of social institutions and of the research community. The very different presentation of otherwise rather similar trends is central to our argument and should become clearer in the course of the discussion.

The evolution of cohabitation in Quebec has more in common with the experience of certain European countries than it does with the Anglo-Saxon world, in the sense that cohabiting unions have become a socially acceptable alternative to marriage as the context for family life. By the early 1990s in Quebec, almost as many babies were born within a common-law union as in a marriage, and less than one quarter were born to couples who had not lived together before marrying (Marcil-Gratton, 1998). Quebec francophones were at the forefront of these changes, and by 1998, less than one quarter of babies were born within marriage in two of the most rural, francophone administrative regions of Quebec (Institut

---

[1] Why pledge our troth before a minister? Let's not be inscribed in a register! Translated from French (Dumas & Bélanger, 1997).

de la Statistique du Quebec, 2000). Evidently, the society producing such statistics is also very different from those cited by Smock and Gupta, where it is not unusual for cohabiting partners to wish to "pass as married." In Quebec, the opposite is more likely to occur, with married couples passing themselves off as cohabiting! French Canadian married women under the age of 50 rarely refer to *mon mari* (my husband), using instead such terms as *mon conjoint* (my partner) or *mon chum* (untranslatable!). A ring on the appropriate finger may indicate that its bearer is in a committed relationship, but does not indicate its legal status. Moreover, few married women adopt their husband's name, with evident repercussions for children, whose surname gives no clue as to the legal status of their parents' union, thereby removing any stigma attached to it. With a much smaller proportion of babies born to cohabiting couples elsewhere in Canada, this distinctive behavior makes Quebec an extraordinary laboratory within North America for family research, and probably explains much of the different perspective on cohabitation.

CONTRASTING ATTITUDES TOWARD COHABITATION: THE INSTITUTIONAL PERSPECTIVE

The Quebec experience of cohabitation, however, cannot account for the different levels of "institutionalization" of cohabitation in Canada and the United States described by Smock and Gupta. The fact that Canada adjusted to this social reality much more fully than the United States is rooted in the approach taken to it from the start, long before cohabitation had become commonplace even in Quebec. As early as the census of 1971, for example, Statistics Canada instructed cohabiting couples to declare themselves as "married"; in all the published census tables, therefore, cohabiting couples and families were classified with those who had married. Even in 1971, therefore, an unmarried couple with children was classified as a two-parent rather than a single-parent family, as is the case still today for U.S. Census publications.

This different approach is mirrored in the treatment of cohabitation within the law with the result that "in the U.S., cohabitation remains much less institutionalized than marriage," while in Canada "all conjugal unions are now almost fully equivalent under Canadian federal law" (Smock & Gupta, chap. 4, p. 71). From the early 1970s, the Canadian legal system adopted the "equivalent-to-marriage" approach to cohabitation, and legislated accordingly. In Canada, the problem of institutionalizing cohabiting unions stems not from the issue of whether or not cohabiting and married couples should be given equal treatment (although this has been the object of some debate, as is seen later), but from how to define a cohabiting union. Although the marriage ceremony provides a clear marker of the start of a marital union, "the more amorphous nature of cohabitation poses problems for legislators in defining which cohabitation relationships will be covered by the legislation in question" (Holland, 2001, pp. 1–5). In the absence of a marriage contract, a criterion of duration (1 or 3 years) is generally required to define a cohabiting union (although this may be waived if the couple has a child).

In other words, in the United States cohabitation appears to have been equated with "going steady," a transient state that would either terminate or transform into marriage; from this perspective, there was no need to adapt the institutional and legal apparatus to it. Canada, on the other hand, by viewing and treating cohabiting unions as equivalent to marriage from the start, has been more prepared for the way in which these unions are evolving on both sides of the border toward an alternative, and not simple a prelude, to marriage. This attitude has also given the Canadian government greater control over these noncontractual unions. The fact that couples in cohabiting unions have been able to claim federal tax credit for their dependent partners since 1993 was mentioned by Smock and Gupta as an example of the equivalence of cohabiting and married unions. An important effect of this particular clause (and probably the motivation behind it) was, in fact, to close tax loopholes previously open to cohabiting couples!

Adapting to cohabitation in Canada has not been as harmonious as it might at first appear. Smock and Gupta mention that many areas of family law, such as laws governing union dissolution and child support, remain under provincial jurisdiction, and it is here that differences in viewpoints appear. Alberta and Quebec, for example, are among the few provinces not providing for support obligations for cohabiting couples at separation. Both provinces are reluctant to admit total equality for married and cohabiting unions, but from entirely opposing viewpoints. In Alberta, where marriage is judged the ideal family context, it is felt that additional recognition of cohabitation would simply undermine it further. This attitude appears to be shared by the United States, which had done so little to regulate cohabiting unions that Smock and Gupta suggest that "many cohabiting couples marry as much for the sake of legal clarity and convenience as out of respect for the institution of marriage" (p. 72). In Quebec, on the other hand, the justification for not assimilating cohabitation to marriage came from both the more "traditional" elements of society and the most "modern." The latter argued the case for keeping marriage and cohabitation separate in terms of promoting individual autonomy: Couples chose cohabitation over marriage precisely to avoid the rights and obligations attached to it, and should not therefore have these imposed on them by the state against their wishes (Lepage, Bérubé, & Desrochers, 1992).

Consequently, in Quebec, where cohabitation is the most widespread, it is the least institutionalized. Although cohabiting couples in Quebec enjoy the same social recognition as married couples with regard to many federal and provincial laws and social programs, Quebec's *Code Civil* does not recognize the status of cohabitation, and from a legal point of view cohabiting partners remain single and strangers to one another (Ministère de la Justice, 1995). The term *conjoint* in this case applies only to married couples. While living together, cohabiting couples have the same privileges as married couples; when separated by death or union dissolution, however, the same is not true. In the case of death of one cohabiting partner, the other has no right to any inheritance unless specified in a will, or to life insurance unless named in the contract. On separation, goods acquired during the relationship belong to whoever paid for them, including the family home; no form of spousal support or compensation is offered, except if one partner can prove a contribution to the other partner's wealth, in which case they are treated as business partners rather than spouses.

The need to protect children born within cohabiting unions was addressed through a 1981 reform to the *Code Civil*, which gave equal rights to children whatever the circumstances of their birth. In other words, the rights and obligations with regard to children are now the same for cohabiting parents as for married parents both during the union and at separation. This did not, however, completely resolve the problem, and provide equal protection for children of cohabiting and married parents after separation, as the former continue to suffer from the absence of obligations between parents. Children remaining in the care of a parent with no legal claim on the family home or any other form of support from an ex-partner risk an even greater drop in living standards than that experienced by children whose married parents separate (Dubreuil, 1999). This is one consequence of "incompletely institutionalized" cohabitation, affecting the lives of children in Quebec more than in most other Canadian provinces.

CONTRASTING ATTITUDES TOWARD COHABITATION: THE RESEARCH PERSPECTIVE

Most research on the question of cohabitation, in Canada as much as in the United States, is based on survey rather than census data. Such data became available at much the same time on both sides of the border, and revealed very similar trends in cohabitation in the two countries (Le Bourdais & Marcil-Gratton, 1996). Smock and Gupta demonstrate a comparable evolution in terms of (a) the proportion of couples cohabiting at a given moment in time, (b) the rising percentage of individuals experiencing cohabitation in successive generation, and (c) the proportion of couples living together before marrying. However, it was not until the mid-1990s that published research in the United States not only acknowledged cohabitating unions as anything but "a short-run alternative to marriage" or a "prelude to marriage" (Cherlin, 1992, p. 236), but started to recognize it as a component of family life (Bumpass & Raley, 1995; Bumpass, Raley, & Sweet, 1995). In the 1980s and early 1990s, births to cohabiting parents were either termed *premarital* and explained away as "little more than an artefact of the timing ceremony," or *nonmarital*, on the assumption (presumably) that the union would be short-lived, and leave the baby in the same situation as those born outside a conjugal union (Bumpass & Sweet, 1989, p. 258).

In an article published in 1995, Bumpass and Raley recognized that one "can no longer discuss family structure or family transitions sensibly when using only marital statuses and transitions" (p. 107) and started to evaluate the impact on research of not having done so in the past. Merging births to single mothers and to cohabiting couples in an "out-of-wedlock" birth category, the most common practice in U.S. family research, has had profound consequences. First, as Bumpass demonstrated, it has completely skewed figures on single-parent, intact, and stepfamilies, overestimating the prevalence and duration of single-parent families, and underestimating these measures for intact and stepfamilies (see Bumpass & Raley, 1995; Bumpass, Raley, & Sweet, 1995). This, in turn, must have had an impact on social policies designed to alleviate the problem of poverty faced by many single-parent families and formulated from results of analyses of single parenthood based on these biased data.

In the conclusion, Bumpass and Raley (1995) put their finger on the problem of cohabitation within U.S. family research with the statement that "many people will be uneasy with defining unmarried units with children as *families*" (p. 107; italics added). Cohabitation as conjugal behavior has been as much a part of the research agenda in the United States as it has in Canada. Where research in the two countries diverges is in the analysis of cohabitation as a family behavior—with an apparent reluctance to conceive of the family outside marriage in the United States. This undoubtedly contributes to the lack of U.S. figures in Smock and Gupta's discussion of the effect of cohabitation on family structure.

THE CHANGING NATURE OF COHABITATION

If Waite's Presidential address to the 1995 Population Association of America (PAA) meeting is representative of U.S. family research, the idea that marriage is more beneficial for individuals and for society than cohabitation, and should be promoted as such, prevails (Waite, 1995). Certainly, the figures given by Smock and Gupta arising from Canadian research seem to reinforce this viewpoint. Not only are cohabiting unions in general more unstable than marriages, they remain so even when the couple has had a child—an event that one might assume acts as a marker of commitment for a cohabiting couple. Children born within cohabiting unions in Canada in the 1980s were more than four times as likely to experience parental separation than those born to married couples who had not cohabited prior to marriage. In other words, as Smock and Gupta state, the evidence largely suggests that "cohabitation promotes greater instability in family life" (p. 59).

However, the reality is rather more complex. In Quebec, four out of five young adults start their conjugal life in a cohabiting union, and marriage, far from being a prerequisite to family formation, is not even the modal way. Is it rational in this context to assume that cohabitation is still as selective of the type of individuals who place little value on stable conjugal relationships? Assessing the changing character of cohabitation and its impact on family structure is a complex process, given that the very nature of cohabitation makes it difficult to compare with marriage. Cohabitation, unlike marriage, covers the whole range of unions from "going steady" to fully committed long-term relationships; some types are likely to include children, whereas others are highly unlikely to. Moreover, as Bumpass and Lu (2000) pointed out, "trends in disruptions between couples with and without children need not even move in the same direction" (p. 34). They suggested using a measure of disruption timed from the formation of a family with children as the only way to assess and compare the stability of two-parent families—in other words, from the moment the first child is born to the couple.

This is precisely the method we employed in two studies of family disruption in Quebec and Canada (Desrosiers & Le Bourdais, 1996; Le Bourdais, Neill, & Marcil-Gratton, 2000). We discuss the most recent study in some detail here, as it provides interesting insights into the evolution of both marriage and cohabitation over time. The study was based on information collected from female respondents of the 1995 General Social Survey, who had become mothers within an intact family (i.e., within a union with their child's father). Fig. 7.1 shows the evolution through time of the type of conjugal union within which first children were born, comparing Quebec with the rest of Canada. Before 1970, throughout Canada, almost all intact families were established by married couples who had not previously cohabited. This proportion dropped to two thirds outside of Quebec, and to one third within Quebec by the end of the century. By this time, more than 30% of first births in intact families in Quebec were to cohabiting partners, more than twice the proportion found elsewhere in Canada.

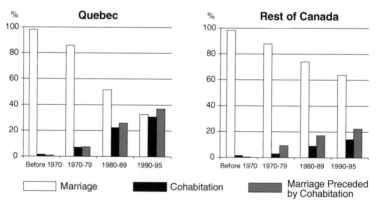

FIG. 7.1   Distribution of intact families, by period of family formation and type of union at first birth, mothers aged 25 to 64 years, Canada. (*Source*: Statistics Canada, 1995 General Social Survey. Based on data from Table 1 in Le Bourdais et al., 2000).

Fig. 7.2 shows how these families fared in terms of their durability from the moment that the first child was born. The cumulative proportions of couples separating are compared for Quebec and the rest of Canada according to the period of family formation. In Quebec, families formed in the 1980s were far less stable than those of the 1970s: Within 10 years of their creation, twice as many families had broken down in the later period. However, information on families formed in the 1990s indicates a reversal of the trend, revealing that at least in the first 5 years these families were as stable as those of the 1970s. The trends in the rest of Canada were more regular through time, showing a slower but steady move toward greater family disruption from one period to the next, to the extent that families formed in the 1990s face a slightly higher risk of breakdown than in Quebec.

The more erratic evolution in Quebec is certainly closely linked to the higher incidence of cohabitation in the province. In Fig. 7.3, the probability of union disruption over time is presented for Canada as a whole, and compares the risk of family disruption associated with different types of conjugal union for families established during the 1970s and 1980s. In the 1970s, choosing cohabitation appears to be the main risk factor, with families formed by couples who lived together before marrying having almost as high a risk of disruption as those who had not legalized their cohabiting union. Ten years later, however, marriage appears the better predictor of union stability, with married-couple families far more stable than cohabiting-couple families, irrespective of whether or not the couple had lived together before marrying.

The question still remains as to where this evolution has left the different family types in Quebec as compared with the rest of Canada. A proportional haz-

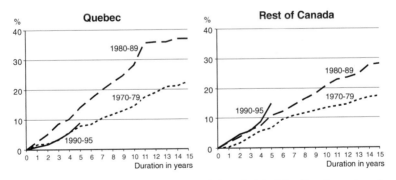

FIG. 7.2 Cumulative proportion of union breakdown in intact families, by region of residence and period of family formation, mothers aged 25 to 64 years, Canada. (Life table estimates; *Source*: Statistics Canada, 1995 General Social Survey. Reproduced from Le Bourdais et al., 2000).

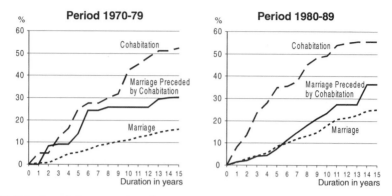

FIG. 7.3 Cumulative proportion of union breakdown in intact families, by period of family formation and type of union at first birth, mothers aged 25 to 64 years, Canada. (Life table estimates; *Source*: Statistics Canada, 1995 General Social Survey. Reproduced from Le Bourdais et al., 2000).

ards model, controlling for a series of variables associated with conjugal and family instability yielded the following results for an interaction variable that combined the effects of region of residence and conjugal pathways (see Table 7.1). Families formed within direct marriage are more unstable in Quebec than elsewhere in Canada. However, in Quebec, married couples who lived together before marriage formed equally stable families as those who did not; in the rest of Canada, these families were 66% more likely to end in parental separation than directly married families. A third difference relates to the relative instability of cohabiting-couple families. In Quebec, the risk of disruption is 2.5 times greater than for other family types, whereas elsewhere in Canada the risk is almost five times as high as that of families created within a direct marriage.

DISCUSSION

Clearly, cohabitation is still evolving, showing signs of growing stability among couples with children as this family type becomes more widespread and socially accepted. In other words, the importance of cohabitation in predicting family disruption seems to be changing over time as society progresses through the stages of the "partnership transition" evoked by Kiernan (chap. 1, this volume). In Quebec, it is now the decision to marry, whether at the start of the relationship or later on, that reduces the risk of family disruption. This suggests that the importance of the "selection" hypothesis in explaining the association observed between cohabitation and union instability is declining while that of the experience of cohabitation itself is increasing. It also suggests that it may be time to change the formulation of the question at the basis of most research on cohabitation: instead of asking

Table 7.1
Risk Ratio of Intact Family Breakdown, by Type of Conjugal Union and Region of Residence[a]

Type of Union	Region of Residence	
	Quebec	Rest of Canada
Direct marriage	1.45	1.00
Marriage preceded by cohabitation	1.46	1.66
Cohabitation	3.47	4.94

Source: Statistics Canada, 1995 General Social Survey. Reproduced from Le Bourdais et al. (2000, Table 2).

[a] The coefficients represent the risk of family breakdown after controlling for the effect of women's sociodemographic characteristics. All coefficients are significantly different at the 0.05 level from the reference category (i.e., direct marriage outside Quebec).

who cohabits and *why*, it may be more appropriate to try and understand who *marries* and why they continue to do so.

As cohabitation moved from being an "avant-garde" phenomenon, chosen by a very small fraction of the population, into a strategy commonly adopted to test the relationship before marriage, into a more enduring form of union and finally into a context for raising children, the nature of both cohabitation and marriage changed. This evolution means that "we can no longer automatically assume. . . that relationships between underlying causes and the behaviour studied are constant across time" (Manting, 1996, p. 55). On the contrary, it is more likely that the impact of given determinants on the formation and dissolution of cohabiting unions alters across generations, as this type of union takes on a new meaning; conversely, the effect of these determinants on direct marriage should also change, as this "option" becomes "increasingly exceptional" over time (p. 55).

Recent research on first union formation in Canada confirms this hypothesis. Namely, it shows that the impact of education and work experience on the choice of cohabitation or marriage to start conjugal life has changed considerably, even having the opposite effect, across generations (Mongeau, Neill, & Le Bourdais, 2000; Turcotte & Goldscheider, 1998). For example, among women belonging to the older cohorts, higher education increased the likelihood of entering a first union through cohabitation and decreased that of entering marriage. Over time, educated women became more rather than less likely to marry, and less rather than more likely to cohabit. For men, education at first increased chances of entering both cohabitation and marriage, but became less important in determining either type of union over time (Turcotte & Goldscheider, 1998).

These results underline the need, stressed by Manting (1996), to pay great attention to the changing influence of the forces underlying the patterns of cohabitation and marriage, if our objective is a better understanding of these two types of unions. We would go one step further, in arguing that these analyses need to be conducted separately for cohabiting unions that involve children. As noted previously, cohabiting unions cover a very wide range of situations, from "going steady" to "raising a family," and there is no evidence that all types are moving in the same direction in terms of the commitment to, and the solidity of, the relationship. Quite the contrary, recent research points to a polarization of behaviors, with a substantial increase in the percentages of both "unstable" and "stable" cohabiting unions (Dumas & Bélanger, 1997), implying that they are selective of different subgroups of individuals. If this is the case, we would expect the impact of given determinants to vary between the two groups.

The co-existence of two types of union that increasingly resemble one another raises the question of their identity: Is cohabitation slowly replacing marriage or is it a new form of union to which are attached different values or attitudes? Gupta's (1999) research on the division of domestic labor between men and women lends support to the first hypothesis, whereas an analysis conducted by LaPierre-Adamcyk, Le Bourdais, and Marcil-Gratton (1999) of the attitudes of Canadian men and women aged 25 to 34 years toward certain aspects of family and professional life, bears out the second position. One problem of both these studies, however, is that they merge all types of cohabiting unions, thereby limiting the insight they can provide on these questions, and confirming the need for more subtle classification of conjugal unions.

All in all, Smock and Gupta's chapter has been highly stimulating, providing much food for thought not only on the differences between the two countries, but also on what they have in common. The insights gained from the process of reflection have made us reassess our own work on the subject and have indicated ways in which our analyses could be improved.

ACKNOWLEDGMENTS

This report has received financial support from the Social Sciences and Humanities Research Council of Canada (SSHRC) and the Institut national de la recherche scientifique (INRS). The authors wish to thank Julie Archambault for preparing the figures.

REFERENCES

Bumpass, L. L., & Lu, H.-H. (2000). Trends in cohabitation and implications for children's family contexts in the United States. *Population Studies, 54,* 29–41.

Bumpass, L. L., & Raley, R. K. (1995). Redefining single-parent families: Cohabitation and changing reality. *Demography, 32,* 97–109.

Bumpass, L. L., Raley, R. K., & Sweet, J. A. (1995). The changing character of stepfamilies: Implications of cohabitation and nonmarital childbearing. *Demography, 32,* 425–436.

Bumpass, L. L., & Sweet, J. A. (1989). Children's experience in single-parent families: Implications of cohabitation and marital transitions. *Family Planning Perspectives, 21,* 256–261.

Cherlin, A. (1992). Marriage, cohabitation, sexual behavior, and childbearing in North America. In *The Peopling of the Americas.* Proceedings of the International Union for the Scientific Study of Population conference (pp. 223–243). Veracruz: IUSSP.

Desrosiers, H., & Le Bourdais, C. (1996). Progression des unions libres et avenir des familles biparentales. *Recherches féministes, 9,* 65–83.

Dubreuil, C. (1999). L'union de fait au Québec: Inexistence dans le Code civil. *Cahiers québécois de démographie, 28,* 229–236.

Dumas, J., & Bélanger, A. (1997). *Report on the demographic situation in Canada 1996.* Ottawa: Statistics Canada.

Gupta, S. (1999). The effects of marital status transitions on men's housework performance. *Journal of Marriage and the Family, 57,* 700–711.

Holland, W. (2001). Introduction to cohabitation: The law in Canada. In W. Holland & B. Stalbecker-Pountney (Eds.), *Cohabitation: The law in Canada* (pp. 1-1–1-47). Toronto: Carswell (3rd release. Original introduction published 1995).

Institut de la Statistique du Québec. (2000). Data from the statistical data section of their website: www.stat.gouv.qc.ca.

LaPierre-Adamcyk, É., Le Bourdais, C., & Marcil-Gratton, N. (1999). Vivre en couple pour la première fois: La signification du choix de l'union libre au Québec et en Ontario. *Cahiers québécois de démographie, 28,* 199–227.

Le Bourdais, C., & Marcil-Gratton, N. (1996). Family transformation across the Canadian/American border: When the laggard becomes the leader. *Journal of Comparative Family Studies, 27,* 415–436.

Le Bourdais, C., Neill, G., & Marcil-Gratton, N. (2000). L'effet du type d'union sur la stabilité des familles dites "intactes." *Recherches sociographiques, 41,* 53–74.

Lepage, F., Bérubé, G., & Desrochers, L. (1992). *Vivre en union de fait au Québec* (3rd ed). Quebec: Les Publications du Québec.

Marcil-Gratton, N. (1998). *Growing up with Mom and Dad? The intricate family life courses of Canadian children,* Ottawa: Statistics Canada.

Manting, D. (1996). The changing meaning of cohabitation and marriage. *European Sociological Review, 12*, 53–65.

Ministère de la Justice. (1995). *Vivre à deux*. Quebec: Les Publications du Québec.

Mongeau, J., Neill, G., & Le Bourdais, C. (2001). Effet de la précarité économique sur la formation d'une première union au Canada. *Cahiers québécois de démographie, 30*, (forthcoming).

Turcotte, P., & Goldscheider, F. (1998). Evolution of factors influencing first union formation in Canada. *Canadian Studies in Population, 25*, 145–173.

Waite, L. (1995). Does marriage matter? *Demography, 32*, 483–507.

III

What Is the Long- and Short-Term Impact of Cohabitation on Child Well-Being?

8

The Implications of Cohabitation for Children's Well-Being

Wendy D. Manning
Bowling Green State University

Research examining the well-being of children often relies on the parents' marital status as a way to understand the context in which children are raised. Marital status provides information about the potential number of caretakers and may imply certain characteristics or qualities of the child's family life. The importance of parents' marital status is reflected in the extensive research attention to the implications of the end of marriage on children's well-being. This emphasis on marital status was appropriate when relatively few children ever lived in cohabiting unions. However, the shift in children's experience in cohabitation requires that cohabitation be considered in new research on child well-being (Bumpass & Lu, 2000). Currently, there are relatively few published papers on this topic but it is an emerging research arena evidenced in part by a growing number of national conference presentations on the topic.

This new recognition of cohabitation forces researchers to consider not only whether cohabitation influences child outcomes but also what matters about cohabitation. Much of the literature is based on the structural questions of the benefits or costs of being raised by one parent versus two parents or married versus unmarried parents. However, it may be more important to consider the nature of the parents' relationship or parenting practices rather than simply focus on the number of parents. Here I review the recent literature with the goal of providing direction for a new research agenda on cohabitation and child well-being.

This chapter is divided into four sections. I begin with a basic discussion of the trends in cohabitation as a family living arrangement for children. Next, I discuss why cohabitation may influence child outcomes. Then I review findings from empirical research that specifically focuses on the effect of cohabitation on children's social and economic well-being. Finally, I present limitations and challenges for future work on the effects of cohabitation on children.

COHABITATION AS A FAMILY STRUCTURE

Traditionally, cohabitation has been viewed as a childless union that only affects adults, but cohabitation frequently involves children (U.S. Bureau of the Census, 1999). The U.S. Bureau of the Census draws on Current Population Survey data and reports that in 1998, 36% of cohabiting households included children under the age of 15. In 1980, 27% of cohabiting households included children (U.S. Bureau of the Census, 1999). The growth rate in cohabiting households has been substantially greater among households with children than those without children.

Children in the United States are increasingly likely to spend some of their lives living in a cohabiting parent family. In 1990, approximately 2.2 million, or 3.5%, of children were living in a cohabiting parent family (Manning & Lichter, 1996). A more comprehensive take on this issue is what proportion of children will ever spend time in a cohabiting union. Bumpass and Lu (2000) estimated that two fifths of children in the United States are expected to experience a cohabiting-parent family at some point during their childhood. These estimates vary some-what depending on data source and method (see Graefe & Lichter, 1999). Chil-dren born during the early 1990s are estimated to spend 9% of their lives in co-habiting unions (Bumpass & Lu, 2000).

Until recently, children living in cohabiting-parent families were treated as children living in single-parent families because one or both of their parents were unmarried. As a result, the understanding of single-parenthood is misrepresented by ignoring cohabitation as a living arrangement. In fact, children who are living in two-parent cohabiting families have been assumed to be living with one parent. A considerable and growing proportion (12%) of single mothers were living with cohabiting partners (London, 1998). Furthermore, substantial proportions of un-married mothers are having children while cohabiting. In the early 1990s, 40% of nonmarital births were born to women who were cohabiting and these levels have increased from 25% in the early1980s (Bumpass & Lu, 2000).

Switching to the child's perspective demonstrates the percentage of children living in cohabiting parent families. In 1990, 1 in 12 children who were living with unmarried mothers lived in a cohabiting couple family (Manning & Smock, 1997). Perhaps even more striking is that 35% of children in single-father families were living with their father and his cohabiting partner (Eggebeen, Snyder, & Manning, 1996).

Children in cohabiting-parent families could be living with two biological parents, whereas others may be living with one biological parent and his or her cohabiting partner, akin to a stepfamily. Bumpass (1994) reported that among children in cohabiting-parent families about 40% live with two biological parents and 60% of children are living with one biological parent. In contrast, children living in married-couple families are largely living with two biological parents (81%; Norton & Miller, 1992). Based on the literature that distinguishes stepfamilies from two-biological parent families, the implications of cohabitation for children's lives should depend on whether they are living with two biological parents or one biological parent and their parent's partner.

The experiences of cohabitation for children vary considerably according to race and ethnicity. Cohabitation appears to be a more central part of the family-building process (formation of unions and fertility) for Hispanics than Whites or

Blacks (e.g., Brines & Joyner, 1999; Bumpass & Lu, 2000; Clarkberg, 1999; Loomis & Landale, 1994; Manning, 1999; Manning & Smock, 1995). McLanahan and Casper (1995) reported that children are more likely to be present in minority cohabiting couple households (67% of Blacks and 70% of Hispanics) than in White cohabiting couple households (35%). In 1990, 8% of Puerto Rican children, 5% of Mexican-American and Black children, and 3% of White children were living in cohabiting-parent families (Manning & Lichter, 1996). However, these single point estimates do not reflect differences in children's lifetime experiences in cohabitation. Minority children are more likely to spend some of their lives in cohabiting-parent families than white children. About half (55%) of African-American children, 40% of Hispanic children, and 30% of White children are expected to experience a cohabiting-parent family (estimates computed from Bumpass & Lu, 2000).[1] The biological relationship of children in cohabiting families to their parents varies for race and ethnic groups. Hispanic children in cohabiting-parent families more frequently live with their biological father (72%) than do White (40%) or Black (39%) children (Clark & Nelson, 2000).

Is the situation in the United States unique? The answer appears to be no. In fact, the United States is somewhat of a "laggard" in this dimension of cohabitation. Cohabitation and parenting are not as often combined in the United States as in other industrialized countries. The clear leader is Sweden. In Sweden, half of firstborn children were born to cohabitors and nearly all (88%) of premarital births were to women who were cohabiting (Heuveline, Timberlake, & Furstenberg, 2000; Kiernan, 1999). The levels in the United States are probably most comparable to West Germany. In the early 1990s, 11% of children in the United States were born to cohabiting parents (Bumpass & Lu, 2000; Heuveline et al., 2000). Yet, premarital childbearing is more heavily composed of fertility that occurs while cohabiting in most European nations than in the United States.

The implications of these patterns and trends are that in the United States cohabitation is growing as an arena for family building (Manning, 1999; Raley, 1999). To some extent, the meaning of cohabitation is dependent on whether children are present or not (Casper & Sayer, 1999; Manning & Smock, 1999; Smock, 2000). Yet, it is important to note the considerable variation in these patterns that exist along several dimensions including: parental education, martial history, race and ethnicity (Astone, Schoen, Ensminger & Rothert, 1999; Brown, 2000c; Bumpass & Lu, 2000; Manning, 1999). Further investigation of the implications of cohabitation for children is required to develop a comprehensive view of cohabitation and parenting.

---

[1] Estimated by summing the proportion of children born between 1990 and 1994 who were born to cohabiting mothers and the product of the proportion of children born outside of cohabitation with mothers who later cohabited and the proportion of children not born in cohabiting unions for each race and ethnic group (Tables 4 and 5 in Bumpass & Lu, 2000).

WHY COHABITATION MATTERS?

Cohabitation is expected to influence the lives of children differently than both marriage and singlehood. The reasons why these differences exist are likely due to the nature of cohabiting unions as well as the characteristics of cohabiting couples. Perhaps the most direct route through which families influence children is via parenting practices and there appears to be differences in parenting according to family type.

Nature of Cohabiting Unions

Cohabiting unions are typically characterized as coresidential unions of short duration that lack institutionalization. First, by definition cohabiting couples are sharing a residence so children in cohabiting-couple families have access to two potential caretakers and income providers. In this sense cohabiting couple families are structurally similar to married couple families. This may prove to be beneficial for children when the alternative is living with one parent raising his or her child alone. At the same time, children may be negatively influenced by a cohabiting partner who is not legally tied to the family.

The average duration of cohabiting unions is about 2 years (Bumpass, 1998) and this is quite short in contrast to marriages. Yet, in almost half of these cases the couple continues to live together, 53% of cohabiting couples married their partner within 5 years of cohabitation (Bumpass & Lu, 1998). Only about one sixth of cohabitations last 3 years or more and only one tenth last 5 years or longer (Bumpass & Lu, 1998). The short life span of cohabiting unions suggests that most children born or living with cohabiting couples will experience a quick change in their living circumstances, in some circumstances into more stable family living arrangements, marriage (this topic is discussed further later). In fact, the duration of cohabiting unions is considerably longer when children are born into the union (30 months) than when no children are born into the union (16 months; Manning, Smock, & Majumdar, 2000). However, the duration of cohabitation does not approach the stability of marriages. In any case, the relatively higher levels of instability may lead to negative outcomes for children. For example, Wu and Martinson (1993) reported that it is the number of transitions experienced during childhood and not the specific family structures that determine the odds of having a premarital birth. Alternatively, the short duration of cohabitation may keep children from experiencing highly conflictual families. Amato, Loomis, and Booth (1995) reported that children suffer more from highly conflictual families than from marital disruption.

A third feature of cohabitation is the lack of institutionalization. Cohabitation is not institutionalized in part because it is not broadly sanctioned by the government or society, and it lacks defined family roles and language to refer to family members. The societal roles and expectations of cohabiting partners are not clearly established (Nock, 1995). Cherlin (1978) characterized remarriages as an incomplete institution because of the lack of language to refer to family members. Cohabitation suffers from a similar institutional barrier. Thus, children living with cohabiting parents may not be as well as integrated into a family as children living with married parents. Also, the legal rights and responsibilities of cohabiting partners to their children and one another remains unspecified by state statute or case law (Durst, 1997; Seff, 1995; Wisensale & Heckart, 1993). This has implications for obligations and rights of nonresident parents as well as resident cohabiting partners.

Parenthood remains a key element in differentiating the institutions of marriage and cohabitation. Cohabiting women are less likely to have children than married women (Loomis & Landale, 1994; Raley, 1999) and the gap in fertility rates has remained constant since 1980 (Raley, 1999). Cohabiting women are more likely to have children than their never-married counterparts living alone (Bachrach, 1987; Manning & Landale, 1996; Musick, 1999).[2] An indicator of the lack of institutionalization of cohabitation as a family-building arena is the level of unplanned childbearing in cohabiting unions. The children born into cohabiting parent families are more likely to be unplanned than children born into married couple families (Manning, 1999). Children born to cohabitors are more likely to be planned than children born to unmarried women living alone (Manning, 1999; Musick, 1999). As a result, children born into cohabiting-parent families may suffer some negative health outcomes or developmental outcomes due to their planning status. The literature indicates that maternal health-related behaviors differ according to the planning status of the child (e.g., Brown & Eisenberg, 1995; Joyce, Kaestner, & Korenman, 2000). The mediating effects of planning status on the relationship between union status and child outcomes and development (social, physical, emotional, cognitive) remains unexplored. The lack of institutionalization of cohabitation as a context for family formation may result in negative effects of cohabitation on children's well-being.

Characteristics of Cohabiting Couples

Children raised in cohabiting-couple families may experience different developmental outcomes in part because of their parents' economic circumstances and psychological or social well-being. This provides information about the environment or context that children are raised. The general characteristics of cohabiting couples are reviewed in more depth by Smock and Gupta (chap. 4, this volume) and discussed in Seltzer (2000a) and Smock (2000).

The question that emerges in all studies that contrast family structures are whether observed differences between family types (cohabiting couple, single,

---

[2] See Seltzer (2000), Musick (1999), and Raley (1999) for in-depth discussions of cohabitation and nonmarital fertility.

and married couple) are a result of their current family living arrangements or rather their current living arrangements are a response to their socioeconomic and psychological characteristics (see Smock, 2000). These selection issues are not resolved here but some hints about this process are detected by examining how characteristics of couples are related to union formation.

Socioeconomic Differentials

Children raised in cohabiting-parent families have parents with lower education levels and lower earnings than children in married couple families and parents with greater education levels and earnings than children in single-parent families (Manning & Lichter, 1996). Childbearing during cohabitation is more common for more disadvantaged women, the odds of having a child while cohabiting are greater if the mother is younger, has a low education level, and is not working full-time (Manning, 1999). Bumpass and Lu (2000) reported that 21% of children born to women with less than 12 years of education were born to cohabiting parents, and only 1% of children born to women with a college degree were born to cohabiting parents. They argued that increases in fertility in cohabiting unions are driven by women with the lowest education levels. Similarly, other research that examines the formation of cohabiting stepfamilies indicates that children who have mothers with lower education levels are more likely to experience cohabitation (Bumpass & Lu, 2000; Graefe & Lichter, 1999). Overall these results are consistent with findings from other studies that do not focus on children and compare the economic standing of cohabiting, single, and married couples (e.g., Bumpass & Sweet, 1989; Cohen, 1999; Rindfuss & VandenHeuvel, 1990).

It does not necessarily follow from these comparisons that cohabitation causes poorer social or economic circumstances. The evidence indicates that men with poorer economic prospects and economic instability are more likely to decide to cohabit than marry (Clarkberg, 1999). Additionally, among cohabitors the transition to marriage occurs for those with the best economic circumstances (Manning & Smock, 1995; Smock & Manning, 1997). In fact, Landale and Forste (1991) argued that cohabitation is an alternative form of marriage among the disadvantaged, suggesting that family formation will occur more frequently among those facing the worst economic circumstances. Taken together, these results suggest that selection into marriage occurs for only those possessing the best economic prospects.

Psychological Differentials

The psychological well-being of cohabitors has been contrasted with that of married adults and singles with regard to many dimensions including depression, happiness, relationship quality or happiness, health, violence, and alcohol problems (Brown & Booth, 1996; Brown, 1999, 2000b; Horwitz & White, 1998; Ross,

1995; Stets & Strauss, 1989; Stets, 1991; Waite & Joyner, 1999). At the bivariate level, significant differences frequently exist according to family type. Yet, once other individual and relationship characteristics are accounted for these differences are often diminished (e.g., Brown, 1999; Brown & Booth, 1996; Horwitz & White, 1998; Ross, 1995; Waite & Joyner, 1999). Selection processes can be attributed for some portion of these differences because factors such as relationship unhappiness, violence, and anticipated instability are negatively associated with marriage among cohabitors (Brown, 2000a; DeMaris, 2000). Thus, those individuals left cohabiting will not compare favorably to married couples. To some extent, cohabitation itself may be associated with some negative psychological outcomes because of the nature of the cohabiting union (instability and lack of institutionalization), but this has not been empirically evaluated.

Rarely have these studies specifically focused on cohabiting families with children (see Brown, 2000b, for an exception), children are usually included simply as a control variable. Brown's (2000b) analysis of mental health, measured by depression, indicates that married and cohabiting couples without children have similar depression levels. Yet among parents (couples with children), cohabitors exhibit higher levels of depression than marrieds (Brown, 2000b). Children in these cohabiting-parent families may be negatively influenced by their parents' poorer mental health status. Further work examining whether children influence parental well-being as well specific comparisons of how parenting cohabitors compare to parenting marrieds or singles is warranted.

Parenting Differentials

Parenting behavior has direct implications for children's developmental outcomes. Only a few studies have distinguished the parenting behaviors of cohabitors from married couples and/or single parents (Clark & Nelson 2000; Dunifon & Kowaleski-Jones, 2000; Thomson, McLanahan, & Curtin, 1992). Each study addresses different aspects of parenting: Clark and Nelson focused on the more negative aspects (arguments and aggravation), whereas Dunifon and Kowaleski-Jones highlighted maternal emotional support and cognitive stimulation. Thomson et al. based their work on parental activities, supervision, and supportiveness.

The definition of family types differs across studies. Thomson et al. (1992) defined step- and cohabiting-parent families as those with no biological children present,[3] whereas Clark and Nelson (2000) created four categories of families: two-biological parent married, two-biological parent cohabiting, one-biological parent married, one-biological parent cohabiting. Dunifon and Kowaleski-Jones (2000) employed an innovative strategy by accounting the number of years in each family type.

---

[3] Significance tests were conducted with two-biological parent families as the reference group. The discussion of comparisons between married and cohabiting stepfamilies or cohabiting and single-parent families are not based on results of significance tests.

In two-biological parent families, parental aggravation[4] does not differ between married and cohabiting families and marital status does not influence whether parents and children disagree often (Clark & Nelson, 2000). Other measures of parenting are not available for comparisons of children in two-biological cohabiting and married parent families.

In stepfamilies, marital status does affect the frequency of arguments (Clark & Nelson, 2000). Also, the level of parental aggravation differs such that aggravation is higher in cohabiting stepfamilies with younger children and higher in married stepfamilies with older children (Clark & Nelson, 2000). Analysis of measures of paternal involvement indicates that stepfathers spend more time in organized youth activities than cohabiting stepfathers, but few differences exist in the activities in the home (Thomson et al., 1992). Similar results were reported by Buchanan, Maccoby, and Dornbusch (1996), who found that married stepfathers and cohabiting-stepfathers were involved in similar activities with children. Children living with stepfathers in cohabiting-parent families and those in married-parent families share similar maternal and paternal responses (Thomson et al., 1992). The level of parental control is similar for children living in cohabiting stepfamilies and married stepfamilies (Buchanan et al., 1996). In the National Survey of Families and Households (NSFH), children in married-couple stepfamilies experience somewhat fewer rules (supervision and television) than children living in cohabiting-couple stepfamilies (Thomson et al., 1992).

Comparisons of parenting in unmarried mother families with a cohabiting partner and those without suggest that few differences exist. Thomson et al. (1992) found that children in cohabiting-parent families eat breakfast less often together but otherwise they share similar activities with their mother as children in single-mother families. The maternal positive response to children is lower in cohabiting than in single-mother families but the negative responses are similar for both family types (Thomson et al., 1992). Maternal emotional support is reported to be not statistically different for cohabiting and single mothers (Dunifon & Kowalski-Jones, 2000). The cognitive stimulation is similar for single and cohabiting Black mothers and is more negative for White children in married or cohabiting families than in single-mother families (Dunifon & Kowaleski-Jones, 2000). The supervision and control over children are alike in cohabiting and divorced single-mother families (except for television; Thomson et al., 1992).

---

[4] Parental aggrevation is measured by questions about anger, bother, how hard child is to deal with, and parents' sacrifice to meet child's needs.

CHILDREN AND THE STABILITY
OF COHABITING UNIONS

A commonly cited limitation of cohabitation for children's well-being is the insta-bility of cohabiting unions (e.g., Poponoe & Whitehead, 1999). It has been docu-mented that cohabiting unions are quite short in duration, lasting on average 2 years (Bumpass, 1998). Yet, to understand the implications for children one needs to know more about the duration of cohabiting unions that include children, as well as directly contrast the duration of cohabiting unions from the child's per-spective.

To begin, children born during cohabitation or prior to cohabitation do not hasten or delay the end of their parents' cohabiting union (Manning, 2000). These results suggest that the high levels of instability of cohabiting unions are not caused by children.

A key limitation of most work on stability of cohabiting unions is the defini-tion of the end of the union. Almost all of the evidence indicating that cohabita-tion is unstable uses the traditional method of conceptualizing the end as when the union stops either by marriage or by dissolution of the relationship (e.g., Graefe & Lichter, 1999). However, this method does not take into account that the parents' union is still intact if they marry. Unlike marriage, cohabitations can end in two ways, marriage or separation. Almost half of cohabiting unions result in marriage (Bumpass, 1998), indicating that the legal status of the relationship has shifted but the relationship has not ended. Most prior studies define the end of the relation-ship as the point the cohabitation ends (marriage or separation). It measures whether the cohabiting union ends or not and is termed a *union-based* measure. In this case, the possible outcomes are that the union has remained intact, ended in sepa-ration, or ended in marriage.

Graefe and Lichter (1999) used the National Longitudinal Survey of Youth (NLSY) and single-decrement life tables[5] to demonstrate that children born into cohabiting unions experience a transition out of that union fairly quickly. Their estimates indicate that by 5 years of age 60% of children born into cohabiting unions had moved into a married-couple family, 28% moved into a single-mother family and 12% remained in their parents cohabiting union (Graefe & Lichter, 1999).

Another conceptual end point is important—the end of the parents' relation-ship. This end point is key, especially from the perspective of children: the termi-nation of the coresidential relationship, whether or not the parents marry. This can be operationalized as the date they stopped living together; the end of the relation-ship is defined as the date of separation for those who do not marry and the date of divorce or legal separation for those cohabiting couples who marry. This approach

---

[5] Single-decrement tables do not take into account the competing risk of other events. In the case of cohabitation, the single-decrement tables of marriage do not account for the probability of separation.

allows an examination of the stability of their parents' relationship in marriage as well as cohabitation. Landale and Hauan (1992) applied this technique to their analysis of the family life course of Puerto Rican children. This measure establishes whether the relationship has ended or not and is referred to as a *couple-based* measure. An implicit assumption in prior work is that the transition to marriage leads to stability for cohabiting couples but marriage may not guarantee a stable future. Indeed, Graefe and Lichter (1999) reported that 17% of children who first moved to a married-couple family had experienced the end of that marriage by age 5.

Applying a couple-based measure of stability Manning et al. (2000) used the National Survey of Family Growth to contrast the experiences of paternal instability for children born to cohabiting and married couples. Research tends to lump different kinds of cohabiting families together and I argue that it may be understandable why cohabiting stepfamilies are unstable, but the comparison that needs to be made is that between the two-biological parent cohabiting couple family and the two-biological parent married couple family. The multivariate analyses provide support for the claims that cohabiting unions are less stable for children than marriages and this is true for Black, White, and Hispanic children. These results are consistent with findings based on Puerto Rican children born in the mid-1980s. Landale and Hauan (1992) reported that children born into informal or cohabiting unions experience higher odds of dissolution than children born into marriages.

The relative benefits of marriage are further examined in two ways. First, does parental marriage promote greater couple stability for children born into cohabiting families? The movement into marriage for children born into cohabiting unions provides some buffer against parental disruption for children. Yet once we account for timing of marriage parental marriage does not protect Hispanic children born into cohabiting unions from instability. Thus, Hispanic children born to cohabiting parents who married experience similar levels of disruption as children whose parents did not marry.

Second, the benefit of marriage for children of cohabitation is evaluated by contrasting instability among children born to cohabiting parents whose parents married and those born into married-couple families. Children born to cohabiting parents who marry experience similar levels of instability as children born into married families. Yet the timing of marriage is an important factor. Among Black children, the marriage of cohabiting parents promotes stability and equalizes the experiences of children born to cohabiting versus married parents. In contrast, marriage timing does not provide the same buffer for Hispanic and White children. Accounting for timing of marriage reveals that Hispanic and White children born to cohabiting parents who marry are more likely to experience their parents' disruption than children born into marriage.

The stability of parental relationships (cohabitation and marriage) has also been evaluated for children living in stepfamilies those who share a residence with only one biological parent (Bumpass, Raley, & Sweet, 1995). Analyses based on the NSFH reveal that children living in married-couple stepfamilies and cohabiting-couple stepfamilies share similar odds of disruption (Bumpass et al., 1995). Thus, cohabitation is just as stable of a living arrangement as marriage for children living with only one biological parent.

COHABITATION AND CHILD OUTCOMES

The literature on the implications of cohabitation has begun to grow rapidly. Yet, to date only a limited number of published papers examine children's social well-being in cohabiting-parent families (e.g., Buchanan et al., 1996; Hanson, McLanahan, & Thomson, 1997; Thomson, Hanson & McLanahan, 1994). Published work on the economic implications of cohabitation is more common (e.g., Bauman 1999; Brandon & Bumpass, 2001; Carlson & Danziger, 1999; Manning & Lichter, 1996; Winkler, 1993, 1997). New work has been presented at national conferences due to the recognition of cohabitation as a potentially important family type and the availability of new data.

Here, I discuss data limitations and analytic concerns. Then I focus on a series of five outcomes. First, I discuss the social outcomes typically addressed, such as behavior and emotional problems and social interactions. Second, I consider academic performance or achievement. The third topic examined is the association between cohabitation and child abuse. Fourth, I present results from projects focusing on both resident and nonresident father involvement. Finally, I discuss the indicators of economic well-being, including poverty, material hardship, family wealth, and welfare use. Overall, children from cohabiting-parent families appear to possess some unique social developmental behaviors as well as economic circumstances.

Data and Family Type Comparisons

Data used in these projects include the NSFH, NLSY, the National Longitudinal Survey of the High School Class of 1972 (NLS–72), National Survey of American Families (NSAF), Survey of Income and Program Participation (SIPP), U.S. Census, Current Population Survey (CPS), the Fragile Family project, and a few specific regional data collections. Each data source contains advantages and disadvantages making no one source optimal.

Central concerns with each data source are the number of cohabiting-parent families and the measure of cohabitation employed. For example, the NSFH is nationally representative and contains two waves of data but has only a limited number of cohabiting unions with children (N=125; Thomson et al., 1994). Their cohabiting-parent families are equivalent to stepparent families, one-biological parent and the parent's cohabiting partner. The number of cases used for a similar analyses that includes children from two-biological cohabiting parent families are not reported (Hanson et al., 1997), but based on Bumpass (1994) it appears there are approximately 100 two-biological parent families. The NLSY contains rich panel data but includes only yearly measures of cohabitation making it difficult to detect short-term unions and whether the same union remained intact across interviews. Also, it is hard to determine who is represented in these data because it is based on young mothers (14–21 years old) in 1979. The NLS–72 is based on the 1972 high school graduation cohort. It provides in-depth prospective data but it contains only one cohort of children who all graduated from high school. This is particularly problematic with regard to analyses of cohabitation and parenting because women with the lowest levels of education are most likely to cohabit and have children within cohabitation (Bumpass & Lu, 2000; Manning, 1999). The NSAF data are new, cross-sectional, and include questions about cohabitation status. Yet, these data do not include retrospective histories of family living arrangements or date of cohabitation. The SIPP data are a longitudinal panel that includes excellent economic data, but prior to 1996 the SIPP data only included inferred measures of cohabitation. Since 1990, the Census and the 1995 CPS have included unmarried partner as a relationship category in the household roster.[6] This provides basic descriptive information but lacks data on family histories and relationships of children to the cohabiting partner. The Fragile Family project is based on interviews with mothers in hospitals shortly after the birth of their child. To date, data have been collected in a few cities but have the potential to speak to outcomes for young children in certain metropolitan areas.

An important advantage of these data sources is that they enable researchers to include a wide array of control variables. Most of the work discussed here is based on multivariate analyses. The papers commonly include controls for socio-economic status, race, and poverty. More refined analyses that seek to understand more about the mechanisms underlying family structure differentials and include other measures, such as parenting practices (Hanson et al., 1997; Thomson et al., 1994), home environment (Dunifon & Kowaleski-Jones, 2000), or relationship quality (Buchanan et al., 1996).

An informed understanding of the implications of cohabitation requires a keen awareness of the comparison group. Often, researchers are interested in whether married families are better for children than cohabiting-parent families. Yet, simply accounting for marital status ignores the importance of the biological relationship to the child. For example, if the goal is to determine the effect of marriage on children it is not appropriate to compare married-couple stepfamilies to two-biological cohabiting parent families. Both married- and cohabiting-couple families should be separated into those with two-biological parents and only one-biological parent (stepfamilies). The same issue is important when the comparison group

---

[6] See Casper and Cohen (2000) for a discussion of indirect estimates of cohabitation.

is unmarried parents. The common question posed is whether children fare better living with just their mother or their mother and her cohabiting partner. Again the answer may depend on whether the cohabiting partner is the biological parent of the child or not. In my review of the literature, I attempt to distinguish both marital status and biological relationship by making three sets of comparisons: two-biological cohabiting versus two-biological parent married families; stepparent married couple versus stepparent cohabiting couple families; and single unmarried mother families versus cohabiting mother families.

In some studies, family type differentials can only be approximated because tests of statistical significance have not been estimated. This is due in part to sample size limits or family type is included largely as a control variable and not of substantive interest to the researchers. Dunifon and Kowaleski-Jones (2000) included significance tests between cohabiting stepfamilies and single-mother families as well as differences in the biological relationship of the cohabiting partner to the child in cohabiting-parent families. Clark and Nelson (2000) focused on two-parent families and test for statistical differences in parents' marital status among two biological parent families as well as stepfamilies. Hanson et al. (1997) included two-biological parent families as the reference category permitting contrasts of married and cohabiting two-biological parent families. Thomson et al. (1994) used two-biological parents as their reference category preventing analyses of statistical differences between cohabiting and married stepfamilies. Morrison's (2000) work targets children of divorce and contrasts how children in cohabiting and married stepfamilies fare.

Most often, previous studies examine children's current living circumstances (e.g., Clark & Nelson, 2000; Thomson et al., 1994). At times, researchers account for duration in these types of families (Dunifon & Kowaleski-Jones, 2000), but this is rare. As a result, most of the information about the effects of cohabitation is based on how intact cohabiting unions influence child outcomes. Few data sources can be used to address questions of how prior transitions in and out of particular families influence child outcomes. A key exception is Morrison's (1998, 2000) work as she accounts for stability of remarriage or cohabitation, duration of union, and prior experience with cohabitation. This is a central issue that deserves further attention.

Behavior and Emotional Problems

Behavior problems are measured using indicators of school-related problems and several components that are sometimes indexed together (using a behavior problem index or subscales of behaviors) or analyzed separately. They typically include measures of the child's temperament, externalizing, internalizing, sociability, and initiative. A key shortcoming is that all of these analyses are restricted to children who are at least age 5 and do not include information about very young children.

Two Biological Parents

Analyses of behavior problems in the NSAF data reveal no significant differences between children living with two-biological parent married and cohabiting-parent families (Clark & Nelson, 2000). More refined analyses show that greater behavioral problems are experienced by Hispanic children in cohabiting parent than married parent families. Hanson et al. (1997) found that children in two-biological cohabiting parent families have statistically similar externalizing, internalizing, sociability, and initiative scores as children in two-biological married parent families.

The research focusing on school behaviors yields similar results. There are no significant differences in the odds that a child from a two-biological married or cohabiting-parent family engaged in school behavior problems (Hanson et al., 1997). Analyses focusing on whether the child was expelled or suspended from school as the dependent variable indicate a few differences between married and cohabiting two-biological parent families (Clark & Nelson, 2000). Further analyses of the NSAF data show race/ethnic and age differences in some of these patterns (Clark & Nelson, 2000).

Stepfamilies

Some of the children who are living in cohabiting-parent families may not be living with the biological father, and it is more appropriate to compare their well-being to children in stepparent families. Children in cohabiting-parent families and stepfamilies in the NSFH appear to have similar levels of behavioral problems after controlling for parenting and socioeconomic characteristics (Hanson et al., 1997; Thomson et al., 1994).[7] These results are confirmed by Clark and Nelson (2000), who showed that overall children living in cohabiting-partner stepfamilies and married-couple stepfamilies share statistically similar levels of behavior problems. Morrison (1998) reported similar findings in her NLSY analysis of the change in problem behaviors among children in remarried versus cohabiting parent families. She found that children of divorce living in married stepfamilies and cohabiting stepfamilies share statistically similar levels of reported behavior problems. Moreover, Morrison (2000) reported that children from divorced families who remained in a stable cohabitation scored as well on externalizing and internalizing indicators as children in stable remarriages.

Yet, some evidence indicates that children living in stepfamilies are negatively influenced by the presence of a cohabiting partner. Older Hispanic children in cohabiting stepfamilies exhibit greater behavior problems than older Hispanic children in married stepfamilies. Children in cohabiting-parent stepfamilies have higher odds of being suspended or expelled from school, these differences were

---

[7] The authors focus on intact married couple families and use this category for their reference group. Statistically significant differences among the other family types were not reported in the paper and cannot be inferred.

statistically significant for White and Hispanic children (Clark & Nelson, 2000). Gender differences in adjustment are presented in Buchanan et al.'s (1996) analysis of children who experienced their parents' divorce in the mid-1980 in two counties in California. They found that girls who live with their mother's cohabiting partner experience similar behavior problems as those who live with their mother's spouse. Boys experience greater adjustment problems when their mother cohabited, but these differences are explained by the quality of the parent–child relationship and level of parental supervision and control (Buchanan et al., 1996).

Unmarried-Parent Families

The final contrast is how children in cohabiting-parent families fare in contrast to children in unmarried-parent families. This is not the goal of the Thomson et al. (1994) or Hanson et al. (1997) papers, but the coefficients suggest similar involvement in problem behaviors for children from cohabiting and married-parent stepfamilies. Also, Morrison's (1998) fixed effects analyses of NLSY data demonstrate that those children living with divorced, single parents have statistically similar levels of behavior problems as children in cohabiting parent families. A comparable analytic strategy using the NLSY data and relying on total number of years in each family type reveals that children in two-parent families have better social interactions than children in one-parent families, and the benefit from two parents exists regardless of the type of union (Dunifon & Kowaleski-Jones, 2000).

Cognitive Behaviors

Several indicators of cognitive behavior are included in the literature: school performance, grade point average (GPA), Peabody Individual Achievement Tests (PIAT) in subject areas, and school engagement.

Two Biological Parents

Dunifon and Kowaleski-Jones (2000) concluded that among children living with two biological parents, children in cohabiting- and married-couple families share similar levels of academic achievement.[8] Yet, among White girls, it appears there is an added value of having a biological father married to the mother. Similarly, children from married and cohabiting two-biological parent families possess statistically equivalent school performance and GPA scores (Hanson et al., 1997). The effects of family type on school engagement are quite similar for children in married and cohabiting two-biological parent families (Clark & Nelson, 2000), but there are some differences for young White children and older Hispanic children.

---

[8] Tests of statistical differences between years spent in marriage and cohabitation are not presented.

Stepfamilies

Overall, children in cohabiting and married stepfamilies have statistically similar school engagement (Clark & Nelson, 2000). Further analyses indicate that older Hispanic and white children living in cohabiting stepfamilies have lower school engagement than their counterparts in married stepfamilies. Furthermore, Morrison (2000) found that among children from disrupted marriages, those in stable cohabitations and remarriages have statistically equivalent math and reading PIAT scores. Yet, once controlling for cohabitation prior to remarriage, children living in stable cohabiting unions score worse on reading and the same on math as children in stable remarriages. Among children living in stepfamilies, children in cohabiting-parent families appear to have lower academic performance than children in married stepfamilies (Hanson et al., 1997; Thomson et al., 1994), but statistical differences are not estimated.

Unmarried-Parent Families

Academic achievement of children from cohabiting-parent families is significantly higher than that of children in single-parent families (Dunifom & Kowaleski-Jones, 2000). Yet, Black girls benefit from the presence of their mother's cohabiting partner only on math and reading scores. The reading scores do not differ for Black girls living with just their mother and those living with their mother's cohabiting partner. School performance appears slightly lower among children in cohabiting one-biological parent families than divorced unmarried mother families (Hanson et al., 1997; Thomson et al., 1994), but these differences are not statistically tested.

Child Abuse

The relationship between child abuse and family structure is an important topic that deserves careful attention. Popenoe and his colleagues drew on the findings from two research papers (Margolin, 1992; Whelan, 1993) as part of the basis for their claim that cohabitation presents a "clear and present danger" for children (Popenoe & Whitehead, 1999, p. 1). While there may be some merit to the argument that cohabitation presents a physically dangerous environment for children, the empirical evidence supporting this claim is quite weak. Due to the weight that these studies have been given in publications about the merits of cohabitation and the limited number of studies on child abuse in cohabitation, I carefully review the evidence here.

The Margolin (1992) study is based on two samples. The first sample consists of interviews with mothers of children born between 1984 and 1990 in an Iowa county and includes 20 cohabiting mothers. This sample is further limited to seven cohabiting mothers who relied on their cohabiting partner for nonparental caregiving in the last week. These seven cases are the basis of further analyses that estimate the expected level of child abuse given the number of hours of care they provide. The second sample is drawn from cases of physical abuse by nonparents between 1985 and 1986 in Iowa. The majority (64%) of these children abused by nonparents were abused by their mother's boyfriend. Unfortunately, Margolin (1992) was unable to distinguish between the effects of a nonresident boyfriend and cohabiting partner. The results are far from conclusive about abuse and cohabitation, and should be considered quite tentative.

The second study (Whelan, 1993) is often cited as evidence of the high incidence of child abuse in cohabiting-parent families. This project is based on child abuse between 1982 and 1988 in Great Britain. The conclusions about child abuse are based on analyses that contrast the proportion of children living in cohabiting-parent families to the proportion of child abuse cases that occur in cohabiting-parent families. The conclusions about child abuse are based on the experiences of only 131 children and 32 children from cohabiting-parent families. These results are based on a minimal number of cases with data from over a decade ago in a different cultural context. Thus, these results should be interpreted with extreme caution and other researchers should not base their understanding of cohabitation on these results.

Despite the shortcomings of both of these studies, child abuse is a central concern and certainly the association between cohabitation and child abuse is an important avenue for future research. Further research should consider children's experiences with parental aggression and parental violence toward one another. Once researchers have accounted for both marital status and biological relationship to the child it will be valuable to know more about the differences in child abuse according to family type.

Father Involvement

Children's welfare is influenced by the extent of father involvement in their lives. Only limited research attention has been paid to resident fathers in cohabiting-parent families and slightly more notice has been given to nonresident father involvement.

Resident Fathers

Married, cohabiting, and single parents all share quite similar values about fatherhood roles (Waller, 1999). Using data from seven cities in the Fragile Families Project, Waller reported that regardless of union status, men and women view fatherhood roles (financial, teacher, discipline, protection, affection, caring) in a similar manner. To date, the only project that contrasts the involvement of married versus cohabiting biological fathers is an analysis of Puerto Rican children (Landale and Oropesa, forthcoming). They find that children in married and cohabiting parent families at birth experience similar levels of paternal involvement and financial support. As discussed previously, stepfathers spend more time in activities outside the home than cohabiting stepfathers but with regard to participation in activities within the home, supervision, and paternal response cohabiting and married stepfathers are quite similar (Thomson et al., 1992). These results are confirmed by Buchanan et al. (1996), who found that children of divorce engage in similar activities with their mother's cohabiting partner as her spouse. Yet, they found that children living with a cohabiting partner report lower acceptance of the partner's authority and feel less close to the cohabiting partner than their mother's spouse (Buchanan et al., 1996).

Fathers' *actual* involvement in unmarried mother families varies across union types (Carlson & McLanahan, 2000; Landale & Oropesa, forthcoming). Puerto Rican children in cohabiting-parent families receive more father involvement and financial support than children in single-mother families (Landale & Oropesa, forthcoming). These results are confirmed in preliminary results from the Fragile Families Project. Unmarried mothers who are cohabiting receive more financial support and other types of assistance during their pregnancy than do unmarried women who are not cohabiting (Carlson & McLahanan, 2000). Furthermore, their paper indicates that fathers who are cohabiting with their child's mother have higher odds of visiting the mother of the child, having his name on the birth certificate, and sharing the father's last name. Carlson and McLanahan (2000) also reported that mothers who are cohabiting have greater desire for the father to be involved in raising the child. These results are not based on the complete set of cities from the Fragile Families Project but they are indicative of patterns of father involvement in unmarried mother families.

Nonresident Fathers

Increasingly, fathers are living apart from their children and are "fathering from a distance." Their abilities to father and remain involved with their children may depend on the living arrangements of the parents at the time of the child's birth. Researchers focus on the social as well as economic ties of nonresident fathers to their children.

Seltzer (2000b) employed both waves of the NSFH and her results are based on bivariate comparisons. She found that weekly visits occur slightly more often among fathers who are cohabiting at the time of the child's birth than fathers who are married or living alone. Yet, when contact is measured by whether any visitation occurred, children born in cohabiting unions are less likely to see their father than children born in marriage and more likely than children born to single parents. Cooksey and Craig (1998) reported similar results with respect to monthly visits. Using the second wave of the NSFH, they find that children born in cohabiting families see their fathers less often than children born in married couple families. However, when they focus on how often nonresident-fathers talk with their children, no significant differences exist between men who had children in marriage, cohabitation, or alone (Cooksey & Craig, 1998). Evidence from Canada indicates that children born into cohabiting-parent families are half as likely to maintain contact net of custody, child support agreement, tension between parents, and time elapsed since disruption (Marcil-Gratton, Bourdais, & La Pierre-Adamcyk, 1999).

Cooksey and Craig (1998) also included measures for fathers' current living circumstances and report that fathers who are cohabiting at the time of interview are significantly less likely to visit monthly than fathers who are married but appeared to be as likely to visit as fathers who are single. In contrast, their analyses of weekly father–child talks show no statistical differences based on fathers' current living arrangements.

Financial support, measured by payment of any child support, occurred less often among fathers who were cohabiting when the child was born than fathers who were married (Seltzer, 2000b). Fathers who had children with unmarried mothers are more likely to pay child support to those they lived with than those they did not (Seltzer, 2000b). Analyses of children in Canada generally confirm these findings and test these relationships in a multivariate framework (Marcil-Gratton & Bourdais, 1999). The parents of children born in cohabiting unions are less likely to seek out court orders for support and if they had agreements former cohabitors are less likely to pay regularly than parents of children born in marriage.

Economic Consequences

Definitions of Family

Official poverty estimates are based on family income and the cohabiting partner is not considered part of the family. Researchers have recognized that cohabiting partners contribute financially to the family (e.g., Edin & Lein, 1997; Manning & Lichter, 1996; Morrison & Ritualo, 2000; Winkler, 1993). Recently, the National Academy of Sciences recommended that the definition of family be expanded such that cohabiting partners' income be included as part of family income when estimating poverty levels (Citro & Michael, 1995). Each approach represents an extreme. The official estimates assume that the partner provides nothing, and the expanded family definition assumes that the partner shares equally with all family members. It is unlikely that either of these simple assumptions accurately reflects the circumstances experienced by cohabiting families (Bauman, 1999).

The inclusion the cohabiting partner's income as part of the family income makes a substantial difference in the poverty levels of children in cohabiting-parent families (Manning & Lichter, 1996). Their analysis of the 1990 Public Use Microdata Samples (PUMS) data indicate that poverty rates of children in unmarried families in 1990 were quite high, close to 50%. When the male partner's income is treated as part of the family income and he is counted as part of the consuming unit, about 31% of children in cohabiting-parent families are living in poverty, compared with 44% when the partner is excluded from the family (see also Bauman, 1999; Carlson & Danziger, 1999; Manning & Smock, 1997).

Economic Well-Being

Children living in cohabiting-couple families fare worse economically than their counterparts in married couple families, but fare better than children living with single mothers (Manning & Lichter, 1996). Living with two parents does not guarantee economic security, and the parents of children in married couple families possess considerably stronger socioeconomic resources than cohabiting parents. Morrison and Ritualo (2000) focused on children's well-being after parental divorce. They find that the gains from remarriage and cohabitation are similar and that cohabitation and remarriage do equally well at restoring the income of children to predivorce levels. Yet the absolute levels of income are lower for children in cohabiting than remarried parent families.

Another measure of economic uncertainty is material hardship and indicates whether there were times when a household did not meet its essential expenses. Using the SIPP data, Bauman (1999) found that income from cohabiting partners did significantly less to alleviate material hardship than did the income from a spouse. These findings suggest that cohabiting and married individuals may not share their income in the same manner. It appears that children in cohabiting-parent families could potentially benefit less from their parent's cohabiting partner than they would from their parent's spouse. However, Winkler (1997) found that those cohabiting families with a shared biological child exhibit more pooling than those without children.

Family wealth has been argued to be a more appropriate measure of children's economic well-being and is defined as the current market value of assets. It indexes consumption providing a more direct indicator of resources that can be invested in children (Hao, 1996). Bivariate comparisons indicate that cohabiting families with children have lower levels of wealth than married couple or stepparent families with children and similar levels of wealth as single-parent families (Hao, 1996). Yet, once duration, number of children, education, marital history, and community conditions are controlled cohabiting-parent families and intact biological families share similar levels of wealth and children in cohabiting-parent families experience higher wealth than single-parent children (Hao, 1996).

Welfare

Part of welfare reform has called for encouraging the formation and mainte-nance of two-parent families. Cohabiting-parent families represent a growing family form but it may not be the two-parent family form envisioned by the architects of welfare reform. Cohabitation is a type of two-parent family that is often not con-sidered in research on welfare. Moffitt, Reville, and Winkler (1998) have exam-ined the state-level Aid to Families with Dependent Children (AFDC) eligibility rules for cohabiting families. If the cohabiting male was biologically related to the child, the family was treated like a married-couple family. The treatment of chil-dren in married- and cohabiting-parent families when the children are biologi-cally related to both partners or spouses is quite similar. However, if the male was not biologically related to the child, children in cohabiting families were not treated the same as children in stepfamilies. In stepfamilies, male income was counted against the welfare grant. In cohabiting-partner families, his income was not counted against the grant in many states. Some variation existed across states, but often, his contribution was ignored (Moffitt et al., 1998). As a consequence, children in stepfamilies formed by marriage were treated differently from children in stepfamilies formed by cohabitation. It is now important to learn more about the treatment of children in cohabiting unions in Temporary Assistance for Needy Families (TANF). It may be difficult to chart these changes with the devolution of welfare to the state-level (see Primus & Beeson, chap. 12, this volume).

Analyses of PUMS data indicate that children living in a cohabiting couple family are slightly less likely (24%) to receive AFDC than children living with single mothers (30%; Manning & Lichter, 1996). A much more detailed examina-tion of welfare receipt and family type illustrates some key differences in welfare receipt based on biological relationships between cohabiting partners and chil-dren. Brandon and Bumpass (2001) relied on the SIPP data to examine differ-ences in types and rates of public assistance for various types of families. Not surprisingly, levels of AFDC receipt are highest for children living with only their mother (predicted probabilities equal 0.22). Children living with their biological mother and her cohabiting partner also have high levels of AFDC receipt with predicted probabilities of 0.18. Their odds of welfare receipt are almost twice as high as for children living with two biological cohabiting parents. Children resid-ing in households with married parents experienced the lowest probabilities of welfare receipt, half as high as two-biological cohabiting parent families. These empirical results basically reflect the eligibility rules outlined by Moffitt et al. (1998). At the same time, we can see considerable variation in how children in cohabiting families are treated under the former welfare system.

DISCUSSION

Many children will spend some part of their lives in a cohabiting-parent family. Knowledge about the implications of cohabitation for children's lives has recently begun to increase. Interestingly, this subject was outlined as being important in the mid-1980s by Blanc (1984):

> Further inquiry into nonmarital cohabitation, especially its effects on fertility, on society as a whole and on parents and their children will be accomplished by detailed studies on the nature of the cohabitational union, on the couples who have children within cohabitational relationships, and on the extent to which this phenomenon has become a socially acceptable lifestyle. (p. 191)

I argue that it is important to investigate the biological relationship of parents to children as well as the parents' relationship to each other. Children enter cohabiting unions by being born to cohabiting parents or by moving into a cohabiting-parent family. Children born to cohabiting parents are typically born into two-biological parent families, whereas children who move into cohabiting-parent families most often live with only one biological parent. The evidence to date is not yet conclusive but suggests some basic patterns. Children born in cohabiting unions experience greater rates of parental instability than children born in marriages, but children in stepfamilies with a married or cohabiting parent face similar odds of dissolution (Bumpass et al., 1995; Landale & Hauan, 1992; Manning et al., 2000).

The relationship between cohabitation and children's outcomes are briefly reviewed. Generally, the marital status of biological parents does not have much impact on children's social well-being. Children in cohabiting-parent families have similar behavior and emotional problems as children in married-parent families (Clark & Nelson, 2000; Dunifom & Kowaleski-Jones, 2000; Hanson et al., 1997; Morrison, 2000; Thomson et al., 1994). The school achievement and engagement are reported to be fairly similar for children in married/and cohabiting-parent families, with a few differentials for young White and older Hispanic children (Clark & Nelson, 2000). The findings related to school problem behaviors are somewhat mixed with Hanson et al. (1997) reporting no differentials and Clark and Nelson (2000) finding significant differentials. The receipt of AFDC is almost two-times greater in two biological parent cohabiting than married families (Brandon & Bumpass, 2001).

Children in married and cohabiting stepfamilies fare equivalently well with regard to behavioral and emotional problems (Clark & Nelson, 2000). They also generally share similar levels of school engagement and achievement scores (Clark & Nelson, 2000; Morrison, 2000). Children living in cohabiting-stepparent families have greater school behavior problems than children in married stepfamilies (Clark & Nelson, 2000) and there are some greater adjustment problems experienced by boys (Buchanan et al., 1996). The evidence on child abuse has been used to argue against cohabitation as an arena in which to raise children (Margolin, 1992) but the evidence is not conclusive and requires more rigorous evaluation. The economic gains to remarriage and cohabitation are quite similar but the absolute levels of well-being are lower for children in cohabiting-parent than married-parent families (Morrison & Ritualo, 2000).

Among children in unmarried-parent families, those living with cohabiting parents have similar behavior problems and social interactions as children with married and single parents (Clark & Nelson, 2000; Dunifom & Kowaleski-Jones, 2000; Morrison, 2000; Thomson et al., 1994). In fact, academic achievement is greater in some cohabiting than in single-parent families (Dunifon & Kowaleski-Jones, 2000). Children living in cohabiting-parent families experience improved economic circumstances and equivalent wealth in contrast to children living in single-mother families (Hao, 1996; Manning & Lichter, 1996). The receipt of AFDC is somewhat lower among children living in cohabiting families with one biological parent than children living in single-parent families (Brandon & Bumpass, 2001).

Increased attention has been paid to the issue of father involvement but hardly any research has examined differences among resident fathers. Resident father involvement with children is quite similar for children in married- and cohabiting-parent stepfamilies (Buchanan et al., 1996; Thomson et al., 1994) but the children's reports of relationships with their parent's new spouse-partner depend on the parent's marital status (Buchanan et al., 1996). Children in cohabiting-parent families appear to receive much more father attention than children in other unmarried parent family types (Carlson & McLanahan, 2000).

The disadvantage of being born to a cohabiting parent seems to emerge once the child and father live apart. Children born to cohabiting-parent families experience lower levels of nonresident father involvement for measures of visitation and child support payments than children born in marriage (Cooksey & Craig, 1998; Seltzer, 2000a). The frequency of verbal contact with nonresident children does not appear to depend on the father's union status at the time of the child's birth (Cooksey & Craig, 1998). These findings may signal the longer term influence of cohabitation on children's lives.

In Cherlin's (1999) Population Association of America presidential address "Going to Extremes: Family Structure, Children's Well-Being, and Social Science" he argued that understanding the effects of family structure presents several challenges. Researchers examining family structure have to be cautious and not treat family structure as if it is an "epiphenomenon" (Cherlin, 1999). Family structure alone does not guarantee extreme negative or positive outcomes, but instead has to be considered in the context of the life of the child. Additionally, to understand family structure researchers need to do more than simply report significant differences. For example, significant differences may exist for some outcomes at the aggregate level but relatively few children may experience the outcome of interest. Alternatively, there may be no significant difference in the relationship between family structure and a child outcome at the aggregate level but family structure may matter more or less among certain types of individuals. This calls for a more person-centered approach rather than a variable-oriented examination of the influence of families on children's well-being.

There are several limitations to this body of work that provide opportunities for new research. An important one is the inability to disentangle selection issues. This is a common problem in research on family structure. It is hard to determine whether family structure causes observed differentials or whether unmeasured factors are responsible for the association between family structure and these outcomes (see Cherlin, 1999). Research needs to evaluate the characteristics of individuals who decide to enter cohabitation and remain cohabiting as well as how cohabitation itself may impact children through potential changes in their parent's attitudes or behaviors. It seems as if the observed differentials could not be completely explained by selection or unmeasured factors but this remains to be empirically evaluated.

Most of these studies are based on static rather than dynamic measures of family structure. Often, data limitations force researchers to use only the current living arrangements of children. The upshot of this approach is that children in stable cohabiting unions and stable marriages are compared. The results of research on the behavioral, emotional, and academic outcomes indicate few differentials for children from cohabiting- and married-couple families. The explanation may be that these are all relatively stable family types. This literature does not include an in-depth examination how the experience of cohabitation (stable or unstable) influences children's lives. An exception is Morrison (1998, 2000), who was able to include detailed measures of family experiences by using the NLSY. For example, she found that accounting for mother's prior cohabitation experience attenuates differentials in the reading outcomes of children in stable cohabiting unions and remarriages. Further analysis of how both unstable and stable cohabitations and marriages influence children is warranted

Data limitations prevent examinations of the long-term implications of cohabitation. Until recently, this question was not of interest because so few children had spent time in cohabiting-parent families. The new generation of children is facing the highest odds of ever experiencing parental cohabitation. A new avenue of research is to consider how children's experiences in cohabiting-parent families influence their own young adult outcomes. In this sense, family history will need to be broadened to include cohabitation.

Conclusions about the effect of cohabitation on children's lives should explicitly account for variability in the experiences of children in cohabiting families. The odds children experience cohabitation differ according to race and ethnicity as well as parents' socioeconomic status and marital history (Brown, 2000c; Bumpass & Lu, 2000). Some researchers examine age and race differences in the effects of cohabitation on child outcomes (Clark & Nelson, 2000;

Dunfion & Kowaleski-Jones, 2000; Manning & Lichter, 1996). More careful attention to variations will provide a more accurate and complete portrayal of children's experiences in cohabiting-parent families.

A broader scope of child outcomes needs to be studied. A shortcoming of the prior research on social and psychological outcomes has been an emphasis on outcomes for older children (over the age of 6). Most of the children who live with two-biological cohabiting parents are young children under the age of 4 (Bumpass, 1994) and suggests that measures of the well-being appropriate for young children are necessary. To date, few researchers have examined the implications of cohabitation for children's physical health outcomes. One exception is a project that examines the mechanisms underlying generational differences in birth weight and infant mortality among Puerto Rican mothers (Landale, Oropesa, Llanes, & Gorman, 1999). They reported no significant differences in the effects of union status on infant health outcomes. Given the association between maternal behavior and planning status, more attention should be paid to how planning status and cohabitation experience influence children's health outcomes.

The research conducted should not be simply descriptive but attempt to analyze the mechanisms that underlie the patterns of behavior. We need to know not only whether differences exist but why do the differences exist. For example, why do children in cohabiting-parent families fare worse than children in two-biological parent families. Theoretically driven research will help ensure an emphasis on mechanisms or processes and as a result help to identify the sources of similarities and differences.

The policy environment governing children's lives has been shifting. Father involvement is more often legalized and enforced. The implication of formalizing father involvement for families that are not legally bound together is intriguing (Seltzer, 2000a). Welfare reform poses new questions about the treatment of cohabiting-parent families. Should they be treated as marriage equivalents and should policies differentiate among cohabiting families based on their biological relationship to children. Brandon and Bumpass (2001) demonstrated the importance of accounting for biological relationships of children as AFDC receipt ranges from a low of 0.08 among two-biological cohabiting parent families to much higher levels for one-biological parent cohabiting families (0.18). New incentives to encourage and stabilize marriages are becoming popular. Are these incentives going to also promote the formation and maintenance of two-parent cohabiting families? Policymakers need to clarify how cohabiting families are treated and recognize cohabitation as a potentially viable family form. As a result, policies will be identified to help disadvantaged children regardless of family type.

The understanding of cohabitation can benefit from turning to other social contexts. Researchers often look to western Europe as a source of information about potential future trends for two reasons. First, the levels of cohabitation are generally higher in Europe and speak to future trends. Second, scholarship on cohabitation was more advanced in Europe than in the United States. Yet, it is unlikely that the patterns of partnering and parenting in the United States will ever match that of Sweden or many other European countries. In Sweden, the majority of first-born children are born into cohabiting unions and almost all nonmarital childbearing occurs to cohabitors. However, researchers in the United States cannot rely on European research as a guide to understand how cohabitation influences children's lives. European scholars rarely consider the effects of cohabitation on children's lives in part because the levels of cohabitation and fertility in cohabiting unions are quite high. Some further attention to the effects of cohabitation on children's lives in Europe may be helpful for understanding cohabitation in the United States.

Cohabitation is a family type that is still rapidly changing. In a relatively short time span, the proportion of young adults experiencing cohabitation rose, the percentage of cohabiting unions ending in marriage declined, and the percentage of children born into cohabiting families increased (Bumpass, 1998; Bumpass & Lu, 2000). Research has to keep pace with these changes and recognize that conclusions about cohabitation may be quite short-lived as cohabitation continues to evolve.

ACKNOWLEDGMENTS

This chapter has benefited from my collaboration with Pamela Smock. Many of the ideas presented here are the result of ideas we developed together in our work. She has challenged and encouraged me to work "outside the box." In addition, I have been fortunate to have many patient and bright colleagues who have engaged in discussions about my research. I appreciate the contributions made by Peggy Giordano, Susan Brown, Monica Longmore, Al DeMaris, Kelly Raley, Laura Sanchez, and Susan Stewart to this chapter.

REFERENCES

Amato, P. R., Loomis, L. S., & Booth, A. (1995). Parental divorce, marital conflict, and offspring well-being during early adulthood. *Social Forces, 73*, 895–914.

Astone, N. M., Schoen, R., Ensminger, R., & Rothert, K. (1999 March). *The family life course of African American men.* Paper presented at the annual meeting of the Population Association of America, New York.

Bachrach, C. (1987). Cohabitation and reproductive behavior in the U.S. *Demography, 24*, 623–637.

Bauman, K. (1999). Shifting family definitions: The effect of cohabitation and other nonfamily household relationships on measures of poverty. *Demography, 36*, 315–325.

Blanc, A. K. (1984). Nonmarital cohabitation and fertility in the United States and Western Europe. *Population Research and Policy Review, 3*, 181–193.

Brandon, P., & Bumpass, L. (2001). The role of paternity in patterns of welfare receipt among children living with unmarried mothers. *Journal of Family Issues, 22*, 3–26.

Brines, J., & Joyner, K. (1999). The ties that bind: Commitment and stability in the modern union. *American Sociological Review, 64*, 333–356.

Brown, S. (1999 March). *Why are cohabitors prone to violence?* Paper presented at the annual meeting of the Population Association of America, New York.

Brown, S. (2000a). Union transitions among cohabitors: The role of relationship assessments and expectations. *Journal of Marriage and the Family, 63*, 833–846.

Brown, S. (2000b). The effect of union type of psychological well-being: Depression among cohabitors versus marrieds. *Journal of Health and Social Behavior, 41*, 241–255.

Brown, S. (2000c). Fertility following marital dissolution: The role of cohabitation. *Journal of Family Issues, 21*, 501–524.

Brown, S., & Booth, A. (1996). Cohabitation versus marriage: A comparison of relationship quality. *Journal of Marriage and the Family, 58*, 668–678.

Brown, S., & Eisenberg, L. (1995). *The best intentions: Unintended pregnancy and the well-being of children and families*. Washington, DC: National Academy Press.

Buchanan, C. M., Maccoby, E. E., & Dornbusch, S. M. (1996). *Adolescents after divorce*. Cambridge, MA: Harvard University Press.

Bumpass, L. (1994 December). *The declining significance of marriage: Changing family life in the United States*. Paper presented at the Potsdam International Conference, Postdam, The Netherlands.

Bumpass, L. (1998). The changing signficance of marriage in the United States. In K. O. Mason, N. Isuya, & M. Choe (Eds.), *The changing family in comparative perspective: Asia and the United States* (pp. 63–79). Honolulu: East-West Center.

Bumpass, L., & Lu, H. H. (2000). Trends in cohabitation and implications for children's family contexts. *Population Studies, 54*, 29–41.

Bumpass, L. L., Raley, K., & Sweet, J. A. (1995). The changing character of stepfamilies: Implications of cohabitation and nonmarital childbearing. *Demography, 32*, 1–12.

Bumpass, L. L., & Sweet, J. A. (1989). National estimates of cohabitation. *Demography, 26*, 615–625.

Carlson, M., & Danziger, S. (1999). Cohabitation and the measurement of child poverty. *Review of Income and Wealth, 45*, 179–191.

Carlson, M., & McLanahan, S. (2000 March). *Parents' relationship quality and father involvement in fragile families*. Paper presented at the annual meeting of the Population Association of America, Los Angeles, CA.

Casper, L. M., & Sayer, L. C. (1999 March). *Cohabitation transitions: Different attitudes and purposes, different paths.* Paper presented at the annual meeting of the Population Association of America, Los Angeles, CA.

Cherlin, A. J. (1978). Remarriage as an incomplete institution. *American Journal of Sociology, 84,* 634–650.

Cherlin, A. J. (1999). Going to extremes: Family structure, children's well-being, and social science. *Demography, 36,* 421–428.

Citro, C., & Michael, R. (1995). *Measuring poverty.* Washington, DC: National Academy Press.

Clark, R., & Nelson, S. (2000 March). *Beyond the two-parent family.* Paper presented at the annual meeting of the Population Association of America, Los Angeles, CA.

Clarkberg, M. (1999). The price of partnering: The role of economic well-being in young adults' first union experiences. *Social Forces, 77,* 945–968.

Cohen, P. N. (1999 May). *Racial-ethnic and gender differences in returns to cohabitation and marriage: Evidence from the current population survey.* Paper presented at the annual meeting of the Population Association of America, Washington, DC.

Cooksey, E., & Craig, P. (1998). The paternal characteristics of nonresidential fathers. *Demography, 35,* 217–228.

DeMaris, A. (2000) Till discord do us part: The role of physical and verbal conflict in union disruption. *Journal of Marriage and the Family, 62,* 683–692.

Dunifon, R., & Kowaleski-Jones, L. (2000 March). *Who's in the house? Effects of family structure on children's home environments and cognitive outcomes.* Paper presented at the annual meeting of the Population Association of America, Los Angeles, CA.

Durst, R. (1997). Ties that bind: Drafting enforceable cohabitation agreements. *New Jersey Law Journal, 147,* S13–S14.

Edin, K., & Lein, L. (1997). *Making ends meet: How single mothers survive welfare and low-wage work.* New York: Russell Sage Foundation.

Eggebeen, D., Snyder, A., & Manning, W. (1996). Children in single-father families in demographic perspective. *Journal of Family Issues, 17,* 441–465.

Graefe, D. R., & Lichter, D. (1999). Life course transitions of American children: Parental cohabitation, marriage, and single parenthood. *Demography, 36,* 205–217.

Hanson, T. L., McLanahan, S., & Thomson, E. (1997). Economic resources, parental practices, and children's well-being. In G. J. Duncan & J. Brooks-Gunn (Eds.), *Consequences of growing up poor* (pp. 190–238). New York: Russell Sage Foundation.

Hao, L. (1996). Family structure, private transfers, and the economic well-being of families with children. *Social Forces, 75,* 269–292.

Heuveline, P., Timberlake, J., & Furstenberg, F. (2000). *Similarities and diversity in children's family structure experiences: An international comaprison.* Paper presented at the annual meeting of the American Sociological Association, Washington, DC.

Horwitz, A., & White, H. (1998). The relationship of cohabitation and mental health: A study of a young adult cohort. *Journal of Marriage and the Family, 60,* 505–514.

Joyce, T., Kaestner, R., & Korenman, S. (2000). The effect of pregnancy intention on child development. *Demography, 37,* 83–94.

Kiernan, K. (1999 March). *European perspectives on non-marital childbearing.* Paper presented at the annual meeting of Population Association of America. New York.

Landale, N. S., & Forste, R. (1991). Patterns of entry into cohabitation and marriage among mainland puerto rican women. *Demography, 28,* 587–607.

Landale, N., & Hauan, S. (1992). The family life course of Puerto Rican children. *Journal of Marriage and the Family, 54,* 912–924.

Landale, N.S., Oropesa, R. S., Llanes, D., & Gorman, B. (1999) Does Americanization have adverse effects on health?: Stress, health habits, and infant health outcomes among Puerto Ricans. *Social Forces, 78,* 613–641.

Landale, N. S., & Oropesa, R.S. Father involvement in the lives of mainland Puerto Rican children: Contributions of nonresident, cohabiting, and married fathers. *Social Forces,* forthcoming.

London, R. (1998). Trends in single mothers' living arrangements from 1970 to 1995: Correcting the current population survey. *Demography, 35,* 125–131.

Loomis, L., & Landale, N. (1994) Nonmarital cohabitation and childbearing among Black and White American women. *Journal of Marriage and the Family, 56,* 949–962.

Manning, W. (1999). *Childbearing in cohabiting unions: Racial and ethnic differences.* Paper presented at the annual meeting of the Population Association of America, New York.

Manning, W. (2000). *Children and the stability of cohabiting couples* (working paper). Center for Family and Demographic Research, Bowling Green State University.

Manning, W., & Landale, N. (1996). Racial and ethnic differences in the role of cohabitation in premarital childbearing. *Journal of Marriage and the Family 58,* 63–77.

Manning, W. & Lichter, D. (1996). Parental cohabitation and children's economic well-being. *Journal of Marriage and the Family, 58,* 998–1010.

Manning, W., & Smock, P. (1995). Why marry? Race and the transition to marriage among cohabitors. *Demography, 32,* 509–520.

Manning, W., & Smock, P. (1997). Children's living arrangements in unmarried-families. *Journal of Family Issues, 18,* 526–544.

Manning, W., & Smock, P. (1999). New families and nonresident father-child visitation. *Social Forces, 78*, 87–116.

Manning, W., Smock, P., & Majumdar, D. (2000 November). *Children's experience with parental stability.* Paper presented at the annual meeting of the National Council of Family Relations, Minneapolis.

Marcil-Gratton, N., & Bourdais, C. L. (1999). *Custody, access and child support: Findings from the national longitudinal survey of children and youth.* Paper presented to the Child Support Team, Department of Justice, Canada.

Margolin, L. (1992). Child abuse by mothers' boyfriends: Why the overrepresentation? *Child Abuse & Neglect, 16*, 541–551.

McLanahan, S., & Casper, L. (1995). Growing diversity and inequality in the American family. In R. Farley (Ed.), *State of the union: America in the 1990's* (pp. 1–45). New York: Russell Sage Foundation.

Moffitt, R., Reville, R., & Winkler, A. (1998). Beyond single mothers: Cohabitation and marriage in the AFDC program. *Demography, 35*, 259–278.

Morrison, D. R. (1998 March). *Child well-being in step families and cohabiting unions following divorce: A dynamic appraisal.* Paper presented at the annual meeting of the Population Association of America, Chicago.

Morrison, D. R. (2000 March). *The costs of economic uncertainty: Child well being in cohabitating and remarried unions following parental divorce.* Paper presented at the annual meetings of the Population Association of America, Los Angeles, CA.

Morrison, D. R., & Ritualo, A. (2000). Routes to children's economic recovery after divorce: Are maternal cohabitation and remarriage equivalent? *American Sociological Review, 65*, 560–580.

Musick, K. (1999). *Determinants of planned and unplanned childbearing among unmarried women in the United States* (Working Paper No. 99-09). Center for Demography. Madison, WI: University of Wisconsin-Madison.

Nock, S. L. (1995). A comparison of marriages and cohabiting relationships. *Journal of Family Issues, 16*, 53–76.

Norton, A. J., & Miller, L. F. (1992). *Marriage, divorce, and remarriage in the 1990's.* (Current Population Report, pp. 23–180). Washington, DC: U.S. Bureau of the Census.

Popenoe, D., & Whitehead, B. (1999). Should we live together? What young adults should know about cohabitation before marriage. The National Marriage Project. Rutgers, The State University of New Jersey.

Raley, K. (1999 March). *Then comes marriage? Recent changes in women's response to a nonmarital pregnancy.* Paper presented at the annual meeting of the Population Association of America, New York.

Rindfuss, R., & VandenHeuvel, A. (1990). Cohabitation: A precursor to marriage or an alternative to being single? *Population and Development Review, 16*, 703–726.

Ross, C. (1995). Reconceptualizing marital status as a continuum of social attachment. *Journal of Marriage and the Family, 57*, 129–140.

Seff, M. (1995). Cohabitation and the law. *Marriage and Family Review, 21*, 141–168.

Seltzer, J. (2000a). Families formed outside of marriage. *Journal of Marriage and the Family, 62*, 1247–1268.

Seltzer, J. (2000b). Child support and child access: Experiences of divorced and nonmarital families. In J. T. Oldham & M. S. Melli (Eds.), *Child support: The next frontier* (pp. 69–87). Ann Arbor: University of Michigan Press.

Smock, P. J. (2000). Cohabitiation in the United States. *Annual Review of Sociology, 26*, 1–20.

Smock, P. J., & Manning, W. D. (1997). Cohabiting partners' economic circumstances and marriage. *Demography, 34*, 331–341.

Stets, J. (1991). Cohabiting and marital aggression: The role of social isolation. *Journal of Marriage and the Family, 53*, 669–680.

Stets, J., & Straus, M. (1989). The marriage license as a hitting license: A comparison of assaults in dating, cohabiting, and married couples. *Journal of Family Violence, 41*, 161–180.

Thomson, E., Hanson, T., & McLanahan, S. (1994). Family structure and child well-being: economic resources vs. parental behavior. *Social Forces, 73*, 221–242.

Thomson, E., McLanahan, S. S., & Curtin, R. B. (1992). Family structure, gender, and parental socialization. *Journal of Marriage and the Family, 54*, 368–378.

U.S. Bureau of the Census. (1999). http://www.census.gov/population/socdemo/ms-la/tabad-2.txt

Waite, L. J., & Joyner, K. (1999). Emotional and physical satisfaction in married, cohabiting, and dating sexual unions: Do men and women differ? In E. Laumann & R. Michael (Eds.), *Sex, love, and health in America: Private choices and public policies* (pp. 239–269). Chicago: The University of Chicago Press.

Waller, M. (1999 June). *High hopes: Unmarried parents' expectations about marriage at the time of their child's birth.* Paper presented at the Fragile Families and Welfare Reform Workshop, Madison, WI.

Whelan, R. (1993). *Broken homes and battered children: A study of the relationship between child abuse and the family type.* London: Family Education Trust.

Winkler, A. (1993). The living arrangements of single mothers with dependent children: An added perspective. *The American Journal of Economics and Sociology, 52*, 1–18.

Winkler, A. (1997). Economic decision-making by cohabitors: Findings regarding income pooling. *Applied Economics, 29*, 1079–1090.

Wisensale, S., & Heckart, K. (1993). Domestic partnerships: A concept paper and policy discussion. *Family Relations, 42,* 199–204.

Wu, L., & Martinson, B. (1993). Family structure and the risk of a premarital birth. *American Sociological Review, 58,* 210–232.

9

Cohabitation and Child Development

Ariel Kalil
University of Chicago

In chap. 8, Manning presents a clear and comprehensive summary of the available research on the nature and characteristics of cohabiting unions and the potential effects of cohabitation on children's development. The number of studies that directly address child well-being in cohabiting unions is quite sparse. Moreover, the available evidence provides but a snapshot of some differences among children in cohabiting unions relative to other living arrangements, along only a few of many relevant dimensions of development. I agree with her conclusion that much more information is needed about how cohabitation relates to children's well being. In my view, future research could begin to address the question of "how" by progressing along one of several different pathways. Here, I focus on the role of individual differences, both among children and among types of cohabiting unions, as well as the role of family functioning and relationships.

INDIVIDUAL DIFFERENCES AMONG CHILDREN

Psychologists are interested in the active role of children in their own environments, and in trying to understand why some children adapt positively to certain experiences, whereas others do not. The small number of papers available for Manning to review did not systematically test the role of individual differences in the pattern of associations between cohabitation and children's developmental outcomes. A relative lack of average effects, however, could mask important differences that occur for certain subgroups. Studies of children from divorced and remarried families reveal great diversity in children's responses to marital transitions. Drawing from the larger family structure literature, there is reason to believe that effects could vary according to different attributes of the child. I briefly mention children's developmental status; children's personality, temperament, gender, and race/ethnicity are likely to be important as well.

Numerous aspects of child development could be related to the experience of cohabitation. In my view, an orientation toward examining effects for children at different ages would further the understanding of which outcomes are the most relevant. To give a simple example, given what is known about the deleterious effects of poverty in early childhood (Duncan & Brooks-Gunn, 1997), findings on cohabitation's ability to restore family income following a family structure dis-

ruption (Morrison & Ritualo, 2000) are especially relevant to the study of cohabitation among mothers of young children. On the other hand, if one is interested in
how cohabitation is associated with adolescents' orientation toward marriage and
family formation, one should look to the work of Axinn and Thornton (2000),
who find that attitudes toward cohabitation link parental divorce to children's
cohabiting behavior. Children who spend substantial amounts of time in cohabiting unions may develop specific expectations about the role of marriage and cohabitation in their own lives.

Similarly, different types of parental investments are relevant at different periods of the child's life. These range from the appropriate response to infants'
needs, to the scaffolding and stimulation that promote children's self-regulation
and cognitive development during childhood, and on to the family management
practices that monitor behavior and support identity formation during adolescence.
Virtually nothing is known about whether and how cohabitation affects parents'
ability to invest in their children at different developmental stages.

VARIATION IN COHABITING UNIONS

Manning argues that an informed understanding of the implications of cohabitation requires an awareness of the comparison group, pointing out that researchers
need to be mindful of both the marital status of the parents as well as each adult's
biological relationship to the child. To this list, I add the gender of the cohabitors.
As Manning reports, although single-father families are far less common than
single-mother families, children living in single-father families are four times as
likely to share that residence with their father's cohabiting partner than are children living with unmarried mothers. A recent paper by Case and Paxson (2000)
presents some intriguing findings that might be relevant for this issue. Case and
Paxson found that children living with biological fathers and stepmothers were
significantly less likely to have routine doctor and dentist visits, or to have a place
for usual medical care, or to wear seatbelts, relative to children living with their
birth mother. These findings suggest that stepmothers (and, perhaps by extension,
cohabiting female partners) do not, by and large, "invest" in children's lives and
highlight one potential pathway to different developmental outcomes for children
depending on the nature of the cohabiting arrangement. Of course, there are additional kinds of investments that would be important to measure and to determine
whether different kinds of cohabitors are more or less likely to make them.

Case and Paxson also found, however, that among children living with stepmothers, those who had regular contact with their birth mothers did not have worse
health care relative to that reported for children who resided with their birth mothers. In other words, the effects of the family structure arrangements were moder-
ated by children's relationships with their nonresident mothers. Related research
on children in divorced and stepfamily arrangements shows that noncustodial

mothers are more likely to be actively involved and influential in their children's lives than are nonresidential fathers (Hetherington, Bridgess, & Insabella, 1998). These findings highlight the importance of not only identifying the gender of the cohabitors, but also accounting for the multiple caregivers in the child's life.

Additional variations among cohabiting unions are also important. Manning presents three sets of comparisons in her discussion of child development outcomes: (a) bio-married versus bio-cohabiting parents (two biological caregivers, distinguished by their marital status); (b) stepmarried versus step-cohabiting parents (one biological and one nonbiological caregiver, distinguished by their marital status); and (c) unmarried alone versus unmarried cohabiting parents (biological relationship of cohabitor not distinguished). However, there is reason to believe that interesting differences might emerge from a three-way comparison, for example, between unmarried single; unmarried-biological cohabitor; and unmarried-step-cohabitor. Other differences could emerge if we compared short- and long-term cohabitors. Future research on child well-being in cohabiting unions will need to account for these and other distinctions.

A Note on Selection Issues

Manning discusses the selection issue from the adults' perspective; suggesting that cohabitors with limited economic prospects, and perhaps those with greater psychological difficulties, are less likely to marry. It should also be recognized that characteristics of the children themselves affect, and might also be affected by parents' propensity to cohabit or to end a cohabiting union through marriage. Studies have shown that children whose parents would eventually divorce showed higher levels of behavior problems prior to the occurrence of the divorce itself (Cherlin et al., 1991). In the context of cohabiting unions, one scenario might be that children's health or behavior problems reduce the likelihood that cohabiting parents will marry; in turn, the experience of protracted coresidence could produce additional effects on the children's subsequent development.

THE ROLE OF FAMILY FUNCTIONING

Nearly all of the available studies on cohabitation and children's outcomes examine child development as a function of current living arrangements. A central concern for future research is to understand how transitions into and out of a particular family structure affect children's development, and to identify the relevant mediating factors. As in much of the research on family structure, it may be that cohabitation promotes some types of family functioning that are beneficial for children's development (e.g., two adults provide higher levels of monitoring and control), whereas other aspects diminish children's well-being (e.g., boundary ambiguity or conflict between cohabitors and children) such that the net effect on child well being is washed out. One recent study found that single mothers' transitions into cohabiting or marital unions (which were treated equivalently) decreased levels of mothers' harsh discipline toward their adolescent children; however, remarriage or repartnering also reduced mothers' time with children (Thomson, Mosley, Hanson, & McLanahan, 2001). A focus on constellations of parenting behavior or family functioning, or different kinds of children (i.e., person-centered vs. variable-centered analyses) might be useful to address these issues.

A focus on family functioning underscores the need to study the child's experience in relation to multiple caregivers in his or her life. Evidence indicates that the quality of relationships in cohabiting partnerships differs from marital partnerships. Carlson and McLanahan (2000) reported that relative to married mothers, mothers in unmarried cohabiting partnerships reported lower levels of relationship quality with the fathers of their children. Brown (2000) observed that cohabiting parents experience higher levels of depression compared to married parents. These psychological characteristics are important to note as psychologically distressed mothers are more likely to view their role as parent less positively, demonstrate less favorable parenting attitudes, and exhibit less positive and more negative behavior to their children (McLoyd, 1990).

Cohabiting partners might also differ in their parenting behaviors. The literature on stepfamily relationships points to adult–child conflicts that ensue when mothers' new relationship partners assume parental roles (Hetherington et al., 1998). Consistency in parental behavior is also an important determinant of children's well-being (Fletcher, Steinberg, & Sellers, 1999); thus, children's adjustment problems could develop if cohabitors' socialization behaviors are incongruous with those of the mothers' or other caretakers. Finally, ambiguity in setting boundaries or difficulties in negotiating co-parenting roles might produce interadult conflict; there is an extensive literature on the deleterious consequences of marital conflict for children's well-being (Cox, 1999).

Biological Fathers, Social Fathers, and Child Development

Some of the disadvantage of being born to a cohabiting parent seems to emerge once the father is no longer living with the child and the child's mother. Nonresident fathers of children born in cohabiting unions appear to be less involved than nonresident fathers of children born into marriage. This finding is important because nonresident father involvement accounts for some of the disadvantage of living with a single mother (Carlson, 2000). Future research will undoubtedly be concerned with identifying the factors that predict involvement among this group of fathers.

Finally, I offer some recent findings from my own research that examines the associations between the presence of a nonbiological *social father* in a child's life and the child's emotional adjustment (Jayakody & Kalil, 2001). In Jayakody and

Kalil, we used data from a cross-section of approximately 700 never-married, low-income Black mothers with preschool children. Results from this study are relevant to the discussion of cohabitation and child development given the socio-economic and demographic characteristics of the sample and the high prevalence of social fathers identified by the mothers of the children. Mothers identified social fathers as men who played an important role in their child's life and who were "like a father" to their daughter or son.

Approximately two thirds of the mothers in the sample reported that their children had a social father; most of these men were the mother's current partner or boyfriend (a smaller number were male relatives of the child's), and most of the children interacted with their social fathers frequently—50% saw him almost daily and only 9% saw him less often than once a week.

To begin our work, we examined the association between social father presence and absent biological father involvement. As noted previously, this issue is relevant given the role of absent biological father involvement in child well-being. In this sample, the presence of a boyfriend social father was inversely related to the level of absent biological father involvement. In contrast, absent biological father involvement was not associated with the presence of a male relative social father.

These results could imply that absent biological fathers limit their involvement when mothers have boyfriends who act as social fathers, or that high levels of biological father involvement lessen the need for such social fathers. Whatever the direction of effects, this hints at some underlying competition between the two men, a competition that is not present with male relative social fathers. Further exploration of the relationship dynamics underlying this association is warranted and may be relevant for the study of cohabitation and child development. If cohabiting males "push" absent fathers out of the picture, then the presence of cohabitors could compound the deleterious effects on child development associated with the absence of the biological father.

Our next question examined the association between social father presence and children's emotional adjustment. Our multivariate regression models controlled for a host of relevant maternal and child characteristics, absent biological father involvement, and the quality of the home environment. Net of all of these factors, children whose mothers report the presence of a boyfriend social father were reported to have significantly lower levels of emotional adjustment. In contrast, the presence of a male relative social father was not correlated with children's emotional adjustment.

The cross-sectional nature of the data did not allow us to discern the direction of these effects. On one hand, mothers who have less well-adjusted children might be more likely to introduce a male role model in the hope of stabilizing or improving children's behavior or achievement. On the other hand, when mothers have boyfriends who act like fathers, children may display less mature behavior. This subgroup of men who lack legal and biological ties to the family might compete with children for the mother's time and attention. Or, perhaps the presence of a boyfriend social father reflects a transition in family relationships that the child has experienced that is associated with poor adjustment. Many of these issues are likely relevant for the study of cohabitation and child development.

SUMMARY

The findings from Manning's review of the literature point to several directions for future research. Studies will need to attend to the ways in which individual differences interact with cohabitation to produce different outcomes for children. These individual differences include characteristics of the children as well as the cohabitors themselves. Moreover, we need to understand the role of the cohabiting relationship from a family systems perspective (Cox & Paley, 1997); recognizing not only the nature of cohabitors' affective ties and interactions with children, but also their relationships with other family members, in addition to the conjoint influence of the adults' relationships on the child's well-being. Finally, future research needs to adopt a dynamic view of cohabitation and child well-being, given the rapidly changing demographics of cohabitation, the concomitant changes in social mores that these changes might be expected to produce, and the fluid nature of cohabiting unions themselves.

ACKNOWLEDGMENTS

I thank Marcy Carlson and Rukmalie Jayakody for their comments.

REFERENCES

Axinn, W., & Thornton, A. (2000). The transformation in the meaning of marriage. In L. Waite (Ed.), *The ties that bind: Perspectives on marriage and cohabitation* (pp. 147–165). New York: Aldine de Gruyter.

Brown, S. (2000). The effect of union type on psychological well-being: Depression among cohabitors versus marrieds. *Journal of Health and Social Behavior, 41*, 241–255.

Carlson, M. (2000). *Family structure, father involvement, and adolescent behavioral outcomes.* Manuscript submitted for publication.

Carlson, M., & McLanahan, S. (2000). *Parents' relationship quality and father involvement in fragile families.* Unpublished manuscript. Princeton, NJ: Bendheim-Thoman Center for Research on Child Wellbeing. Princeton University.

Case, A., & Paxson, C. (2000). *Mothers and others: Who invests in children's health?* Unpublished manuscript. Princeton, NJ: Research Program in Developmental Studies. Princeton University.

Cherlin, A., Furstenberg, F., Chase-Lansdale, P.L., Kiernan, K., Robins, P., Morrison, D., & Teitler, J. (1991). Longitudinal studies of the effects of divorce in children in Great Britain and the United States. *Science, 252,* 1386–1389.

Cox, M. (1999). Marital conflict, parent-child relationships, gender, and outcomes for young adults in families. In A. Booth, A. Crouter, & M. Shanahan (Eds.), *Transitions to adulthood in a changing economy* (pp. 103–108). Westport, CT: Praeger.

Cox, M., & Paley, B. (1997). Families as systems. *Annual Review of Psychology, 48,* 243–267.

Duncan, G., & Brooks-Gunn, J. (1997). *Consequences of growing up poor.* New York: Russell Sage Foundation.

Fletcher, A., Steinberg, L., & Sellers, E. (1999). Adolescents' well-being as a function of perceived interparental consistency. *Journal of Marriage and the Family, 61,* 599–610.

Hetherington, E. M., Bridgess, M., & Insabella, G. M. (1998). What matters? What does not? Five perspectives on the association between marital transitions and children's adjustment. *American Psychologist, 53,* 167–184.

Jayakody, R., & Kalil, A. (2001). *Social fathering in low-income African American families with preschool children.* Manuscript submitted for publication.

McLoyd, V. (1990). The impact of economic hardship on Black families and children: Psychological distress, parenting, and socioemotional development. *Child Development, 61,* 311–346.

Morrison, D., & Ritualo, A. (2000). Routes to children's economic recovery after divorce: Are cohabitation and remarriage equivalent? *American Sociological Review, 65,* 560–580.

Thomson, E., Mosley, J., Hanson, T., & McLanahan, S. (2001). Remarriage, cohabitation, and changes in mothering. *Journal of Marriage and the Family, 63,* 370–380.

10

Of Fathers and Pheromones: Implications of Cohabitation for Daughters' Pubertal Timing

Bruce J. Ellis
University of Canterbury, New Zealand

One of the most dramatic implications of cohabitation for children's lives is its relation to biological family composition. Children living in married-couple families are about twice as likely as children living in cohabiting-parent families to live largely with both biological parents (81% vs. 40%; Manning, chap. 8, this volume). Conversely, children living in cohabiting-parent families are about three times as likely as children living in married-couple families to live with a biologically unrelated parent (60% vs. 19%; Manning, chap. 8, this volume). Furthermore, given the short life span of cohabiting unions, even children who currently live with both biological parents in cohabiting families are likely to experience changes in the biological composition of their families in the future.

Although I concur with Manning's assertion that "the implications of cohabitation for children's lives should depend on whether they are living with two biological parents or one biological parent and their parent's partner" (p. 122), the fact is that most cohabiting-parent families are not biologically intact families. Thus, children in cohabiting families are at increased risk of biological father absence and stepfather presence. In this chapter I discuss some possible consequences of biological father absence, stepfather presence, and father involvement on daughters' pubertal development.

OVERVIEW

The onset of pubertal development has typically been viewed as an important marker of the transition into adolescence and is accompanied by major social and cognitive changes (Conger, 1984; Feldman & Elliot, 1990). Variations in the timing of pubertal maturation—in levels of physical and sexual development of adolescents in comparison to their same-age peers—has received considerable research attention. The most consistent finding to emerge from the literature is that early onset of puberty in girls is associated with negative health and psychosocial outcomes. In particular, early maturing girls are at greater risk later in life for breast cancer (e.g., Kampert, Whittemore, & Paffenbarger, 1988 & Vihko & Apter, 1986) and unhealthy weight gain (e.g., Ness, 1991; Wellens et al., 1992); have higher rates of teenage pregnancy (e.g., Manlove, 1997; Udry & Cliquet, 1982); are more likely to have low birthweight babies (Scholl et al., 1989); and tend to show more disturbances in body image, to report more emotional problems such as depression and anxiety, and to engage in more problem behaviors such as alcohol consumption and sexual promiscuity (e.g., Caspi & Moffitt, 1991; Flannery, Rowe, & Gulley, 1993; Graber, Lewinsohn, Seeley, & Brooks-Gunn, 1997; Mezzich et al., 1997; Susman, Nottleman, Inoff-Germain, Loriaux, & Chrousus, 1985).

Although a good deal is now known about the sequelae of variations in pubertal timing in girls, relatively little is known about the social and psychological antecedents of this variation. Recent theory and data (e.g., Belsky, Steinberg, & Draper, 1991; Ellis & Garber, 2000; Ellis, McFadyen-Ketchum, Dodge, Pettit, & Bates, 1999; Graber, Brooks-Gunn, & Warren, 1995) suggest that family composition and family processes during childhood may influence the physiological mechanisms that initiate and control pubertal development. In this chapter I discuss my ongoing research on two community samples of adolescent girls who have been followed prospectively during childhood. This research tests predictions derived from an evolutionary model of individual differences in pubertal timing. These predictions concern the relations between family composition, quality of family relationships, and individual differences in the timing of pubertal maturation.

THE BELSKY, STEINBERG, AND DRAPER EVOLUTIONARY MODEL OF PUBERTAL TIMING

Belsky et al. (1991) proposed an evolutionary model of psychosocial influences on the timing of puberty. They posited that "a principal evolutionary function of early experience—the first 5–7 years of life—is to induce in the child an understanding of the availability and predictability of resources (broadly defined) in the environment, of the trustworthiness of others, and of the enduringness of close interpersonal relationships, all of which will affect how the developing person apportions reproductive effort" (p. 650). Drawing on the concept of sensitive-period learning of reproductive strategies, Belsky et al. suggested that humans have evolved to be sensitive to specific features of their early childhood environments, and that exposure to different environments biases children toward acquisition of different reproductive strategies. Children whose experiences in and around their families of origin are characterized by relatively high levels of stress (e.g., scarcity or instability of resources, father absence, negative and coercive family relationships, lack of positive and supportive family relationships) are hypothesized to develop in a manner that speeds rates of pubertal maturation, accelerates sexual activity, and orients the individual toward relatively unstable pairbonds.

In essence, Belsky et al. (1991) proposed that the context of early rearing "sets" the person's reproductive strategy in a way that was likely to have functioned adaptively in that context in the environments in which humans evolved. Over the course of our natural selective history, ancestral females growing up in adverse family environments may have reliably increased their reproductive success by accelerating physical maturation and beginning sexual activity and reproduction at a relatively early age, without the expectation that paternal investment in childrearing would be forthcoming, and without the precondition of a close, enduring romantic relationship (Belsky et al., 1991). As Chisholm (1996) suggested, "when young mammals encounter conditions that are not favorable for survival—i.e., the conditions of environmental risk and uncertainty indexed by emotional stress during development—it will generally be adaptive for them to reproduce early" (p. 21).

MATERNAL DEPRESSION, MARITAL AND FAMILY STRESS, AND DAUGHTERS' PUBERTAL TIMING

My first goal was to test the hypothesis that girls whose experiences in and around their families of origin are characterized by relatively high levels of stress would develop in a manner that speeds rates of pubertal maturation. In Ellis and Garber (2000), we tested this hypothesis in a longitudinal data set focusing on development of psychopathology in adolescence. It has been well established in past research that major psychopathologies, such as mood disorders and substance abuse, are strongly predictive of marital discord, conflictual relationships with children, and divorce (Beach & Nelson, 1990; Cummings & Davies, 1994; Downey & Coyne, 1990). In this research, we tested the specific prediction that a history of mood disorders in mothers predicts earlier timing of pubertal maturation in daughters, and that this relation is mediated by stressful family relationships and father absence.

This prediction was supported in a short-term longitudinal study of 87 adolescent girls and their mothers. In the primary test of the model, we found that a history of mood disorders in mothers predicted earlier pubertal timing in daughters, and that this relation was fully mediated by levels of stress in the mothers' romantic relationship and biological father absence (Ellis & Garber, 2000), as shown in Fig. 10.1. In total, these results provided support for the evolutionary model of pubertal timing proposed by Belsky et al. (1991) linking stressful family environments to earlier puberty in girls and extended the model to include maternal psychopathology as a more distal predictor of marital and family dysfunction and pubertal timing.

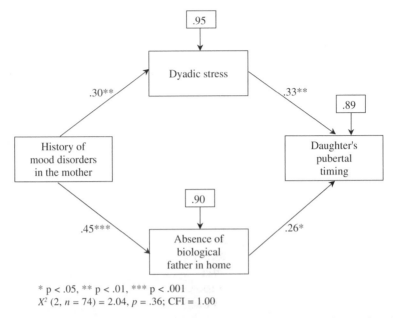

FIG. 10.1   Path analysis of daughters' pubertal timing. *Source*: Ellis and Garber (2000).

STEPFATHER PRESENCE AND DAUGHTERS' PUBERTAL TIMING

Although the relations between family environment and pubertal timing are intriguing, they beg the most interesting question: What is the mechanism? How does family environment influence pubertal timing? One possibility is that girls reared in homes without their biological fathers present may experience earlier sexual maturation because of increased exposure to unrelated adult males, especially stepfathers and mothers' dating partners. Research on a variety of mammalian species (e.g., mice, cows, pigs, tamarins) indicates that exposure to pheromones produced by unrelated adult male conspecifics accelerates female pubertal development (Izard, 1990; Sanders & Reinisch, 1990; Ziegler, Snowdon, & Uno, 1990). Research on humans has also provided definitive evidence of regulation of women's reproductive functioning by pheromones (Stern & McClintock, 1998). If, consistent with the animal literature, human females possess physiological mechanisms that accelerate pubertal maturation in response to pheromonal stimulation by unrelated adult males, then exposure to stepfathers and mothers' dating partners, rather than absence of the biological father per se, should most strongly predict early pubertal timing in girls.

We sought to test this hypothesis in the study of maternal depression and daughters' pubertal timing (Ellis & Garber, 2000). We began by identifying a subset of girls who were living in homes without their biological fathers. Some of these girls had a significant alternative father figure in their lives (i.e., a stepfather or mother's cohabiting partner). We then examined the relation between length of exposure to the alternative father figure and pubertal timing. If exposure to unrelated adult males causes accelerated pubertal development in girls, then greater duration of exposure to unrelated father figures (rather than duration of father absence per se) should be associated with earlier pubertal timing. This prediction was supported (Ellis & Garber, 2000), as shown in Table 10.1. In total, the younger the daughter at the time of the father figure's arrival, the earlier her pubertal timing. In contrast, there was not a relation between age of daughter when the biological father moved out and timing of pubertal maturation. These data are consistent with the hypothesis that exposure to the pheromones of unrelated adult males accelerates girls' pubertal development.

As discussed in Manning's chapter, children who live in cohabiting-parent families are about three times as likely as children living in married-couple families to be exposed to a biologically unrelated parent. This exposure changes the pheromonal environment of the child, which may in turn influence pubertal and sexual development.

Table 10.1

Timing of Biological Father Absence and Father Figure Presence Correlated with Seventh-Grade Pubertal Timing in Daughters

Timing of Biological Father Absence and Father Figure Presence	n	Pubertal timing
Age of daughter when biological father moved out of home	47	-.13
Age of daughter when first alternative father figure came into her life	31	-.37*

*$p < .05$
Source: Ellis and Garber (2000).

THE ROLE OF BIOLOGICAL FATHERS IN REGULATION OF DAUGHTERS' PUBERTAL DEVELOPMENT

The other side of the coin is that a close relationship between a biological father and daughter may slow down speed of pubertal development. Belsky et al. (1991) hypothesized that girls who have warm, supportive relationships with their families will experience later pubertal timing. Graber et al. (1995) and Steinberg (1988) each presented longitudinal data that are consistent with this hypothesis. This again raises the question: What is the mechanism? How could warm, positive family relationships delay pubertal development? One possibility is inhibition of pubertal development through pheromonal exposure to the biological father (Hoogland, 1982; Surbey, 1990). There is some evidence in the animal literature that the presence of closely related adult males inhibits reproductive maturation in females (and may function as an incest avoidance mechanism). In prairie dogs, for example, first ovulation is delayed in females who remain in contact with their biological fathers (Hoogland, 1982).

In a second study, my colleagues and I (Ellis et al., 1999) examined the role of father involvement in regulation of daughters' pubertal timing in an 8-year longitudinal study of 173 girls and their families. Quality of family relationships were assessed prior to girls' entry into kindergarten, based on both interviews with the mother and, for a subsample of families, on direct behavioral observations in the home. Pubertal timing was subsequently assessed when girls were in the seventh grade. The general goal of the study was to test the hypothesis that more negative and coercive (or less positive and harmonious) early family relationships provoke earlier reproductive development in adolescence. In relation to the pheromonal hypothesis, we examined (a) whether daughters who spent more time with their biological fathers early in life tended to experience later pubertal timing and (b) whether quality of father-daughter relationships predicted daughters' pubertal timing more strongly than did quality of mother-daughter relationships. If exposure to the biological father's pheromones inhibits pubertal development, then girls who spend more time in the care of their biological fathers should experience later puberty, and fathering effects should uniquely predict daughters' puberty above and beyond mothering effects.

The clearest finding to emerge from this research was that it was the absence of warm, positive family relationships, rather than the presence of negative, coercive family relationships, that forecast earlier pubertal development in girls (see Table 10.2). These relations emerged (a) even though there was an 8-year time period between measurements, (b) even though the correlations were across independent data sources (interview reports and behavioral observations of family relationships vs. daughters' self-reported pubertal timing), and (c) whether quality of family relationships was assessed indirectly through mother-based interviewer reports or directly through home observations.

Table 10.2
Correlations Between Positive and Negative Family Relationships Factors
and Seventh-Grade Pubertal Timing in Daughters

Family relationships factors	n	Pubertal timing
Factors derived from interview with mother		
Positive family relationships	157	-.31***
Negative family relationships	157	-.03
Factors derived from home observations		
Positive family relationships	40	-.45**
Negative family relationships	40	-.16

**p< .01   ***p< .001
Source: Ellis et al. (1999).

The pheromonal hypothesis is inherently difficult to test because paternity is uncertain. Blood tests for misassigned paternity in men suggest that the putative father is not the biological father in anywhere from 2% to more than 25% of families, depending on the population under study (e.g., Bellis & Baker, 1990; Flinn, 1988a; Pothoff & Whittinghill, 1965). In our study, we collected mother-reports on the amount of time spent by the "father" in child care. Unfortunately, we did not specifically inquire about the biological relation of the "father" to the child. There were 107 putatively biologically intact families in the sample at the beginning of the study. In this subsample, more time spent by the father in child care when the daughters were 4 to 5 years old predicted less pubertal development by daughters in the seventh grade, $r(107) = -.24, p < .05$. Furthermore, within the subset of these families in which the girls continued to live with their biological fathers through adolescence (and thus were not exposed to stepfathers), more time spent by the father in child care during the first 5 years still predicted later pubertal timing in the seventh grade, $r(78) = -.30, p < .01$ (Ellis et al., 1999). These data are at least consistent with the hypothesis that increased pheromonal exposure to biological fathers inhibits sexual maturation. However, it is also likely that girls who have high-investing fathers in the home tend to begin sex and dating at a later age (e.g., Flinn, 1988b; Hetherington, 1972) and thus have less pheromonal exposure to male dating partners in early adolescence.

Another relevant line of evidence is the comparison of the influence of mothers and fathers on daughters' pubertal timing. If fathers have a special pheromonal influence on daughters timing of pubertal development that mothers do not have,

Table 10.3
Hierarchical Multiple Regressions: Comparison of Father-Effects
and Mother-Effects on Daughters' Pubertal Timing ($n = 40$)

Variables	R^2 Change	F Change	β	t
Father-effects model[a]				
Step 1	.12	2.63		
Mother-Daughter			-.36	-2.21*
Affectionate-Positivity				
Mother-Daughter			-.02	-0.13
Coercive Control				
Step 2	.09	3.98*		
Father-Daughter			-.36	-2.00*
Affectionate-Positivity				
Mother-effects model[b]				
Step 1	.30	8.17***		
Father-Daughter			-.53	-3.70***
Affectionate-Positivity				
Father-Daughter			-.36	-2.56*
Coercive Control				
Step 2	.01	0.49		
Mother-Daughter			-.12	-0.70
Affectionate-Positivity				

[a] Effects of father-daughter affectionate-positivity, controlling for mother-daughter affectionate-positivity and mother-daughter coercive control.
[b] Effects of mother-daughter affectionate-positivity, controlling for father-daughter affectionate-positivity and father-daughter coercive control.
* $p \leq .05$ *** $p < .001$
Source: Ellis et al. (1999).

then the quality and quantity of father-daughter relationships, more than mother-daughter relationships, should affect pubertal timing. We only had comparable data on the quality of mother-daughter and father-daughter relationships in the behavioral observation subsample ($n = 40$ families). Of these families, 33 were biologically intact. Families were observed in their homes over two 2-hour sessions around dinner time. Mothers and fathers were coded on both levels of affectionate-positivity and coercive control displayed toward daughters. We found that more father-daughter affectionate-positivity and more mother-daughter affectionate-positivity each predicted less pubertal development by daughters in the seventh grade (Ellis et al., 1999). Most relevant, even after controlling for the two mother-daughter variables, father-daughter affectionate-positivity still significantly incremented the prediction of daughter's pubertal timing. The converse was not true of mother-daughter affectionate-positivity (Table 10.3).

In total, these data indicate that the effects of maternal caregiving on daughters' pubertal timing were redundant with the effects of paternal caregiving, whereas the effects of paternal caregiving contributed uniquely to the prediction of daughters' pubertal timing. Additionally, as shown in second hierarchical regression (Table 10.3), more father-daughter affectionate-positivity and more father-daughter coercive control each significantly predicted later pubertal timing in daughters when entered simultaneously into the regression equation (Step 1; $R^2 = .30$). These data suggest that more father-daughter interaction per se (whether positive or negative) may be associated with later pubertal maturation in daughters. These findings, which highlight a potentially important role for father-daughter relationships in the regulation of daughters' pubertal timing, are broadly consistent with the hypothesis that pheromonal exposure to the biological father inhibits pubertal development in daughters.

CONCLUSION

One of the most striking features of cohabiting families is their instability. As Manning points out in her chapter, "The average duration of cohabiting unions is about 2 years (Bumpass, 1998) and this is quite short in contrast to marriage. . . The short life span of cohabiting unions suggests that most children born or living with cohabiting couples will experience a quick change in their living circumstances" (p. 124). One implication is that girls who are born or living with their biological fathers in the context of cohabiting-parent families are less likely to remain living with their biological fathers throughout childhood. Another implication is that girls in cohabiting-parent families are more likely to be exposed to biologically unrelated father figures. Both of these conditions may lead to earlier pubertal development in girls and associated health and psychosocial risks. The two studies reviewed in this commentary each underscore a potentially important role for fathers and father figures in regulation of girls' pubertal development. Cohabitation introduces substantial variability into the number, type, and duration of father-daughter relationships over the course of childhood.

REFERENCES

Beach, S. R. H., & Nelson, G. M. (1990). Pursuing research on major psychopathology from a contextual perspective: The example of depression and marital discord. In G. H. Brody & I. E. Sigel (Eds.), *Methods of family research: Biographies of research projects: Vol. 2 clinical populations* (pp. 227–259). Hillsdale, NJ: Lawrence Erlbaum Associates.

Bellis, M. A., & Baker, R. R. (1990). Do females promote sperm competition? Data for humans. *Animal Behaviour, 40*, 997–999.

Belsky, J., Steinberg, L., & Draper, P. (1991). Childhood experience, interpersonal development, and reproductive strategy: An evolutionary theory of socialization. *Child Development, 62*, 647–670.

Bumpass, L. (1998). The changing significance of marriage in the United States. In K. Oppenheim Mason, N. Isuya, & M. Choe (Eds.), *The changing family in comparative perspective: Asia and the United States* (pp. 63–79). Honolulu: East-West Center.

Caspi, A., & Moffitt, T. E. (1991). Individual differences are accentuated during periods of social change: The sample case of girls at puberty. *Journal of Personality and Social Psychology, 61*, 157–168.

Chisholm, J. S. (1996). The evolutionary ecology of attachment organization. *Human Nature, 7*, 1–38.

Conger, J. J. (1984). *Adolescence and youth.* New York: Harper & Row.

Cummings, E., & Davies, P. (1994). Maternal depression and child development. *Journal of Child Psychology and Psychiatry, 35*, 73–112.

Downey, G., & Coyne, J. (1990). Children of depressed parents: An integrative review. *Psychological Bulletin, 108*, 50–76.

Ellis, B. J., & Garber, J. (2000). Psychosocial antecedents of variation in girls' pubertal timing: Maternal depression, stepfather presence, and martial and family stress. *Child Development, 71*, 485–501.

Ellis, B. J., McFadyen-Ketchum, S., Dodge, K. A., Pettit, G. S., & Bates, J. E. (1999). Quality of early family relationships and individual differences in the timing of pubertal maturation in girls: A longitudinal test of an evolutionary model. *Journal of Personality and Social Psychology, 77*, 387–401.

Feldman, S., & Elliot, G. (Eds.) (1990). *At the threshold: The developing adolescent.* Cambridge, MA: Harvard University Press.

Flannery, D. J., Rowe, D. C., & Gulley, B. J. (1993). Impact of pubertal status, timing, and age on adolescent sexual experience and delinquency. *Journal of Adolescent Research, 8*, 21–40.

Flinn, M. V. (1988a). Mate guarding in a Caribbean village. *Ethology and Sociobiology, 9*, 1–28.

Flinn, M.V. (1988b). Parent-offspring interactions in a Caribbean village: Daughter guarding. In L. Betzig, M. Burgerhoff Mulder, & P. Turke (Eds.), *Human reproductive behaviour* (pp. 189–200). Cambridge: Cambridge University Press.

Graber, J. A., Brooks-Gunn, J., & Warren, M. P. (1995). The antecedents of menarcheal age: heredity, family environment, and stressful life events. *Child Development, 66,* 346–359.

Graber, J. A., Lewinsohn, P. M., Seeley, J. R., & Brooks-Gunn, J. (1997). Is psychopathology associated with the timing of pubertal development? *Journal of the American Academy of Child and Adolescent Psychiatry, 36,* 1768–1776.

Hetherington, E. M. (1972). Effects of father absence on personality development in adolescent daughters. *Developmental Psychology, 7,* 313–326.

Hoogland, J. L. (1982). Prairie dogs avoid extreme inbreeding. *Science, 215,* 1639–1641.

Izard, M. K. (1990). Social influences on the reproductive success and reproductive endocrinology of prosimian primates. In T. E. Ziegler & F. B. Bercovitch (Eds.), *Socioendocrinology of primate reproduction* (pp. 159–186). New York: Wiley-Liss.

Kampert, J. B., Whittemore, A. S., & Paffenbarger, R. S. (1988). Combined effects of childbearing, menstrual events, and body size on age-specific breast cancer risk. *American Journal of Epidemiology, 128,* 962–979.

Manlove, J. (1997). Early motherhood in an intergenerational perspective: The experiences of a British cohort. *Journal of Marriage and the Family, 59,* 263–279.

Mezzich, A. C., Tarter, R. E., Giancola, P. R., Lu, S., Kirisci, L., & Parks, S. (1997). Substance use and risky sexual behavior in female adolescents. *Drug and Alcohol Abuse, 44,* 157–166.

Ness, R. (1991). Adiposity and age of menarche in Hispanic women. *American Journal of Human Biology, 3,* 41–48.

Pothoff, R. F., & Whittinghill, M. (1965). Maximum likelihood estimation of the proportion of nonpaternity. *American Journal of Human Genetics, 17,* 480–494.

Sanders, S. A., & Reinisch, J.M. (1990). Biological and social influences on the endocrinology of puberty: Some additional considerations. In J. Bancroft & J. M. Reinisch (Eds.), *Adolescence and puberty* (pp. 50–62). New York: Oxford.

Scholl, T. O., Hdiger, M. L., Vasilenko, P. III, Ances, I. G., Smith, W., & Salmon, R. W. (1989). Effects of early maturation on fetal growth. *Annals of Human Biology, 16,* 335–346.

Steinberg, L. (1988). Reciprocal relation between parent-child distance and pubertal maturation. *Developmental Psychology, 24,* 122–128.

Stern, K., & McClintock, M. K. (1998). Regulation of ovulation by human pheromones. *Nature, 392,* 177–179.

Surbey, M. (1990). Family composition, stress, and human menarche. In F. Bercovitch & T. Zeigler (Eds.), *Socioendocrinology of primate reproduction* (pp. 71–97). New York: Liss.

Susman, E. J., Nottleman, E. D., Inoff-Germain, G. E., Loriaux, D. L., & Chrousos, G. P. (1985). The relation of relative hormonal levels and physical development and social-emotional behavior in young adolescents. *Journal of Youth and Adolescence, 14,* 245–264.

Udry, J. R., & Cliquet, R. L. (1982). A cross-cultural examination of the relationship between ages at menarche, marriage, and first birth. *Demography, 19,* 53–63.

Vihko, R. K., & Apter, D. L. (1986). The epidemiology and endocrinology of the menarche in relation to breast cancer. *Cancer Survey, 5,* 561–571.

Wellens, R., Malina, R., Roche, A., Chumlea, W., Guo, S., & Siervogel, R. (1992). Body size and fatness in young adults in relation to age at menarche. *American Journal of Human Biology, 4,* 783–787.

Ziegler, T. E., Snowdon, C. T., & Uno, H. (1990). Social interactions and determinations of ovulation in tamarins (Saguinus). In T. E. Ziegler & F. B. Bercovitch (Eds.), *Socioendocrinology of primate reproduction* (pp. 159–186). New York: Wiley-Liss.

11

Child Well-Being in Cohabiting Families

Susan L. Brown
Bowling Green State University

Cohabitation has fundamentally altered the meaning of family and the measures of family structure. Researchers can no longer rely on marital-based family classification schemes. The categories of married-couple families, remarried stepfamilies, and single-parent families mask substantial variation due to the proliferation of cohabitation. Most two-biological parent couples are married, but some are cohabiting. A considerable proportion of stepfamilies are formed through postmarital cohabitation, rather than remarriage. And, many single mothers and even more single fathers actually reside with cohabiting partners. Approximately 75% of children born to single mothers and 20% of children born to married mothers are expected to spend some time in a cohabiting family before age 16 (Bumpass & Lu, 2000). Children will spend an increasing share of their childhoods in cohabiting unions and a decreasing share in marriages (Bumpass & Lu, 2000). Clearly, research on family structure effects on children cannot afford to ignore the significance of cohabitation.

Manning (chap. 8, this volume) argues convincingly for distinguishing among children by both the biological status of the parent-child relationship and the marital status of the biological parent(s). These distinctions are complex and perhaps even somewhat tedious, but are necessary if one wishes to adequately capture the growing diversity of American families in research. In fact, further distinctions might be required for family-level analyses, including differentiating children in the household who are from prior unions versus children from the present union. And, there may be important differences between cohabiting stepfamilies that involve a never-married versus divorced parent. The role of nonresident fathers—whether they were cohabiting with the mother at the time of the child's birth or the child now resides with the mother and her cohabiting partner—largely has been neglected to date, but merits careful consideration as 40% of nonmarital births occur to cohabiting mothers and many children experience postmarital cohabiting stepfamilies following parental divorce (Bumpass & Lu, 2000).

Manning's review is exhaustive and provides a comprehensive examination of both the demography of children in cohabiting families and the effects of this living arrangement on a variety of child outcomes. As she notes, very little is known about the influence of cohabitation on children; research in this area is still emerging. The earliest study using national data on cohabiting children's outcomes was conducted by Thomson, Hanson, and McLanahan (1994), who found that children residing with cohabiting mothers perform more poorly in school and exhibit more school behavior problems than children living with first-married, remarried, or single-mother parents. Recent work by Clark and Nelson (2000) and Dunifon and Kowaleski-Jones (2000) also indicates that child well-being, measured by cognitive outcomes and behavioral problems, is greater in two-parent first-married families than cohabiting families. In contrast, Morrison (1998) found few effects of remarriage or postmarital cohabitation on children's behavioral problems. In general, it appears that the differences between children in cohabiting versus married two-biological parent families are minimal.

LIMITATIONS OF THE CURRENT LITERATURE

Still, these results are preliminary for many reasons. Manning's chapter draws attention to several deficiencies characterizing the research on children in cohabiting families. Notably, reliance on cross-sectional data means that we are primarily comparing children in stable cohabiting families with children in stable married families. Many analyses are restricted to select samples that do not permit distinctions among cohabiting families, making it difficult to draw conclusions about the implications of cohabitation for children. For instance, work by Morrison (1998, 2000a, 2000b) using the National Longitudinal Survey of Youth (NLSY) data only considers children involved in postmarital unions (i.e., children residing with remarried or divorced, cohabiting mothers) and all of the children in her sample were born to young (14–21 years of age) mothers. The few researchers who have accounted for children's prior living arrangement transitions (Dunifon & Kowaleski-Jones, 2000) also have relied on this sample of children of young mothers from the NLSY, however, the quality of this sample is compromised by incomplete union histories. Respondents are asked at each survey (annually) whether they are cohabiting or married, but whether the current partner or spouse is that from the prior interview or a new one is unknown.

Additionally, children under age 6 have been neglected in analyses of child well-being in cohabiting unions, another omission resulting primarily from data constraints. Consequently, the range of child well-being indicators investigated to date is rather narrow. Research on the effects of family structure on child well-being has conceptualized well-being primarily in terms of school performance (Dunifon & Kowaleski-Jones, 2000; Morrison, 2000a; Thomson et al., 1994) and school behavioral problems (Clark & Nelson, 2000; Morrison, 1998, 2000a; Thomson et al., 1994, although the latter ,1994 also consider child temperament).

And, a limitation characterizing most research on family structure also is evident here: selection. Selection is integral to one's understanding of cohabitation. As recent research has revealed, the positive association between premarital cohabitation and subsequent divorce is largely an artifact of selection (Lillard, Brien, & Waite, 1995). Evidence presented by Manning concerning the types of people who are most likely to have children in cohabiting unions—the less educated—suggests that selection may play a role in determining the circumstances in which cohabitation is a family-building context. Future research must document the role of selection in both the formation of cohabiting families and their effects on children.

Manning also notes that researchers need to develop theoretical explanations for the effects of parental cohabitation on child outcomes. What mechanisms produce observed differences? Apparently, economic factors do not fully explain them. Cohabiting children's poor academic performance and high level of behavioral problems are at least partially a consequence of low levels of parental support and involvement (Thomson et al., 1994). Morrison's (2000a) analysis of child well-being in cohabiting and remarried unions following divorce also supports the importance of parenting behaviors. Economic deprivation does not account for the greater behavioral problems observed for children residing in nonstably remarried families. Instead, both the quantity and quality of parenting are the key mediators of the family structure effect. Emotional support from the mother is associated with child outcomes, according to Dunifon and Kowaleski-Jones (2000), but they do not investigate whether economic factors also account for some of the effects of family structure on child well-being. In summary, family processes, conceptualized here as parenting behaviors, are influential mediators of the effects of family structure on child well-being.

THE SIGNIFICANCE OF PARENTAL WELL-BEING

In addition to parenting behaviors, parental psychological well-being possibly accounts for some of the negative effect of cohabitation on child outcomes. In Brown (2000), I compared the psychological well-being of cohabitors and marrieds. I found that cohabitors are significantly more depressed than their married counterparts, net of a variety of sociodemographic factors. The influence of children on depression interacts with union type such that among marrieds, the presence of either biological or stepchildren is associated with lower levels of depression, whereas among cohabitors, biological and stepchildren increase depression. These findings suggest that the well-being of children residing in cohabiting families may be compromised as parental well-being has a profound impact on offspring (Amato & Booth, 1997). Children living with cohabiting parents are possibly at risk of a variety of adverse outcomes, including poor school performance, behavioral problems, and psychological distress.

My research on adult well-being in cohabiting unions has prompted me to think about the possible implications of cohabitation for children's well-being. I am currently engaged in a project that examines the influence of cohabitation on child outcomes using data from the 1997 National Survey of America's Families (NSAF). The project examines multiple mechanisms through which family structure might affect child well-being, including parental psychological well-being, parent–child relationship quality, and family economic status. After briefly describing this data set, I present some preliminary findings from this project.

DATA

Designed to evaluate the effects of devolution on children and families, the NSAF is a nationally representative sample of the civilian noninstitutionalized population under age 65 that covers topics ranging from child well-being, child care, and child support to health care and insurance coverage, employment and training, and welfare reform. During 1997, interviews were conducted in more than 44,000 households, yielding information on more than 100,000 people, including 34,439 children (for a detailed description of the 1997 NSAF, see Brick et al., 1999). Data on one child under age 6 and one child between ages 6 and 17 were gathered from the most knowledgeable adult (MKA) in the household. In nearly all of the cases, the MKA is a biological or stepparent, typically a mother. A new cross-section was interviewed in 1999, but these data are not yet available. The 1997 NSAF provides possibly the most recent and largest nationally representative sample of children residing with cohabiting parents. These data contain 795 children residing with two biological cohabiting parents and 1,049 children living with a biological parent and a cohabiting partner. There are sufficient numbers of cases of Black, White, and Hispanic children in first-married, remarried, cohabiting, and single-parent families to permit racial/ethnic comparisons. And, a low-income oversample permits detailed economic comparisons by family structure. All results presented here have been adjusted for oversampling to ensure they are representative of the American population as a whole.

I distinguish among seven family types:

1. Two biological married parents
2. Two biological cohabiting parents
3. Married stepfamilies
4. Cohabiting stepfamilies
5. Single mother only
6. Single father only
7. No parents (i.e., other families)

Unfortunately, the data do not permit measurement of duration in various family types or the number of family transitions children have experienced. Fig. 11.1 shows the distribution of the sample. Most children live in two-biological parent married families or single-mother families, but about 2% of children live with two biological cohabiting parents, and nearly 3% live with a biological parent and cohabiting partner. Among all children living with two biological par-

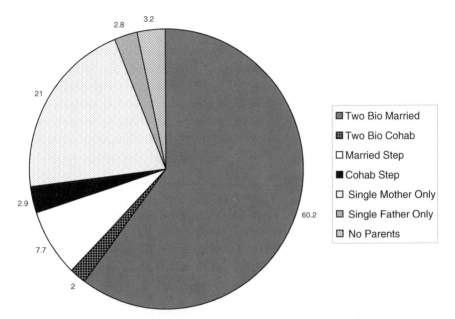

FIG. 11.1 Children's living arrangements.

ents, 3% of their parents are cohabiting, not married. The percentages are considerably higher when one considers stepfamilies—27% of children living with a biological parent and spouse/partner are in cohabiting stepfamilies. And, of all children living with one biological unmarried parent, 17% of these children also reside with their parent's cohabiting partner (results not shown). These figures demonstrate that ignoring cohabitation substantially misrepresents children actual living arrangements—we must account for both biological parentage and parent's marital status.

These data allow us to compare the well-being of children in cohabiting unions to that of children in first-married, remarried, and single-parent families across multiple components of child well-being, including child school engagement and child behavioral and emotional problems among children ages 6 to 17 and, for children under age 6, family outings and being read to. All of these measures are constructed variables in the NSAF data set. The psychometric properties of these measures, namely the quality of the data, internal reliability, and construct validity, are quite good, as discussed in NSAF Methodology Report 6 (Ehrle & Moore, 1999). School engagement assesses the degree to which the child cares about doing well in school, only works on schoolwork when forced, does just enough schoolwork to get by, and always does homework. I use a negative school engagement indicator constructed by NSAF to identify those children with low levels of school engagement. Child behavioral and emotional problems are tapped by separate scales for 6- to 11-year-olds and 12- to 17-year-olds. For both groups, questions measuring the MKA's perceptions of the extent to which the child doesn't get along with other kids, can't concentrate for long, and has been sad or depressed are included in the scales. For 6- to 11-year-olds, the MKA also is asked about whether the child feels worthless and inferior, has been nervous or tense, and acts too young for his or her age. For 12- to 17-year-olds, additional questions tap whether the child has trouble sleeping, lies or cheats, and does poorly at school work. Family outings measures the frequency with which a family member or relative took the child on a fun outing (e.g., going to the park, zoo, grocery store, church). Negative outings for children is a NSAF constructed variable that distinguishes children who are taken on outing two to three times per month or fewer (coded 1) from others (coded 0). A second well-being measure for children under age 6 is the number of times per week the child is read to by a family member. I use the NSAF constructed variable to differentiate children who are read to two times or fewer (coded 1) from other children (coded 0). Parental psychological well-being is tapped by a MKA mental health scale that gauges how often in the past month the MKA felt very nervous, felt calm and peaceful, felt downhearted, was a happy person, and felt so down in the dumps she or he could not be cheered up. I use a derived indicator variable in the data set that is coded 1 for poor mental health and 0 otherwise. Parent-child relationship quality is gauged using an aggravation in parenting scale that includes measures of how often in the past month the MKA felt that the child was much harder to care for than most, the child did things that really bothered the MKA, the MKA was angry with the child, and the MKA felt she or he was giving up more of his or her life for the child's needs. I examine a derived indicator variable that is assigned a value of 1 for a child living with an MKA who is highly aggravated and 0 otherwise.

RESULTS

The results presented below are descriptive, but they highlight some of the complexities surrounding the attempts to decipher the relation between family structure and child outcomes. Additionally, they offer new information about children in cohabiting families and how they compare to children in other living arrangements. I begin by examining the composition of children in cohabiting families and then I turn to family structure differences in parent and child well-being.

Fig. 11.2 shows the racial/ethnic composition of children by family structure. Among children living in two-biological parent families, Hispanic and Black children are especially likely to reside with cohabiting parents. In contrast, when one considers children living in stepfamilies, Hispanic children are disproportionately concentrated in married stepfamilies. Not only are there considerable racial differences across family structure, there are also significant differences in racial/ethnic composition between children living in two-biological parent cohabiting

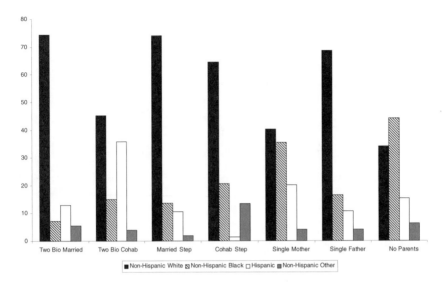

FIG. 11.2   Racial/ethnic distribution by family structure.

families and cohabiting stepfamilies. These results support the notion that researchers must incorporate both biological parentage and marital status in measures of children's living arrangements.

Fig. 11.3 reveals that children residing in cohabiting families are considerably poorer than their counterparts in married families. In fact, cohabiting children more closely resemble children living in single-mother families; only about one quarter are at 200% or above the poverty line. These patterns are consistent with those found by Manning and Lichter (1996) using 1990 Census data.

Turning now to parent psychological well-being, Fig. 11.4 shows the percentage of parents who are psychologically distressed. Note that the percentage of distressed MKAs is about 40% greater in two-biological parent cohabiting families than two-biological parent married families. Similarly, distress among MKAs of children in cohabiting stepfamilies is about 40% higher than distress among MKAs of children in married stepfamilies. The percentage of distressed MKAs in cohabiting stepfamilies is essentially the same as that in single-mother families, suggesting that the presence of a partner who is not a biological parent of the child does not enhance parental well-being. Distress varies markedly by cohabitation type. Almost 30% of MKAs in cohabiting stepfamilies are distressed versus nearly 20% in two-biological parent cohabiting families, which supports the assertion that not all cohabiting unions are alike—biological parentage is important.

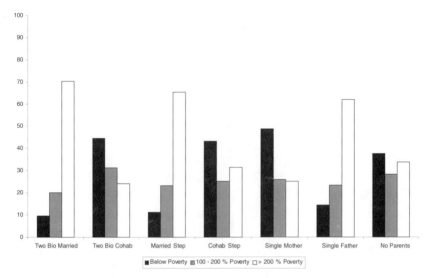

FIG. 11.3   Poverty status by family structure.

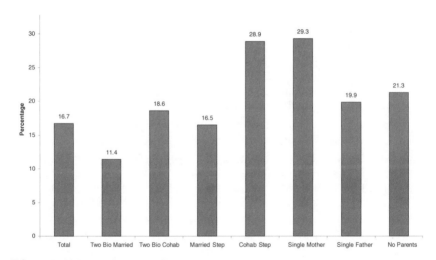

FIG. 11.4   MKA psychological distress.

180

Similar results are obtained when we consider the percentage of MKAs who are aggravated in parenting, although the differences between two-biological cohabiting families and cohabiting stepfamilies are much smaller (see Fig. 11.5). MKAs of children in married families are substantially less likely to be aggravated in parenting than are MKAs of children in cohabiting or single mother families.

Fig. 11.6 shows the percentage of children by family structure who have low levels of school engagement. Negative school engagement is higher in stepfamilies than two-biological parent families, although within this latter category, negative engagement is slightly more common among children in cohabiting families. Children in cohabiting stepfamilies and single-mother families are about equally likely to be disengaged from school, at nearly 30%.

Emotional and behavioral problems are more common among children residing with two-biological cohabiting parents than two-biological married parents (see Fig. 11.7). Among adolescents living in stepfamilies, the percentage exhibiting emotional and behavioral problems is twice as high in cohabiting than in married stepfamilies. And, although the percentage of 6- to 11-year-olds in cohabiting families experiencing emotional and behavioral problems does not differ for two-parent versus one-parent living arrangements, among those 12 to 17, there are considerable differences between those residing with two biological cohabiting parents versus one biological cohabiting parent. Within this latter group, almost one in four suffer from behavioral and emotional problems.

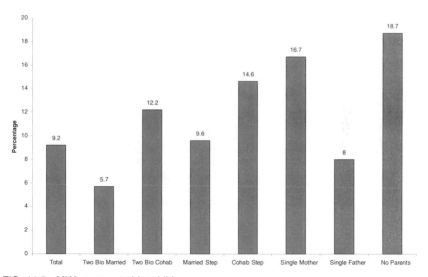

FIG. 11.5 MKA aggravated by child.

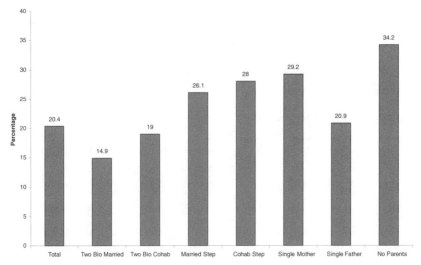

FIG. 11.6   Child's negative school engagement.

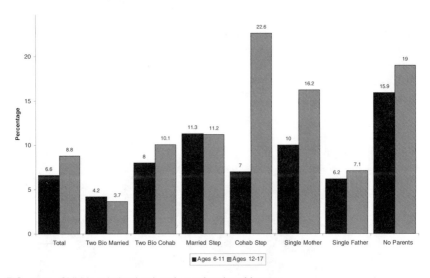

FIG. 11.7   Child has behavioral and emotional problems.

The findings presented above for children ages 6 to 17 as well as those shown by Clark and Nelson (2000), Dunifon and Kowaleski-Jones (2000), Morrison (1998, 2000a, 2000b), and Thomson et al. (1994), are placed in perspective when age distribution by family structure is examined. In Fig. 11.8, it is evident that particularly among children residing with two biological cohabiting parents, the age distribution is highly skewed. Nearly 80% of these children are under age 6. Just over 5% are between the ages of 12 and 17. This distribution makes sense when one considers that most cohabiting unions are short-lived. About 90% survive fewer than five years. Thus, as indicated by Graefe and Lichter (1999) as well as Bumpass and Lu (2000), a majority of children born to cohabiting mothers will experience subsequent living arrangement transitions at young ages. The more balanced age distribution characterizing cohabiting stepfamilies reflects the two possible pathways to this living arrangement: union formation by a never-married parent and her or his partner or union formation by a divorced parent and her or his partner. In the former case, children likely are younger, whereas in the latter case, children are typically older. Finally, the older age distribution characterizing married stepfamilies is perhaps a function of the fact that most divorces and remarriages do not occur when children are very young. The birth of a child tends to deter divorce for a few years (White & Booth, 1985), and divorced parents typically do not remarry for at least a year or two (Ahlburg & DeVita, 1992), meaning that most children living in married stepfamilies are school-aged. Ultimately, this figure clearly demonstrates that the age distribution of children residing in two-biological parent married families, two-biological parent cohabiting families,

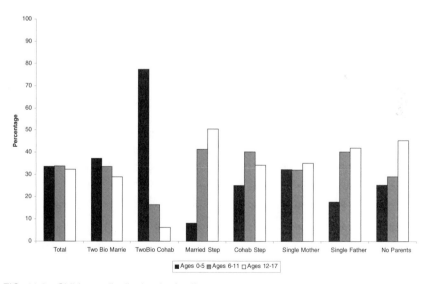

FIG. 11.8   Child age distribution by family structure.

married stepfamilies, and cohabiting stepfamilies are all unique from one another. One needs to keep these differences in mind when considering the effects of family structure on child well-being. Studies to date, which have focused on school-aged children, reveal little about the well-being of children living with two biological cohabiting parents, as most of them are under age 6. Yet, an estimated 1.1 million children under age 6 currently reside with two biological parents[1]. How are they faring?

Figs. 11.9 and 11.10 examine well-being indicators for young children. Fig. 11.9 depicts the percentage of children who are taken on no more than just two or three outings per month. Children in two-parent biological cohabiting families as well as cohabiting stepfamilies and single-mother families are much more likely to have experienced few outings than children in two-biological parent married families and married stepfamilies. Approximately 25% of children living with two-biological parent cohabiting families were taken on no more than a couple of outings, compared with just 15% of those in married-couple families.

Finally, almost one third of children under age 6 in two-biological parent cohabiting families are read to two or fewer times each week, compared to less than 20% in married-couple families and 16% in cohabiting stepfamilies, as shown in Fig. 11.10. The explanation for the dramatic difference between two-parent biological cohabiting families versus cohabiting stepfamilies is not readily apparent, but hopefully will be elucidated in multivariate analyses. At least, these results are supportive of the assertion that all cohabiting families are not alike. It is important to differentiate between two-biological cohabiting families and cohabiting stepfamilies as children's outcomes in these two living arrangements are not always similar.

CONCLUSIONS

Throughout this volume, we have contemplated the significance of cohabitation as a childrearing context and its implications for the well-being of children. One recent estimate indicates that two out every five children will spend some time in a cohabiting family. In fact, 11% of U.S. children are born to a cohabiting mother (Bumpass & Lu, 2000). Yet, very little is known about the effects of parental cohabitation on early childhood outcomes. The high levels of parental psychological distress and aggravation in parenting reported by cohabiting parents suggests that their children may be at risk for a variety of adverse outcomes. The results presented here indicate that children in cohabiting families are doing worse than their counterparts in married families. Indeed, children living in cohabiting families appear more similar to children residing with single mothers both in terms of their poverty status and their well-being outcomes. Notably, school-aged children in two-biological parent cohabiting families seem to be somewhat better off

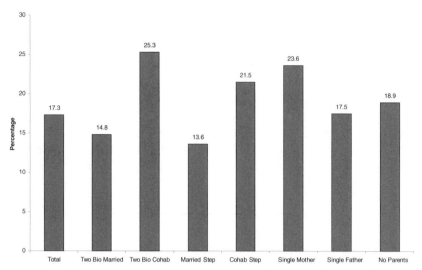

FIG. 11.9   Child taken on two to three outings per month or less.

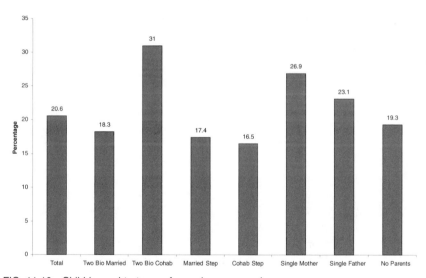

FIG. 11.10   Child is read to two or fewer days per week.

than children in cohabiting stepfamilies. But, an examination of child outcomes among children under age 6 yields the opposite conclusion—children in two-biological parent cohabiting families are less likely to go on family outcomes and are less likely to be read to than children in cohabiting stepfamilies. Clearly, future analyses need to pay close attention to both the child's age and the type of cohabiting union in which she or he resides (i.e., one- vs. two-biological parents). Families with two adults, married or unmarried, biological or nonbiological parents, are not all alike. As children's living arrangements continue to become more diverse and complex, researchers must try to keep up with the changes if we are to truly understand the effects of family living arrangements on children's well-being.

ACKNOWLEDGMENTS

This research was supported in part by the Association for Public Policy Analysis and Management, and the NSAF Small Research Grants Program funded by the Annie E. Casey Foundation. Thanks to Wendy Manning for many engaging discussions about cohabitation and to Meagan Wensinger for her assistance with the figures.

REFERENCES

Ahlburg, D., & DeVita, C. (1992). New realities of the American family. *Population Bulletin, 47*, 1–50.

Amato, P. R., & Booth, A. (1997). *A generation at risk: Growing up in an era of family upheaval*. Cambridge, MA: Harvard University Press.

Brick, P. D., Kenney, G., McCullough-Harlin, R., Rajan, S., Scheuren, F., Wang, K., Brick, J. M., & Cunningham, P. (1999). 1997 NSAF survey methods and data reliability. *NSAF Methodology Reports, No. 1*.

Brown, S. L. (2000). The effect of union type on psychological well-being: Depression among cohabitors versus marrieds. *Journal of Health and Social Behavior, 41*, 241–255.

Bumpass, L. L., & Lu, H. (2000). Trends in cohabitation and implications for children's family contexts in the united states. *Population Studies, 54*, 29–41.

Clark, R. L., & Nelson, S. L. (2000). *Beyond the two-parent family: Behavioral problems among school-aged children living with married biological parents, unmarried biological parents, biological mother and stepfather, and biological mother and her boyfriend*. Paper presented at the annual meeting of the Population Association of America, Los Angeles, CA.

Dunifon, R., & Kowaleski-Jones, L. (2000). *Who's in the house? Effects of family structure on children's home environments and cognitive outcomes.* Paper presented at the annual meeting of the Population Association of America, Los Angeles, CA.

Ehrle, J., & Moore, K. A. (1999). Benchmarking child and family well-being measures in the NSAF. *NSAF Methodology Reports, No. 6.*

Graefe, D. R., & Lichter, D. T. (1999). Life course transitions of American children: Parental cohabitation, marriage, and single motherhood. *Demography, 36,* 205–217.

Lillard, L. A., Brien, M. J., & Waite, L. J. (1995). Premarital cohabitation and subsequent marital dissolution: Is it self-selection? *Demography, 32,* 437–458.

Manning, W. D., & Lichter, D. T. (1996). Parental cohabitation and children's economic well-being. *Journal of Marriage and the Family, 58,* 998–1010.

Morrison, D. R. (1998). *Child well-being in step-families and cohabiting unions following divorce: A dynamic appraisal.* Paper presented at the annual meeting of the Population Association of America, Chicago, IL.

Morrison, D. R. (2000a). *The costs of economic uncertainty: Child well-being in cohabiting and remarried unions following parental divorce.* Paper presented at the annual meeting of the Population Association of America, Los Angeles, CA.

Morrison, D. R., & Ritualo, A. (2000b). Routes to children's economic recovery after divorce: Are maternal cohabitation and remarriage equivalent? *American Sociological Review, 65,* 560-580.

Thomson, E., Hanson, T. L., & McLanahan, S. S. (1994). Family structure and child well-being: Economic resources vs. parental behaviors. *Social Forces, 73,* 221–242.

U.S. Bureau of the Census. (1999). Ch-1. Living arrangements of children under 18 years old: 1960 to present. http://www.census.gov/population/socdemo/ms-la/tabch-1.txt

White, L. K., & Booth, A. (1985). The transition to parenthood and marital quality. *Journal of Family Issues, 6,* 435–449.

IV

How Are Cohabiting Couples and Their Children Affected by Current Policies? What Policies Are Needed for These Individuals?

12

Safety Net Programs, Marriage, and Cohabitation

Wendell E. Primus and Jennifer Beeson
Center on Budget and Policy Priorities

The vast majority of families with children receiving cash welfare assistance are headed by single mothers. In the 65 years since the establishment of the first national welfare benefit program, the demographic profile of families served by low-income programs has changed dramatically. Originally designed to serve a relatively small group of widows and abandoned mothers, welfare has evolved to serve mostly families headed by divorced, separated, or never-married mothers. New research reveals that a significant percentage of single mothers at all income levels—including those who receive welfare—are living with a man to whom they are not married, who may or may not be the father of her children.

The rise in the number of unwed mothers receiving low-income assistance over the last several decades and the increase in cohabitation has motivated policymakers and researchers to question whether welfare and tax policies influence a range of decisions about family, including decisions to marry, have children, or cohabit. Although the findings of academic researchers have been inconclusive, many lawmakers and others continue to express concern that the eligibility and benefit structures of means-tested programs may indirectly encourage single-parent families or discourage marriage. The cornerstone of this argument is that benefits for low-income single mothers are too high relative to benefits for married couple families and that families are better off cohabiting than being married.

This chapter attempts to investigate the validity in that argument. Do tax and transfer programs encourage single parenthood or cohabitation? Are there financial disincentives to marry or incentives for single parents to live together without marriage? Can cohabiting families misreport income more easily than married families? Calculating marriage penalties or bonuses for low-income single parents is more difficult than it may initially appear. Calculations of marriage penalties must take into account the living arrangements of the parents (separate or together), the earnings (if any) of the mother and father, the amount of welfare, food stamps, and other program benefits for which they qualify, their tax filing status, and child support payments, where appropriate. Marriage penalties vary depending on the situation of couples considering marriage. A key variable determining the size of the marriage penalty is whether the couple has children in common. The effects of marriage on disposable income are different for a single mother with a cohabiting partner than for a couple living together with one or more children in common, or a mother and a father living together, each with their own children but no children in common, for example. All of these possible permutations emphasize the need for more subtle analyses of the marriage penalty.

To be clear, this chapter uses the term cohabiting parents to identify two unmarried individuals who are living together and who have a child in common. Cohabiting partner is an individual living with a single parent with no child in common. A stepparent is an individual who may or may not have children of his or her own who is married to a parent living with his or her children. The stepparent may or may not have legally adopted the stepchild.

As shown in Table 12.1, data from the 1997 National Survey of American Families shows that about 1.4 million children live with cohabiting parents and that 1.8 million children live in families with cohabiting partners. The child poverty rate for children living with cohabiting parents is 34%, almost as high as the poverty rate for children in single-mother families. Children in unmarried cohabiting families represent about 15% of all poor children living in two-parent families.

Table 12.1
Child Living Arrangements

Family Type	Number of Children (thousands)	Percent of All Children	Percent Poor
Married Couple	42,594	59.8	7.7
Married Stepparents	5,691	8.0	6.8
Single Mother	15,933	22.4	37.5
Single Father	2,240	3.1	11.7
Cohabiting Parents (Fragile Familie with Common Children)	1,392	2.0	30.2
Single Parent with Cohabiting Partner	650	0.9	17.7
No Parents/Foster Parents/Other	2,700	3.8	31.1

Source: Tabulations of the National Survey of American Families, 1997.

Due to reporting, the number of children living with a single parent with cohabiting partner may be underestimated.

Poverty status is based on social families, which includes income of unmarried partners in determining poverty status. Otherwise poverty definition matches the official definition of poverty. Food stamps and other non-cash benefits are excluded in determining poverty status.

The analyses in this chapter focus on low-income couples with children in common for several reasons: (a) a large number of children are born into these families and they have not received much policy attention, (b) their high poverty rate—there are about 50% more poor children in these families than there are poor children in families where the adults do not have children in common, and (c) the potential to strengthen these families by providing services and ensure that they secure the benefits to which they are entitled.

Calculating marriage penalties for low-income families requires understanding the eligibility requirements, benefit levels, and the program rules for an array of programs serving these families. In this chapter, we describe how eligibility and benefit rules apply to different family combinations, including single-parent families, married-couple families, and single parents who are living with partners. To fully understand how cohabiting couples with children are treated, one must know how they are treated relative to single-parent or married-couple families. These comparisons are made throughout the chapter.

The first section contains a brief review of the literature on whether tax and welfare policies affect family formation.

The second part defines the variables that affect marriage penalty–bonus calculations. It describes the general eligibility rules, benefit levels, and program requirements for a range of safety net programs and describes how those rules have different impacts on different family types.

Next, we define how a marriage penalty-bonus should be calculated and evaluates the marriage penalty for families with different structures in Maryland, California, and Texas. We find that in some cases there are financial disincentives for marriage relative to cohabitation. However, there are financial incentives for both marriage and cohabitation relative to living separately. In general, federal tax policy favors cohabiting families over married families, and two-parent families (both married and unmarried) must meet additional requirements to be eligible for some programs in some states. Two-parent families invariably fare better than single-parent families regardless of whether they marry if the calculation takes into account child support payments and the additional costs associated with maintaining two separate households.

In the final section, we describe the policy implications of the outcome of the marriage penalty or bonus calculations and make several suggestions on how tax and transfer programs should be modified. Our recommendations focus on proposals that will increase services for two-parent families while continuing to support single-parent families. Adding a cohabiting filing status in the IRS code for cohabiting families with children in common would allow the federal government to treat cohabiting couples with children in common the same as married couples. The child support program also could play a greater role in enforcing these rules and making these recommendations administratively feasible.

BACKGROUND AND LITERATURE REVIEW

There is mounting evidence that the structure of many U.S. families is changing in dramatic ways. Cohabitation, or living together without marriage, is on the rise. Using nationally representative data, Bumpass and Lu (2000) found that cohabitation increased dramatically between 1987 and 1995.

Conventional wisdom holds that welfare benefits provide a disincentive to marry. By many indices it would seem that the welfare system has provided low-income mothers with a perverse incentive to remain single. Before 1988, two-parent families—with a few exceptions, such as when a parent was incapacitated—did not qualify for cash assistance in half the states. Even today, the eligibility requirements for two-parent families are more rigorous than for single-parent families in at least 13 states. Setting aside the child support system, if the decision to marry was based solely on short-term income maximization, a low-income pregnant woman may be better off (and would have a more stable income source) if she remained single, cohabited with the father, and collected welfare benefits, than if she married and the father's earnings substantially reduced the size of the welfare check. This calculus is especially true if the father's income were unstable and went unreported to welfare authorities.[1]

However, research has been more equivocal than conventional wisdom. Since the early 1980s, numerous studies have considered whether the presence and size of a welfare check can be tied to marriage rates or likelihood to cohabit. Most results have been inconclusive. Furthermore, no one has conducted a state-by-state analysis linking the benefits to marriage or cohabitation rates, despite the fact that the size of a typical welfare benefit package varies greatly among states.[2]

Evenhouse and Reilly (1999) found that higher welfare benefits increase the incidence of single-mother families and two-adult households in which the man is not the father of the child. Dickert-Conlin and Houser (1999), however, found no correlation between receipt of Aid to Families with Dependent Children (AFDC) and the decision by mothers to not marry.

Researchers have also analyzed the effect of tax policy on marriage rates. Ellwood (1999) found that the combination of the Earned Income Tax Credit and welfare reform has encouraged single parents to work but has had no discernible effect on marriage or cohabitation. Rosenbaum (2000) used large samples from Survey of Income and Program Participation (SIPP) and Current Population Survey (CPS) data and found that tax incentives may have an influence on decision to enter into marriage, but the magnitude of the effect is hard to measure. He also found that it is unlikely that tax incentives influence a decision to end a marriage.

---

[1] This is an overly simplistic calculation of benefits versus penalties of marriage for low-income couples. First, the welfare reform law of 1996 may have changed the calculus of this analysis by strengthening child support collections. Second, as this chapter demonstrates, calculating marriage penalties and bonuses can be enormously complex, depending on living arrangements, earnings, number of children, and so forth.

[2] For a review of studies on the influence of welfare policies and marriage rates, see Moffitt (1998).

Researchers analyzing the effect of various benefits on decisions to marry have had difficulty sorting out the benefits for which different family combinations are eligible. There has been relatively little systematic analysis of how cohabitation is treated by various programs.[3]

A young couple has several choices to make regarding their living arrangements: whether to marry; whether to live together; if they do not live together the mother must decide whether to set up a household separate from her parents. Among other factors, the decision to live separately, cohabit, or marry will be based on the woman's emotional relationship to the father of her child (is he a good partner and a good father?), his ability to contribute financially to the family (can he bring in a steady income?), and how his presence affects her ability to contribute to the family (will he care for the child while she works, will the family continue to be eligible for cash welfare and food stamps?). Whether or not the mother experiences a financial incentive to marry depends on her income, her partner's income, the number of children they have in common, the number of other children present in the family, the level of cash assistance for which the family qualifies, and whether child support will be a factor.

Ellwood and Liebman's (2000) calculation of marriage penalty is representative of the conventional wisdom on marriage penalties. They found that the tax system creates significant marriage penalties for single parents who choose to marry. An analysis by Steurle (1997) estimates that the marriage penalty can be as high as $8,060 under certain circumstances. However, the methodology used to calculate the marriage penalty in this example is problematic. First, this calculation evaluates the tax liability of an unmarried single mother plus a single man (not the father of the children) who are living apart compared with the tax liability of a woman and man who marry and live together. But the calculation does not account for the economies of scale resulting from the maintenance of one household instead of two, and does not differentiate between the impact of the change in living arrangements versus the change in marital status.

Second, the Steuerle and Ellwood and Liebman examples do not take child support payments into account. Child support payments are important especially when comparing the well-being of families where the mother and children are eligible for cash welfare assistance. In most states, mothers do not receive child support payments when they are on welfare because the state retains it as a reimbursement for welfare expenses. However, fathers are still required to pay child support or they accumulate a child support debt owed to the state. The payment of child support increases the cost of remaining separated, even when the parents are cohabiting because child support payments are typically only required when a parent is not residing with the child.[4]

---

[3] One exception to this is a systematic analysis of state AFDC rules by Moffitt, Reville, and Winkler (1994).

[4] If the marriage penalty calculations assume that the two adults do not have a child in common, child support is not a factor.

Third, the loss of Medicaid benefits for the married couple are an important part of the Steuerle calculation. Although Medicaid coverage is an important component of the marriage penalty calculation, it is important to acknowledge that health coverage is not equivalent to cash. The value of health coverage to a healthy family is different than the value of medical coverage to a family with a member who has a health problem or chronic condition requiring substantial medical attention. Steurle's calculation assumes that when working families move from welfare to work they lose Medicaid benefits and do not gain employer-based coverage. Furthermore, as health insurance becomes more universal among low-income families (through expansions of the State Children's Health Insurance Program (SCHIP) and expansions to working parents), provision of health benefits will become a smaller part of the marriage penalty–bonus formula. Finally, one must be cautious about including Medicaid benefits in the marriage penalty formula because many families and individuals do not receive the benefits for which they are eligible. Additionally, families may not understand the full value of these benefits or their eligibility; if that is the case, how could eligibility for benefits influence their decision to live separately from each other or together?

Nevertheless, the calculation of marriage penalties and bonuses should be based on the entire combination of tax and transfer programs, including the child support system. And it should explicitly address the savings associated with maintaining one household rather than two.

In studying the various choices the single mother faces, the challenge for policymakers is deciding whether the tax and transfer system is providing the right package of incentives to help parents make choices that will ultimately benefit them and their child(ren). Despite the mixed research evidence, many lawmakers are convinced that tax and transfer policies do influence decisions to marry or have children. In fact, it may be that the messages that the law sends about how society views marriage are as important as the actual effect on marriage rates.

ELIGIBILITY, BENEFIT LEVELS, AND PROGRAM RULES

This section describes the availability of means-tested programs to married, cohabiting, and single-parent families.

Temporary Assistance for Needy Families

The 1996 welfare reform law requires states to use Temporary Assistance to Needy Families (TANF) to serve needy children and their families, but the law does not define family. Although TANF law grants states greater flexibility to determine eligibility, most states have maintained the same eligibility rules as they did under AFDC.

Under TANF rules, cohabiting parents are treated in much the same way as married parents in all states. TANF rules do, however, make distinctions between one-parent and two-parent families (either married or not) in a number of ways. Several federal- and state-based policies frame how single-parent and two-parent families are treated by TANF, including work requirements, definitions of the assistance unit, income deeming rules, and the treatment of contributions by persons not in the assistance unit.

As of July 1999, 33 states, including Maryland, allow two-parent families to qualify for TANF assistance solely on financial circumstances. However, 17 states do not allow two-parent families to participate in TANF on the same basis as one-parent families. In most of these states, two-parent families that meet the financial eligibility requirements are eligible only if one parent is incapacitated or one parent (or the principal wage earner, if not a parent) is unemployed. These states usually require this second parent to meet an unemployment test.[5] Additionally, a two-parent family's principal wage earner can typically work no more than 100 hours per month to remain eligible, which is known as the "100-hour rule" (U.S. House of Representatives, 1996).

How a state defines the assistance unit has implications for marriage and cohabitation. No state considers cohabiting partners (i.e., the mother's boyfriend) part of the assistance unit if the couple have no child in common. States vary in how they treat stepparents. Twenty states have laws of general applicability, which require stepparents be treated as legally responsible for the stepchildren.[6] In these states, stepparent families are treated the same as two-parent families. In other states, stepparents may not be considered part of the assistance unit. However, states have the ability to reduce the size of the cash grant by counting contributions of cash, food, clothing, or housing assistance from a cohabiting male.

Medicaid

Because of higher income eligibility requirements, the Medicaid program serves more families than does TANF. Before 1996, Medicaid was provided automatically to families receiving welfare. When families applied for welfare benefits, they simultaneously applied for Medicaid, and lost their Medicaid coverage when they left welfare. Medicaid expansions in the late 1980s and welfare reform have severed the automatic link between Medicaid and TANF. States were required to provide Medicaid to families who remained eligible based on income and assets, whether or not they received TANF.

---

[5] A typical test requires the unemployed parent to have received (or have been eligible for) unemployment compensation benefits in at least 6 of 13 quarters ending within a year of applying for TANF.

[6] The duty lasts so long as the stepparent is married to the child's biological parent. A significant number of other states do not have statutes but use the *in loco parentis* doctrine to impose a similar support obligation on stepparents (Morgan, 1999).

Medicaid's eligibility and participation rules treat marriage and cohabitation in the same way TANF does. The 100-hour employment rule that restricts two-parent families participation in TANF in 17 states also affects two-parent families' ability to receive Medicaid. In these states, two-parent families are not eligible to receive Medicaid simply by meeting the financial requirements. One parent must be incapacitated or unemployed (and meet an unemployment test) before qualifying for benefits.

Food Stamps

The federal government is primarily responsible for determining the eligibility rules for food stamps. A family's food stamp benefit is based on the needs of a "food stamp household," which federal law defines as one person or a group of persons living together that usually share food and meals.[7] Their biological or marital relationships are irrelevant. Members of the same household must apply for food stamps together, and their income, expenses and assets are aggregated in determining eligibility and benefits.[8] The eligibility and benefit levels for the food stamp program for all types of two-adult families—married parents, cohabiting parents, a parent plus stepparent, and a single parent plus partner—is equivalent, provided equal income and assets and that each couple applies as a single unit. Yet, there is a possibility for differences in benefits among these different family types. Because the food stamp rules allow certain persons who live together to apply separately, it is technically possible—although perhaps very unlikely—that a single mother with her children could apply as one household and her cohabiting partner (who is not the father of any of her children) could apply as a separate household. The burden of completing a food stamp application, providing necessary documentation and periodically re-certifying eligibility makes it especially unlikely that a couple living together would attempt to maintain separate food stamps households.

Housing

Federal housing programs currently make no distinction based on marital status for either eligibility or rent determination. Because housing assistance benefits all the people who live in the housing, housing programs simply count the income of all people who will live in the unit. However, only 25% to 33% of eligible house-

---

[7] Households comprised entirely of TANF, Supplemental Security Income (SS1), or general assistance participants are automatically eligible for food stamps, although their benefit is still determined by their income and expenses.

[8] Some persons who live together can be considered separate households for the purposes of food stamps, and persons living together receive larger aggregate benefits if they are treated as more than one food stamp household. Persons who live together but buy food and prepare meals separately may apply for food stamps separately except for spouses, parents and their children, and children who live under parental control of a caretaker (except for foster children who may be treated separately). Different food stamp households can live together, and food stamp recipients can reside with nonrecipients.

holds receive housing assistance due to limited supply. To determine income eligibility, housing programs use a ceiling of a percent of the Housing and Urban Development (HUD)-adjusted area median income for a family of that size.[9] After adjusting for family size, both single-parent families, as well as families with two adults (whether married parents, cohabiting parents, parent plus cohabiting partner, or parent plus stepparent) are equally eligible for housing benefits.

Although housing policy does not directly address cohabitation or marital status, the application of rules regarding criminal history may have an effect on cohabitation or marriage. Public housing authorities (PHAs) are permitted to deny applicants on the basis of applicants' criminal histories. Many low-income fathers have criminal records (E. Johnson et al., 1999) and anecdotal evidence suggests that this policy discourages many two-parent families from applying for housing assistance. PHAs are supposed to consider evidence of rehabilitation, recency of criminal conduct, effect on other family members, and other mitigating circumstances. In practice, however, PHAs typically deny applicants with a history that involves drugs or violence, and leave it to the appeal process for the applicant to prove rehabilitation. A father returning to the family from drug-related prison sentence presents the family living in public housing with three choices: the father does not move back in, the father moves in with the family but they do not report his presence to the housing authorities, or the family leaves public housing to find other residence. It seems likely that if a single mother was in a relationship with a man burdened by a criminal record, she would have an incentive to maintain housing in her name only, even if that relationship were long term. Low-income families in these circumstances present policymakers with difficult choices in terms of the best way to help two-parent families stay together without putting communities at a potentially greater risk.

Child Support

Child support policy is relevant mostly to single-parent mothers and the (separated) noncustodial father. To receive child support, a mother must first establish the paternity of the child (if she has never married the father) and secure a child support order. The state is charged with enforcing the order and ensuring that the mother receives child support payments.

The child support enforcement system was originally designed to help recover the costs of providing cash assistance to low-income families, although it is available to families of all incomes. If the custodial child is in a family that is currently receiving welfare, most or all of the child support paid by noncustodial

---

[9] Generally, the maximum income for eligibility is 80% of the HUD-adjusted area median income for a family of that size, with a varying percentage of admissions required to be households with incomes below 30% of adjusted median income depending on the program. In determining rent for public housing (not Section 8 vouchers), public housing authorities may disregard earnings of returning fathers for a period of time, or otherwise seek to encourage two-parent families.

fathers to their needy child is retained by the state and federal government to reimburse it for its welfare expenses. In 16 states, mothers on welfare receive no more than $50 per month of the child support paid by the father. In 31 states, mothers on welfare receive no child support payments at all, even when the father is paying the full amount on time.[10]

In recent years, lawmakers have given the child support system a host of stronger enforcement tools. The combination of paternity establishment requirements, cooperation agreement requirements, automatic wage withholding, and the development of a national directory of new hires has resulted in a system that is much harder for noncustodial parents to avoid. The improved efficacy of the child support system makes it even more appropriate to include child support as part of a marriage penalty formula.

Although one typically thinks of child support in the context of separated parents, there is substantial evidence that some fathers who live with the mother of their children are also paying child support (Pate & Johnson, 2000; Waller & Plotnick, 1999). Cohabiting families may also struggle with child support arrearages, or debt resulting from unpaid child support that may be owed to the state rather than the custodial family. Also, low-income fathers are sometimes charged with the Medicaid costs of child birth if the new mother applies for cash assistance after the birth of the child. If the father moves in with the young family soon after birth, he remains responsible for hospital costs. If this same couple were living together at the time of the birth, and they applied for welfare as a two-parent family, the father would not be responsible for the birthing costs.

As it is currently administered, the child support program gives the welfare agency a key tool to prevent families from misrepresenting themselves. As mentioned previously, if a father has earnings and is living in the family, high effective tax rates on earnings can give the family an incentive to misreport their earnings to welfare authorities. Several years ago, if the mother and children applied for welfare benefits without identifying the presence of the father, the family would end up with substantially more cash and food stamp benefits, and considerably more income, as a result of misreporting themselves. Today, the implications are substantially different. The mother would have to comply with work requirements and cooperate with the child support program, or risk sanctions that may cut off her welfare benefit in its entirety. Even if she initially misreports the presence of the father, the child support agency will investigate and subject the father to the child support program, thus increasing the "cost" of misreporting family living arrangements. Boyfriends can still escape detection but this is probably appropriate since the extent to which income is shared is unknown and there is no way that this can be enforced.

---

[10] State Policy Documentation Project, a joint effort of the Center on Budget and Policy Priorities and the Center for Law and Social Policy. Online at www.spdp.org.

Taxes

Marital status is an explicit factor in determining an individual's state and federal taxes. The federal tax policies most relevant to low-income families are the child exemption, the child tax credit, the nonrefundable dependent care credit, and (perhaps most important) the earned income tax credit (EITC), which provides tax refunds for low-income working individuals and families.

The eligibility rules for the EITC can treat unmarried cohabiting workers more generously than married couples, who must file jointly and count income together. (See Table 12.2.) Depending on the total family income and the distribution of income (as well as the distribution of children) between the man and woman, the EITC can act as either an incentive or a disincentive to live together and can have financial implications on the decision to marry. In the case where cohabiting parents with a child in common each have very low earnings (on Table

Table 12.2
Comparison of Federal Income Tax Liability for Couples with Common Children If They Cohabit or Marry

Mother's Earnings	Father's Earnings	One Child			Two Children		
		Tax Liability if Cohabiting	Tax Liability if Married	Marriage Penalty/ Cohab Bonus	Tax Liability if Cohabiting	Tax Liability if Married	Marriage Penalty/ Cohab Bonus
0	5,000	1,700	1,700	0	2,000	2,000	0
	10,000	2,353	2,353	0	3,888	3,888	0
	15,000	1,984	1,984	0	3,402	3,402	0
	20,000	492	1,047	(555)	2,349	2,349	0
5,000	5,000	1,700	2,353	(653)	2,000	3,888	(1,888)
	10,000	2,353	1,984	369	3,888	3,402	486
	15,000	1,984	1,047	936	3,402	2,349	1,053
	20,000	492	(502)	994	2,349	1,296	1,053
7,500	5,000	2,353	2,353	0	3,000	3,888	(888)
	10,000	2,308	1,584	724	3,843	2,875	968
	15,000	1,939	273	1,666	3,357	1,822	1,534
	20,000	447	(1,262)	1,710	2,304	427	1,877
10,000	5,000	2,353	1,984	369	3,888	3,402	486
	10,000	1,933	1,047	886	3,468	2,349	1,119
	15,000	1,564	(502)	2,066	2,982	1,296	1,686
	20,000	72	(1,638)	1,710	1,929	(475)	2,404
12,500	5,000	2,353	1,584	769	3,888	2,875	1,013
	10,000	1,933	273	1,660	3,468	1,822	1,646
	15,000	1,189	(1,262)	2,451	2,607	427	2,180
	20,000	(303)	(2,012)	1,710	1,554	(1,092)	2,646
15,000	5,000	1,984	1,047	936	3,402	2,349	1,053
	10,000	1,564	(502)	2,066	2,982	1,296	1,686
	15,000	814	(1,638)	2,451	2,232	(475)	2,707
	20,000	(678)	(2,388)	1,710	1,179	(1,468)	2,646
20,000	5,000	492	(502)	994	2,349	1,296	1,053
	10,000	72	(1,638)	1,710	1,929	(475)	2,404
	15,000	(678)	(2,388)	1,710	1,179	(1,468)	2,646
	20,000	(1,428)	(3,138)	1,710	429	(2,218)	2,646

Note: Positive sign indicates a federal tax credit. Negative amounts denoted by a "()." A negative number in the column labeled Marriage Penalty/Cohab bonus signifies a marriage bonus.

12.2, if they each have $5,000 or $7,500 in earnings), they will become eligible for a higher EITC if they marry. However, if either parent has higher earnings, their combined earnings may put them over the income limit for the EITC. In this case, the EITC acts as a financial disincentive to marry and they are financially better off if they simply live together.

Table 12.2 shows the different tax liabilities for low-income cohabiting parents versus married parents. It calculates federal income taxes for a father and mother with different earnings and for one or two children. If the couple is married, they must file as "married, filing jointly" and add together their earnings and report all children as dependents of this one tax filing unit. However, if they cohabit, the higher earner must file as head of household and claim all the children. The other adult files as a single individual and may not claim the childless worker EITC. All of these examples assume that the adults have common children.

The examples in Table 12.2 illustrate that the unmarried cohabiting family's overall income tax liability is usually lower than the married couple family's tax liability. When both parents have earnings, they are almost always better off financially by cohabiting rather than marrying. However, when one of the adults has zero or very low earnings, the family's tax liability is typically the same or is occasionally better off if the adults marry.

The situation is more complicated if both parents are not able to claim the child(ren) to qualify for the EITC. This would occur anytime that the two adults did not have common children. (Until tax year 2000, the cohabiting partner may have been able to claim the child for the EITC because the foster child definition under the EITC statute did not require a formal foster care placement, but it did require the adult to live in the home with the child all 12 months of the year. As of tax year 2000, the EITC eligibility rules deny the EITC to unrelated workers unless an authorized agency, such as a licensed foster care agency, has formally placed the child in the care of such a worker.) Table 12.3 assumes that only the mother can claim the EITC for the examples with one or two children. In the case of three children, the mother brings two children to the relationship and the father brings one child. As the examples in Table 12.3 illustrate, overall there are fewer marriage penalties in this table than in Table 12.2. However, under these assumptions married parents face substantial tax penalties when both parents earn between $10,000 and $20,000 per year.

Recipiency Rates Among Different Family Structures

So far in this section we have seen that the eligibility rules for programs that serve the poor, with the exception of the EITC, make limited or no distinction between cohabiting parents and married parents. Transfer programs provide little incentive or disincentive for a couple (with children in common) that is already living together to marry; but, in some cases, the EITC offers a disincentive to marry.

Table 12.3

Comparison of Federal Income Tax Liability for Couples Without Common Children If They Cohabit Or Marry.

(Examples with one and two children assume they are the mother's; example with three children assumes two are the mother's, one is the father's.)

Mother's Earnings	Father' Earnings	One Child			Two Children			Three Children		
		Tax Liability if Cohabiting	Tax Liability if Married	Marriage Penalty/ Cohab Bonus	Tax Liability if Cohabiting	Tax Liability if Married	Marriage Penalty/ Cohab Bonus	Tax Liability if Cohabiting	Tax Liability if Married	Marriage Penalty/ Cohab Bonus
0	5,000	353	1,700	(1,347)	353	2,000	(1,647)	1,700	2,000	(300)
0	10,000	(391)	2,353	(2,744)	(391)	3,888	(4,279)	2,353	3,888	(1,535)
0	15,000	(1,170)	1,984	(3,154)	(1,170)	3,402	(4,572)	1,984	3,402	(1,418)
0	20,000	(1,920)	1,047	(2,967)	(1,920)	2,349	(4,269)	492	2,349	(1,856)
5,000	5,000	2,053	2,353	(300)	2,353	3,888	(1,535)	3,700	3,888	(188)
5,000	10,000	1,309	1,984	(674)	1,609	3,402	(1,792)	4,353	3,402	951
5,000	15,000	530	1,047	(517)	830	2,349	(1,519)	3,984	2,349	1,635
5,000	20,000	(220)	(502)	282	80	1,296	(1,216)	2,492	1,912	580
7,500	5,000	2,706	2,353	353	3,353	3,888	(535)	4,700	3,888	812
7,500	10,000	1,962	1,584	378	2,609	2,875	(266)	5,353	2,875	2,478
7,500	15,000	1,183	273	910	1,830	1,822	8	4,984	1,822	3,162
7,500	20,000	433	(1,262)	1,696	1,080	427	653	3,492	1,347	2,146
10,000	5,000	2,706	1,984	722	4,241	3,402	839	5,588	3,402	2,186
10,000	10,000	1,962	1,047	915	3,497	2,349	1,149	6,241	2,349	3,892
10,000	15,000	1,183	(502)	1,685	2,718	1,296	1,422	5,872	1,912	3,959
10,000	20,000	433	(1,638)	2,070	1,968	(475)	2,443	4,380	445	3,935
12,500	5,000	2,706	1,584	1,122	4,241	2,875	1,366	5,588	2,875	2,713
12,500	10,000	1,962	273	1,690	3,497	1,822	1,675	6,241	1,822	4,419
12,500	15,000	1,183	(1,262)	2,446	2,718	427	2,291	5,872	1,347	4,525
12,500	20,000	433	(2,012)	2,446	1,968	(1,092)	3,060	4,380	(172)	4,553
15,000	5,000	2,337	1,047	1,290	3,755	2,349	1,406	5,102	2,349	2,753
15,000	10,000	1,593	(502)	2,095	3,011	1,296	1,715	5,755	1,912	3,842
15,000	15,000	814	(1,638)	2,451	2,232	(475)	2,707	5,385	445	4,940
15,000	20,000	64	(2,388)	2,451	1,482	(1,468)	2,949	3,894	(548)	4,441
20,000	5,000	845	(502)	1,347	2,702	1,296	1,406	4,049	1,912	2,136
20,000	10,000	102	(1,638)	1,739	1,958	(475)	2,433	4,702	445	4,256
20,000	15,000	(678)	(2,388)	1,710	1,179	(1,468)	2,646	4,332	(548)	4,880
20,000	20,000	(1,428)	(3,138)	1,710	429	(2,218)	2,646	2,841	(1,298)	4,138

Note: Positive sign indicates a federal tax credit. Negative amounts denoted by a "()." A negative number in the column labeled Marriage Penalty/Cohab bonus signifies a marriage bonus.

Although married and cohabiting couples are equally eligible to receive benefits, cohabiting couples differ from married couples in significant ways. Cohabiting families are less likely to stay together than married-couple families and their residency patterns are more likely to shift (Bumpass & Lu, 2000). For low-income mothers, the decision to include the father in the household (either as a cohabiting or married partner) carries emotional and financial risks. Qualitative research reveals that economics plays a key role in welfare mothers' decisions to marry or to live together. Many mothers enact an informal "pay-and-stay" rule, whereby men are allowed to remain part of the household if they can continue to hold a job in the above-ground economy. Given their extremely limited resources, these mothers are unwilling to continue living with a man who cannot bring in regular, legal wages, especially if his presence threatens her ability to receive TANF or food stamps (Edin, 1999). If someone must go without, it will be the other adult rather than her children. Among couples with unstable residency patterns, the income of a cohabiting mother receiving welfare more closely resembles a single separated mother than that of a married couple.

Even when two parents decide to stay together, either as a cohabiting or married couple, they may face barriers to participation in transfer programs that a single parent does not face. There is widespread belief among poor families that low-income programs serve only single mothers and children. Welfare programs historically have not served two-parent families for a number of reasons, including the belief that welfare encouraged dependency. Furthermore, the history of racially motivated enforcement of "man in the house" rules probably contributes to the perception among low-income communities that two-parent families are ineligible.

Two-parent families (both married and cohabiting) receive benefits at rates lower than single-parent families. Although many states eased their restrictions on serving two-parent families as a result of welfare reform, two-parent families continue to participate at very low rates: of the 2.6 million families receiving welfare in fiscal year 1999, less than 5% were two-parent families (U.S. Department of Health and Human Services, 2000).

When two-parent families are served by the welfare system, their benefits are not disproportionately low compared to single-parent families. However, two-parent families participate in food stamps, housing, Medicaid, and cash welfare assistance at a much lower rate than single-parent families, even when their incomes are similar. Table 12.4 shows program recipiency rates by income level as a percent of the poverty line for different types of families. For example, 37% of single-mother families below the poverty line receive cash benefits, but only 20% of cohabiting parents and 7% of married biological or adoptive couples with incomes below the poverty line receive cash benefits.

Cohabiting partners participate in means-tested programs at about the same rate as single-mother families. This follows from the program eligibility rules where income of the cohabiting partner is not included in determining eligibility

Table 12.4
Program Participation, by Family Type and Income Level

	Poverty Level	Number of Families (thousands)	% Receiving No Cash, Food Stamps, or Housing Benefits	% Receiving Cash Benefits	% Receiving Food Stamps	% Receiving Housing Benefits	% Receiving Housing and Food Stamps	% Receiving Housing and Cash	% Receiving Cash and Food Stamps	% Receiving Cash, Food Stamps and Housing
Single-Mother Families	0-50	1,775	24.2%	44.2%	69.0%	32.4%	26.8%	18.1%	42.6%	17.8%
	51-100	1,856	41.0%	29.7%	50.4%	24.2%	16.9%	10.5%	28.2%	10.2%
	0-100	3,631	32.8%	36.8%	59.5%	28.2%	21.7%	14.2%	35.3%	13.9%
Married Stepparents	0-100	210	43.0%	23.9%	54.1%	13.9%	11.3%	3.4%	23.5%	3.4%
Married Biological/ Adoptive Couples	0-50	620	73.9%	7.6%	23.9%	6.2%	4.3%	1.2%	7.1%	1.2%
	51-100	1,320	71.2%	6.7%	26.7%	4.4%	2.6%	0.6%	6.4%	0.6%
	0-100	1,940	72.1%	7.0%	25.8%	5.0%	3.1%	0.8%	6.6%	0.8%
Cohabiting Couples (Fragile Families with Common Children)	0-100	208	52.3%	17.3%	38.8%	11.8%	5.2%	7.8%	8.9%	1.7%
Cohabiting Partners	0-100	92	19.6%	37.1%	73.3%	25.8%	22.0%	21.3%	33.4%	20.9%
Single-Father Families	0-100	169	59.4%	17.3%	36.9%	18.9%	16.1%	7.6%	16.3%	7.6%

Source: Tabulations of the National Survey of American Families, 1997.

Based on program participation in two consecutive months. Program participation and the number of families with cohabiting partners may be understated because of under-reporting in household surveys.

Poverty status is based on social families, which includes income of unmarried partners in determining poverty status. Otherwise poverty definition matches the official definition of poverty. Food stamps and other non-cash benefits are excluded in determining poverty status.

for TANF and the family is more likely to apply for food stamps. About 50% of poor cohabiting parents and three out of eight cohabiting partners do not receive either TANF, food stamps, or housing benefits. For married families, the percentage receiving neither of those benefits is almost 75%. These percentages are somewhat overstated because of underreporting of program participation in household surveys and because there has been no attempt to model other program requirements such as asset rules. These problems would affect the relative program recipiency rates of different family types somewhat, but would not close the huge disparities in recipiency rates for the different family types below the poverty line as shown in Table 12.4. These recipiency rates represent the percentage of families who receive benefits from a given program at the time of the survey in the current month and are likely to receive them the next month. Recipiency is defined by whether the family has received benefits for two consecutive months— these data do not reflect whether the family received benefits at any time during a calendar year as reported on Census surveys in the CPS.

Table 12.5 shows recipiency rates among different family types in child care and the child support system. The data in this table show the same trends: The recipiency rate in the child-care program is only 10% among poor single-mother families, and even lower among other family types. About 40% of single-mother

Table 12.5
Program Participation of Families With Incomes Below the Poverty Threshold

Family Type	Number of Families (thousands)	% Receiving Child Care Assistance	% with Child Support Orders	% Receiving Child Support
Single-Mother Families	3,631	9.8%	41.8%	24.5%
Married Stepparents	210	6.3%	41.6%	19.5%
Married Biological/Adoptive Couples	1,940	1.3%	3.7%	1.5%
Cohabiting Couples (Fragile Families with Common Children)	208	2.0%	8.9%	4.0%
Cohabiting Partners	92	6.1%	47.6%	17.9%
Single-Father Families	169	0.4%	0.3%	16.8%

Source: Tabulations of the National Survey of American Families, 1997.
Based on program participation in two consecutive months. Program participation and the number of families with cohabiting partners may be understated because of under-reporting in household surveys.
Poverty status is based on social families, which includes income of unmarried partners in determining poverty status. Otherwise poverty definition matches the official definition of poverty. Food stamps and other non-cash benefits are excluded in determining poverty status.

families and married stepfamilies below poverty have a child support order, and about 50% of these families actually receive child support.

Low recipiency rates for two-parent families imply that many of these families are not receiving all of the assistance to which they are entitled. Although the poverty rate for children in two-parent families is much lower than for children in one-parent families, children in two-parent families who are needy are served at much lower rates than children in one-parent families. If children in two-parent families were served at the same rate as children in one-parent families, an additional 1.6 million poor children would receive food stamps and an additional 1.1 million poor children would receive Medicaid.

PUTTING THE RULES TOGETHER: HOW DIFFERENT FAMILIES FARE UNDER LOW-INCOME PROGRAMS

The previous section described how the rules of different low-income programs treat single, married, and cohabiting parents and the variables that affect the calculation of marriage penalties or bonuses. This section puts all these programs and variables together and describes their impact on disposable income for single parents, cohabiting parents, and married parents living in Maryland. It calculates the combined financial impact of TANF, food stamps, child support, and the federal tax code, including the EITC on the disposable earnings of these families, for several hypothetical earnings combinations.

Table 12.6 describes two examples—one case where the mother has no earnings and the man earns $15,000, the other case where the man earns $20,000 and the mother earns $6,000. The table illustrates that holding earnings constant, the family is eligible for substantially different benefits given different assumptions about how the family reports itself to the transfer and tax offices.

If the man is the father of the two children and the parents are unmarried, then Row 1 of each example describes how they should report their situation to the respective offices. In these cases, the man is included in the assistance unit for TANF and food stamps. To accurately describe the family's situation, the father should file as a head of household and total disposable income should be $18,983 and $26,695, respectively, in the two cases. In both of these cases, the father's earnings would make the family ineligible for TANF and reduce or eliminate the family's food stamp benefit compared to the situation where the father is not part of the assistance unit in either program (which is illustrated in Row 4 of each example).

Row 8 of each example shows the disposable income of a married-couple family. If the parents in the first row of each example were to marry, they would face a small marriage bonus of $37; in the second, if the parents were to marry they would face a marriage penalty of $1,852. The TANF and food stamp benefits are the same for the cohabiting couple with children in common (Row 1) and the

Table 12.6
Disposable Income for a Mother and Two Children With a Cohabiting Male in Maryland, 2000

	Male in TANF Filing Unit	TANF Benefit	Male in Food Stamp Unit	Food Stamp Benefit	Tax Filing Status Male	Tax Filing Status Female	Federal Income & Payroll Taxes	State Taxes	Total Disposable Income
When Male Earns $15,000 and Female Has No Earnings									
1.	yes	$0	yes	$1,424	HoH	DNF	$2,254	$305	$18,983
2.	no	$5,004	yes	$1,994	HoH	DNF	$2,254	$305	$24,558
3.	no	$5,004	yes	$1,994	Single	DNF	$(2,318)	$(763)	$18,918
4.	no	$5,004	no	$4,020	Single	DNF	$(2,318)	$(763)	$20,943
5.	no	$5,004	no	$4,020	HoH	DNF	$2,254	$305	$26,583
6.	no	$5,004	no	$4,020	Joint	Joint	$2,254	$341	$26,619
7.	no	$5,004	yes	$1,994	Joint	Joint	$2,254	$341	$24,594
8.	yes	$0	yes	$1,424	Joint	Joint	$2,254	$341	$19,020
When Male Earns $20,000 and Female Earns $6,000									
1.	yes	$0	yes	$0	HoH	Single	$695	$0	$26,695
2.	no	$1,104	yes	$0	HoH	Single	$695	$0	$27,799
3.	no	$1,104	yes	$0	Single	HoH	$(1,509)	$(770)	$24,825
4.	no	$1,104	no	$2,951	Single	HoH	$(1,509)	$(770)	$27,776
5.	no	$1,104	no	$2,951	HoH	Single	$695	$0	$30,750
6.	no	$1,104	no	$0	Joint	Joint	$(1,022)	$(136)	$28,897
7.	no	$1,104	yes	$0	Joint	Joint	$(1,022)	$(136)	$25,947
8.	yes	$0	yes	$0	Joint	Joint	$(1,022)	$(136)	$24,843

Note: "DNF" means that parent did not file a tax return; "HoH" means that parent filed as a head of household. Row 1 of each example shows how they should report if the parents are cohabiting and have children in common. Row 3 shows how they should report if the parents are cohabiting and they have no children in common. Row 8 illustrates how the family should report if the parents are married.

married couple (Row 8). The difference in disposable income is the result of federal and state taxes. In the example where the father earns $15,000 and the mother has no earnings, there is only a small difference in taxes because at that income level, the fathers earnings are not high enough for the difference in the standard deduction between filing a joint return and filing as the head of household to impact tax liability at the federal level; at the state level the difference is very small. In the example where the man earns $20,000 and the woman earns $6,000, the difference in tax liability is significant—instead of a federal tax credit of $695 that the parents received as cohabitors, the family has a tax liability of $1,022 if they marry. This large effect is primarily due to the EITC.

If the man is not the father of the children, but lives and eats together with them, then Row 3 in each example represents how they should be reporting themselves to the tax and transfer system. Because the man has no legal obligation to support the children, he would not be included in the TANF unit but would be included in the food stamp unit. This situation leaves the family with the lowest disposable income of all the scenarios: $18,918 in the first example and $24,825 in the second. The couples in this situation would face a small marriage bonus in the first case ($102). In the second case, the couple's income is virtually unchanged. Prior to tax year 2000, this family would have been substantially better off because the man would have been able to claim the children as "foster children" and receive the EITC (assuming he lived with the mother for the entire tax year). Row 2 describes what the families' incomes would be if the tax year 1999 rules were still in effect.

As discussed previously, a family's economic status can be substantially enhanced if the family misreports its true situation to the welfare and tax authorities. However, this decision results in a situation that is problematic for both parents of the child. The father could eventually be served with a child support order for a time period that he was cohabiting with the child and the child's mother. To rectify that problem, the mother would have to admit that she is living with the child's father, thus leaving her vulnerable to charges of welfare fraud. This example underscores the need for low-income separated or cohabiting families to understand the child support and tax and transfer system to avoid situations where they are misrepresenting their actual situation.

Overall, these examples illustrate the complexity of determining what policy toward cohabiting families should be. Calculations of marriage penalties or bonuses vary depending on which situations are being compared—and the extent to which the male is already included in tax and benefit units.

In general, the fact that total family income can vary significantly depending on the actual circumstances of the cohabiting situation is not necessarily undesirable. If the father is living with his children, then presumably income is being shared and means-tested benefits should decline. If the male is in a new relationship and his income is not being shared, then the mother and children should remain eligible for TANF, and total income available to the family should increase.

One reason to look at the combined effect of participation rules is to determine whether or not policies unintentionally favor separated low-income families over cohabiting or married families with children. It is possible that economic incentives could influence a family's choice of living arrangements, although there is little evidence showing that relationship exists. However, if the combined impact of low-income programs provide economic advantage to separated families over cohabiting families, this could have important political implications.

Measuring the Marriage Penalty–Separation Bonus

Studies of the marriage penalty in the tax code examine the difference in the way the code treats families that are cohabiting versus those that are married. These studies typically assume the couple resides together and must make a decision about whether to marry. However, when calculating marriage penalties for low-income single parents, there are a number of additional issues that must be addressed. As Table 12.6 indicates, calculations of marriage penalties must make additional assumptions about whether both parents are participating in various means-tested programs and how they report themselves to these programs, whether their children are in common, or how the male is related to the children, and whether a child support order is established and whether it is paid.

This section compares the impact on disposable income of maintaining separated families versus cohabiting or married families for a number of different income levels. This analysis assumes that the mother and father have two children in common, and no other children. Because most low-income programs make no distinction in the size of the benefits between cohabiting and married families, as the previous section described, this analysis treats cohabiting families and married families the same way in terms of the TANF and food stamp benefits for which they are eligible—the father is always included in the assistance unit. The main difference is that the married family files a joint return, whereas the parents in the cohabiting family file separate returns.

In constructing these illustrative hypothetical examples, several other choices about which programs should be included or excluded from the analysis should be justified. Housing programs were excluded because only a small percentage of poor families actually receive housing benefits. Even a smaller percentage of married or cohabiting families receive housing benefits. For those married or cohabiting families with housing benefits who become separated (and assuming the housing subsidy stays with the custodial family), it would ease the financial loss from the separation. For married or cohabiting families without a housing subsidy, it probably does not affect the decision to separate because of the waiting period involved in securing housing benefits.

This analysis also excludes child care assistance. Child-care expenses are assumed to be zero and not to increase when the family is separated. This is probably unrealistic but if child-care expenses and subsidies were included in the analysis, it would only reinforce the general conclusion that the family is better off when married or cohabiting. Very few families receive child-care assistance. In most cases, this only offsets work expenses and thus does not really make the separated family better off relative to either being married or cohabiting. Child-care arrangements are probably easier to negotiate when there are two adults with work schedules than when there is only one adult with a work schedule (e.g., in instances of sick children, or in terms of compatibility of working hours with child-care provider hours).

A somewhat more difficult decision to justify is the exclusion of the Medicaid program. According to the latest findings from the National Survey of America's Families based on 1999 data, about 22% to 23% of children are uninsured below 200% of poverty. Approximately the same percentage of children are uninsured below poverty as between poverty and 200% of poverty. These estimates are probably somewhat overstated because household surveys miss children who are covered by Medicaid. Additionally, for many children who are uninsured but eligible, Medicaid will provide coverage once medical expenses are incurred.[11]

About 35% of low-income (less than 200% of poverty) adults are uninsured. Clearly, if Medicaid coverage were extended to low-income parents (including noncustodial parents who paid child support), marriage penalties would be lowered. Nevertheless, the fact that almost 80% of children are covered and about 65% of adults have coverage does suggest that in the typical situation, children and parents are covered and this coverage is not necessarily affected when the family structure changes.

The methodology employed in this analysis assumes that if the couple is separated, the noncustodial parent (NCP) lives alone. Many of these NCPs do live with parents or with other adults, and some NCPs have started new families. Although there may be some economies of scale in these situations compared to assuming the NCP lives alone, they probably are not as great as those assumed in the poverty thresholds. Young men may not eat with their parents or roommates, transportation costs are probably different than that of a couple, and the lack of privacy that a man living with others would face led us to assume that if a couple separated, the children would live with mother and the man would live alone (or the economic cost would be equivalent to living alone).

One further issue is weighting to compare the overall disposable income of separated families versus families that are cohabiting or married. The methodol-

---

[11] Although uninsured children have access to some medical care, this lack of coverage does result in fewer visits to doctors and less care than is optimal.

Table 12.7

Detailed Comparison of Disposable Income for a Married, Cohabiting, and Separated Family With Two Children in Common in Maryland, 2000

	Married Total	Cohabiting Total	Separated, Child Support Not paid			Separated, Child Support Fully paid		
			Custodial	NCP	Total	Custodial	NCP	Total
Earnings	20,000	20,000	7,500	12,500	20,000	7,500	12,500	20,000
Payroll Taxes	(1,530)	(1,530)	(574)	(956)	(1,530)	(574)	(956)	(1,530)
Federal Income Tax	2,349	3,843	3,000	(795)	2,205	3,000	(795)	2,205
State Income Tax	0	446	450	(588)	(138)	450	(588)	(138)
Work Expenses	(1,000)	(1,000)	(375)	(625)	(1,000)	(375)	(625)	(1,000)
TANF	0	0	129	0	129	0	0	0
Food Stamps	794	794	2,850	0	2,850	1,674	0	1,674
Child Support Order	N/A	N/A	0	0	0	3,428	(3,428)	0
Disposable Income	20,613	22,554	12,980	9,536	22,516	15,103	6,109	21,212
Percent of Poverty Line	119.1%	130.3%	94.3%	107.3%	97.6%	109.8%	68.7%	99.5%

Note: Parentheses indicate negative numbers—that is, a deducation from gross income. Federal and state taxes are positive in some cases because of Earned Income Credits.

ogy employed in the following tables averages the income expressed as a percentage of the poverty line, weighted by person, rather than a simple average of the two households.[12]

Table 12.7 illustrates in detail the impact of living arrangements and marital status on families' disposable income. This illustrative example assumes both the mother earns $7,500 and the father earns $12,500 per year, for a total of $20,000. The payroll taxes in each case are the same—each parent pays the employee share of the federal payroll tax is always equal to 7.65 percent of earnings for a total of $1,530.

In terms of federal income taxes, the married family is worse off than the cohabiting family but slightly better off than the separated family—for the most part because of the EITC. As the IRS requires, in the cohabiting families with a child in common, the higher earner must claim all the children for the purposes of the EITC. For this cohabiting family, the EITC is based on the father's earnings of

---

[12] For example, the last row in Table 12.7 shows the income as a percent of the poverty line for each of the four scenarios. In the case where the child support order is not paid, the custodial family is at 111% of poverty and the NCP is at 90% of poverty. The "total" column shows income as a percent of poverty weighted per person: the total of three times 111 for the custodial family, plus 90 for the NCP, divided by 4. This results in average of 106% of poverty for disposable income. This method takes into account the number of people whose economic well-being changes when living arrangements change. For example, if a family of four at 100% of the poverty level were to split into an NCP and a custodial family of three, and the NCP remained at 100% of poverty, the custodial family of three would be left at 62% of poverty. It would be incorrect to simply average these two numbers (100 and 62) without weighting them by the number of people in each family because three people are worse off, whereas only one remained at the same level. The simple average equals 81%, whereas the weighted average is 72%.

$12,500, and totals $3,888. For married families, the EITC is calculated based on $20,000 of earnings. The EITC is phasing out at this income range—it is only worth $2,349. For the separated families, the EITC is based on the custodial mother's income of $7,500, which secures a benefit of $3,000 for her.

In terms of state taxes, there is a cohabitation bonus relative to both separated and married families. The married family owes nothing in state taxes, whereas the cohabiting family receives a credit of $446. Separated families owe $138 in state taxes; the custodial parent receives a state EITC, but the father's tax liability exceeds the amount of the credit.

The married and cohabiting families receive a significantly lower food stamp benefit than the separated families. An income of $20,000 still leaves the four-person units eligible for $794 in food stamps. The separated custodial parent earning $10,000 is eligible for $2,850 in food stamps if she does not receive any child support, and $1,674 if she receives a full child support payment. The noncustodial parent is ineligible for food stamps if he does not pay child support, and receives a food stamp benefit of $129 if he does pay child support, because the food stamp program allows him to deduct his child support expenses from his income.

When all elements of income are taken into account, the total amount of disposable income available to these families varies between $22,554 for the unmarried cohabiting family to $20,613 for the married couple family. Evaluated this way, there appears to be a small bonus for separated families relative to married families. However, this is not the best way to measure relative well-being, because total dollars available to separated families does not take into account the cost of maintaining two separate households.

The more appropriate comparison would take into account the economies of scale that cohabiting and married families realize. Describing income as a percentage of the poverty line allows us to standardize for the increased expenses of maintaining separate households. For example, a married couple family of four that is living together reaches the poverty line with an income of $17,310 in 2000. If the family were to split into two households—a single NCP and a custodial family with two children—the total income necessary to keep both households at the poverty level is 33% higher, or $22,633.[13] It is more appropriate to assess how different family combinations fare when income is expressed relative to the poverty line for the household unit, rather than comparing total dollars available to the family members.

When the disposable incomes as a percent of the poverty line of the married, cohabiting, and separated families in Table 12.8 are compared, the cohabiting family is the most well-off. Both the married and the cohabiting family are better off than the separated families as a whole (expressed as income as a percent of the poverty line weighted by person).

---

[13] The poverty threshold for a single individual is $8,880, plus the threshold for a family of three, $13,753, equals $22,633.

Table 12.8

Income Effects (Expressed as a Percentage of the Poverty Line) of Different Family Structures for a Mother, Father, and Two Children in Common in Maryland, 2000

Earnings					Disposable Income as a Percent of the Poverty Line					
					Separated, Child Support Not Paid			Separated, Child Support Fully Paid		
Mother	Father	Combined	Married	Cohab	Mother	Father	Average*	Mother	Father	Average*
0	10,000	10,000	95%	95%	61%	89%	68%	61%	63%	61%
2,500	7,500	10,000	95%	89%	72%	78%	74%	72%	65%	70%
5,000	5,000	10,000	95%	82%	83%	66%	79%	83%	54%	76%
5,000	15,000	20,000	119%	127%	83%	126%	94%	93%	79%	90%
7,500	12,500	20,000	119%	130%	94%	107%	98%	110%	69%	100%
10,000	10,000	20,000	119%	126%	111%	89%	106%	125%	65%	110%
15,000	5,000	20,000	119%	127%	128%	66%	113%	135%	55%	115%
5,000	25,000	30,000	143%	155%	83%	205%	114%	103%	137%	112%
7,500	22,500	30,000	143%	161%	94%	185%	117%	120%	124%	121%
10,000	20,000	30,000	143%	160%	111%	165%	125%	135%	111%	129%
12,500	17,500	30,000	143%	160%	122%	145%	128%	143%	98%	132%
15,000	15,000	30,000	143%	161%	128%	126%	128%	148%	85%	132%
20,000	10,000	30,000	143%	160%	146%	89%	132%	163%	67%	139%
10,000	30,000	40,000	178%	201%	111%	244%	144%	145%	168%	151%
20,000	20,000	40,000	178%	198%	146%	165%	151%	178%	115%	163%
30,000	10,000	40,000	178%	201%	203%	89%	175%	220%	68%	182%.

*This is an average weighted by person.

When income as a percent of the poverty line is used to compare families that are living together and married to those that are separated and living apart, it becomes clear that for these families the current system strongly favors marriage or cohabitation over living separately.[14] Table 12.8 examines the effects on disposable income for a mother, father, and two children in Maryland with combined total earnings between $10,000 and $40,000 under three scenarios—one where the couple is married, a second where the family is unmarried but cohabiting, and two where the family is separated. In one case, the child support order is not paid (or never established), and in the other it is fully paid.[15]

Table 12.8 shows the income effects of different family structures, and indicates that under current law, the married couple is always better off than the average of the custodial family and NCP. It also shows that in many cases, a cohabiting family is better off than a married family. For example, the first row shows the impacts on disposable income when the custodial parent has no earnings and the NCP has annual earnings of $10,000. If this couple lived in one household (either

[14] The appendix includes a version of this analysis where income is expressed in total dollars rather than as a percentage of poverty.

[15] By showing the two extreme examples—where the child support order is not paid and fully paid, this table shows the range of outcomes.

married or unmarried), their disposable income would place them at 95% of the poverty line. If the couple separates and no child support is paid, the custodial family is left at 61% of the poverty line, and the father is at 89% of the poverty line. (However, if paternity and a child support order are established, and the father is not yet paying support, he is building up child support arrearages and risking severe penalties.) The members of this family, on average, are at 68% of the poverty line.

If the same couple is separated and the child support order is fully paid, the custodial family has disposable income of 61% of the poverty line, and the NCP has income of 63% of the poverty line. The weighted average, in this case, is 61% of the poverty line. The family's weighted average is lower if child support is fully paid than if it is not paid because Maryland retains the entire child support payment as a reimbursement for welfare costs. Once the family is off welfare, however, the custodial parent's disposable income increases when child support is paid.

As this example indicates, child support plays an important role in ensuring that the NCP is not significantly better off than the custodial parent and children when the family is separated. However, this outcome requires an effective child support enforcement system. The right-hand portion of the chart shows the outcome when the child support order is fully paid. Because the size of the order for low-income NCPs in Maryland is relatively high, it is probably unrealistic to assume the amount will be paid consistently and in its entirety. Even when the child support order is fully paid, the custodial family is better off financially when married or cohabiting.

If one were to calculate the marriage penalty for a female-headed custodial family and an unrelated male (who is not the father of the children in the custodial family), the marriage penalty on average will be larger than this chart reflects. The reason is that the child support order plays a significant role in lowering the NCP's disposable income when the family is separated or unmarried, thus making the economic incentives for marriage or cohabitation larger. In contrast, if the unrelated male does not have an established child support order, his disposable income will be higher while the family is separated, and will be less likely to have an economic incentive for marriage or cohabitation.

Overall, the table clearly illustrates that in most cases both households of separated families with children face significant marriage or cohabitation bonuses, not marriage penalties as conventional wisdom holds. If they separate, overall levels of income decline.

The examples in Table 12.8 are noteworthy for showing that low-income couples are always better off financially by living together. In every single one of these examples, the average income-to-poverty ratio for the members of the separated family are lower than that where the couple was married or cohabited. Maryland's TANF benefits are close to the average of all the states, with a small earnings disregard policy (U.S. Department of Health and Human Services, 2000). Marriage bonuses are probably larger in states with low benefits.

Table 12.8 also shows that in a few instances the father is better off if the family separates—particularly when he earns most of the money. If this father can avoid the child support system, he is much better off. But if the child support system works as intended, then his income in most of these examples is also lower than when couple lived together either or as a cohabiting relationship. The child support program serves an important purpose of curtailing the father's economic incentives to break up the relationship.

Table 12.9 extends this analysis to two additional states: California, which has a relatively high TANF benefit (the maximum monthly benefit for a family of three is $626), and Texas, which has a relatively low TANF benefit (the maximum benefit for a for a family of three is $201). The conclusion that families that marry or cohabit are better off than separated families when economies of scale are taken into account holds for these states as well. Although families in California have the highest disposable incomes as a percent of the poverty line, and families in Texas have the lowest, the percentage point change in disposable income among the different family types as a percent of the poverty line is fairly constant across the three states, although when the mother has low earnings the marriage bonus is highest in Texas.

For example, if the mother earns $5,000 and the father earns $15,000, and they are married, their disposable income would be 119% of the poverty line in all three states. In Texas, a cohabiting family at the same income level would have a disposable income that is 6 percentage points higher (125% of the poverty line), whereas a separated family would have a disposable income that is 30 percentage points lower (89% of the poverty line). In Maryland, the cohabiting family would have income that is 8 percentage points higher than the married family, and the separated family would have income that is 29 percentage points lower than the married family. Finally, in California the married family is 6 percentage points lower than the cohabiting family, but 21 percentage points higher than the separated family.

POLICY IMPLICATIONS AND SUGGESTED POLICY CHANGES

Preliminary findings of a recent study based on interviews with low-income unwed parents in seven cities indicate that at birth, the vast majority of unwed fathers are strongly attached to their families. More than half of the parents in the study were living together when their child was born, and 80% were romantically involved. More than 75% expected to marry (McLanahan, Garfinkel, & Carlson, 2000). These "fragile families" find themselves at a critical moment at the birth of the child. Many have high hopes for a long-term relationship and rate their chances

Table 12.9

Disposable Income Expressed as a Percentage of the Poverty Line for Married Familes Relative to Cohabiting and Separated Families With Two Children in Maryland, California, and Texas

Earning		Texas			Maryland			California		
			Percentage Point Change if:			Percentage Point Change if:			Percentage Point Change if:	
Mother	Father	Disp. Inc. if Married	Cohabiting	Separated[a]	Disp. Inc. if Married	Cohabiting	Separated[a]	Disp. Inc. if Married	Cohabiting	Separated[a]
0	10,000	91%	0%	-35%	95%	-0%	-33%	112%	0%	-38%
2,500	7,500	91%	-5%	-27%	95%	-6%	-25%	112%	-4%	-25%
5,000	5,000	91%	-11%	-19%	95%	-13%	-19%	112%	-9%	-18%
5,000	15,000	119%	6%	-30%	119%	8%	-29%	119%	6%	-21%
7,500	12,500	119%	9%	-21%	119%	11%	-20%	119%	9%	-13%
10,000	10,000	119%	6%	-12%	119%	7%	-9%	119%	6%	-4%
15,000	5,000	119%	6%	-5%	119%	8%	-4%	119%	6%	-2%
5,000	25,000	149%	7%	-37%	143%	12%	-31%	149%	7%	-36%
7,500	22,500	149%	12%	-28%	143%	18%	-22%	149%	12%	-27%
10,000	20,000	149%	14%	-20%	143%	18%	-13%	149%	14%	-19%
12,500	17,500	149%	15%	-17%	143%	18%	-11%	149%	14%	-15%
15,000	15,000	149%	16%	-17%	143%	19%	-10%	149%	15%	-12%
20,000	10,000	149%	14%	-10%	143%	18%	-3%	149%	14%	-9%
10,000	30,000	189%	4%	-39%	178%	23%	-27%	188%	5%	-33%
20,000	20,000	189%	15%	-26%	178%	20%	-15%	188%	14%	-20%
30,000	10,000	189%	4%	-22%	178%	23%	4%	188%	5%	-19%

[a] Assumes child support order fully paid. Weighted average of the disposable incomes of custodial and noncustodial parents expressed as a percent of the federal poverty line.

of continuing the father's involvement in childrearing as good. Despite these feelings, statistics show that fragile families tend to separate over time. According to 1997 data by the Urban Institute, by the time poor children are in their teens, only 5% live in a fragile family and 59% live with their mother and their father is not highly involved (J. Johnson, 1999).

The growth of cohabitation and the question of how to better serve fragile families presents policymakers with a host of difficult issues. Conservative scholars are eager to push the direction of future welfare reform toward matters of family formation—promoting marriage and discouraging out-of-wedlock births. They point to the link between poverty and single-parent households, and voice concern over a body of research that finds negative effects on children growing up without a father. This view is summed up by Horn, who wrote: "A welfare system that helps single mothers become employed, but ignores the need to promote fatherhood and marriage, may only serve to enable unmarried women to rear children without the presence of the father" (Horn & Bush, 1997).

Many progressives are uncomfortable with a "pro-marriage" agenda, which may stigmatize single parents and restore the negative connotations of "illegitimacy." They are also concerned about the appropriate role of government in promoting marriage and worry that pro-marriage initiatives will ignore domestic violence. On the other hand, both conservatives and progressives are concerned about the effects of family breakup and understand that marriage remains a highly valued and desired status for a most Americans (Ooms, 1998). Additionally, there is mounting evidence that most children fare better in a two-parent environment, if all other factors are equal (McLanahan & Sandefur, 1994).

Current policy mostly ignores the existence of cohabitation. Making policy that factors in the increasingly widespread practice of cohabitation will require a delicate balancing act. As a guiding principle of any policy change, we must ensure that we do not make families substantially worse off because of policy changes, particularly separated families. At the same time, in the case of couples with children in common, we do not want to treat married parents worse than cohabiting parents. Instead, we must provide some incentives for cohabiting relationships to become permanent stable married relationships. Additionally, we must not provide incentives for families to separate from cohabiting or married relationships. Using these principles as guideposts, we suggest the following policies:

- Create a new IRS filing status for cohabiting parents with children in common
- Help fragile families stay together by serving a much greater percentage of cohabiting parents and married-parent families and by educating them about their rights and responsibilities within the safety net system
- Create a strong, universal child support program that recognizes the heterogeneity of nonresident parents
- Ensure that families who separate receive the financial supports they need
- Provide health coverage to all low-income children and their parents

Institute a New Filing Status: Cohabiting Partners
With Children in Common

As the tables in the previous section demonstrated, cohabiting parents with children are treated more generously by the tax system than single parents or even married couples, mainly because filing status is based on marital status. Several bills in Congress attempt to address this for low-income families by increasing the plateau in the EITC for married couples, filing jointly. However, a much simpler way of addressing the fact that cohabiting families are treated more generously is to create a separate tax filing status for cohabiting parents with a common child.

Policymakers should consider reducing the cohabiting bonus by amending how the tax system treats cohabiting families. Changing the tax system for cohabiting families would follow three rules: (a) adults living together with a child in common file as a "cohabiting couple, filing jointly" with essentially the same tax parameters as those for married couples filing jointly; (b) the EITC could always be claimed by a low-income custodial parent, regardless of the earnings of other adults in the household; and (c) the EITC could never be claimed by a nonrelative except when the child is living in a foster care home or under the care of a legal guardian, or where the child welfare or TANF agency is providing support to a relative caretaker, or in a household of multiple filers (e.g., a multiple generation household), the EITC would accrue to the relative caretaker if it resulted in a larger EITC and the custodial parent had lower earnings. (There would be no change in the tax code for couples cohabiting without children.)

The first rule recognizes that long-term, cohabiting couples should have financial benefits similar to those of married couples. This will result in lower EITC benefits for cohabiting low-income couples. Some of this loss in assistance could be offset by insuring that these families receive the food stamps, child care, and other assistance to which the family is entitled. Further expansions of the EITC would also help to offset this loss.

The second rule allows the EITC to function primarily as an earnings subsidy to help low-income custodial parents achieve self-sufficiency. This would eliminate the tie-breaker rule in EITC, without preventing the ability of another adult related to the child to claim both the exemption and the EITC, if it were more beneficial to the family. It would also significantly reduce payment errors associated with the EITC. This proposal is similar to policies recently recommended by the Clinton administration.

Policymakers could also consider providing very modest marriage bonuses that would work in tandem with changing the filing status of cohabiting couples. One way to do this is to increase the EITC plateau for married couples filing jointly. The Administration proposed to increase this plateau by $1,450 for married couple families with two-earners in its Fiscal Year 2001 budget, and it has been incorporated into several tax bills in Congress as well. One could also increase slightly the standard deduction for married couples filing jointly relative to the standard deduction for cohabiting couples with a common child.

The policies advanced thus far assume that the biological parents should be held responsible for the care and economic support of their children. And government should help both parents regardless of their marital or living situation to meet this parental responsibility. What should be the policy for cohabiting couples who do not have children in common? Indirectly, we have suggested several policies that affect these situations. States should examine (perhaps re-examine) their TANF and Medicaid eligibility policies for stepparents and cohabiting partners. Tax policy would explicitly deny EITC and other tax benefits for cohabiting couples without children in common. The EITC could only be claimed by the custodial parent (or other relative caretaker).

Help Fragile Families Stay Together

The second finding of the previous section was the extremely low recipiency rates of cohabiting parent and married parent families in programs providing economic assistance, including food stamps, TANF, housing, and Medicaid. If as a society we believe two parents are better than one, we should make sure that couples who choose to stay together receive all of the economic assistance to which they are entitled. Additionally, these couples need to know their rights and responsibilities within the welfare and child support system.

On the one hand, it seems fairly obvious that there are financial incentives for cohabiting or marrying, because maintaining one household is less expensive than maintaining two. On the other hand, some young couples may suspect it is better to separate, if they know they are unable to access support services as a two-parent family, or if they are unsure of how the TANF and child support system operate. As the tables in this chapter show, calculating the economic impacts of these different decisions can be complex. It seems likely that many fragile families are not aware of all the financial consequences of their decisions around marriage and living arrangements.

For a mother and father who are unmarried at the time of the birth of their child, states should educate both parents about the financial consequences to their welfare benefits if the couple decides to split. Mothers should understand rules about receiving welfare and establishing paternity, the implications for the father of establishing paternity, as well as her rights to receive child support. Fathers should understand how the child support system works, as well as understand their duty to financially and emotionally support their children. Once couples have a clear understanding of the financial implications of their choices to marry or not, or live together or apart, they will be able to make more informed decisions, and will also better understand their rights within the system.

An example of the need for education comes from a case study in California. A new father lived with the mother the first year after his son's birth and paid for most of the family's expenses. After they broke up, he discovered that the mother had been receiving welfare at her mother's address. The result of this unfortunate mistake was the accumulation of a huge arrearage that the father owed to the state (Waller & Plotnick, 1999). In these situations, the welfare and child support agencies should be less concerned with fraud and blaming either partner and more concerned that the fragile family does not separate.

Another way to encourage fragile families to stay together is to make sure they receive all the benefits to which they are entitled. Although many low-income separated parents experience a financial incentive for cohabiting or marrying, states have been unsuccessful at serving eligible two-parent families. The first step to increasing participation is to eliminate all eligibility factors that apply only to two-parent families such as work history and unemployment tests that a second parent must meet in order to participate in TANF and Medicaid in 17 states. States should be required to eliminate all barriers or eligibility restrictions that cause them to serve two-parent families at much lower rates and take affirmative outreach steps. The second step would be to require states to develop a plan to increase participation rates of two-parent families in TANF, Medicaid, and food stamps, and consider penalizing them if they do not increase their two-parent participation rates to approximately the same levels as one-parent families.

Interviews with welfare recipients reveal that the main reason cohabiting couples have difficulty establishing a stable family unit is the inability of the low-income father to bring in steady wages. Some mothers on welfare report that unless her partner is able to bring in a steady income, his presence in the home is a greater burden (Edin, 1999). Although welfare reform emphasized moving mothers on welfare to work, there has not been a coordinated and concentrated effort on also putting low-income fathers to work. Like low-income mothers, fathers need an array of employment and supportive services—such as parenting classes, job placement services, and skills upgrading. But fathers probably find it more difficult than mothers to connect to the social services system. Among policymakers, there is growing acknowledgment that at least some services should be provided to both low-income men and women, which would benefit the entire family. A study of welfare reform in Minnesota found that improving families' financial security through changes in safety net programs improved their chances of becoming and staying married (Knox, Miller, & Genetian, 2000).

If we believe that low-income families could benefit from supports given to low-income fathers, policymakers must then choose which low income fathers should receive services. Both fathers in separated families as well as cohabiting families could benefit from employment supports.

One modest proposal that policymakers could consider is to put cohabiting or married-parent families (in which both parents are unemployed) first in line for a publicly funded job. Although there are very few publicly funded jobs available, giving one of these jobs to one parent in a two-parent family may encourage fragile families to stay together (Knox et al., 2000).

Finally, we might consider home visiting programs modeled after the Nurse Home Visitation Program, a university-based demonstration program developed by David Olds and implemented in Elmira, New York; Memphis, Tennessee; and Denver, Colorado. Another successful program is Healthy Families America that evolved from Hawaii's Healthy Start (Duggan, McFarlane, Windham, Rohde, Salkever, Fuddy, Rosenberg, Buchbinder, & Sia, 1999).

Create a Strong, Universal Child Support Program That Recognizes the Heterogeneity of Nonresident Parents

When it functions properly, the child support system increases the cost of separation substantially, and helps support separated families. Additionally, as the previous analysis indicated, child support plays an important role in ensuring that the NCPs are not significantly better off than the custodial parent and children when the family is separated. A number of policy changes would make the child support system more effective. The child support program should be nearly universal—children have a right to know their father's identity, and have a right to financial and emotional support from him. Paternity should be established for almost all children born out of wedlock. When cohabiting relationships end, absent parents should pay child support through the child support system. Adoption of stronger child support legislation, and higher per-capita expenditures on child support have been shown to increase the program's collection rates and the incomes of single mothers (Garfinkel, 2000). Increasing the number of child support enforcement staff would also help to increase child support collections.

In addition to strengthening enforcement and increasing the number of children covered by the child support system, the current system needs to recognize that NCPs have great disparities in their ability to pay. States should take steps to ensure that child support guidelines are reasonable for low-income NCPs, and that a flexible child support modification process that would take into account the often fluctuating incomes of poor men is in place.[16] States should also increase the amount of child support that is disregarded when calculating a TANF benefit. Increasing the amount of child support that is disregarded would result in a significant improvement in many low-income families' budgets. Currently, a father who pays child support to a child who is receiving welfare faces a near 100% tax rate on his child support payment.[17] At the same time, in calculating TANF benefits, the state should ensure that the earnings disregard of a second parent in a two-parent family is equal to or greater than the disregard of child support payments by an NCP.

---

[16] For more suggestions on how to improve child support system, see Primus and Daugirdas (2000).

[17] Lawmakers are aware of this problem, and have made efforts to address it. The House of Representatives overwhelmingly passed legislation that, among other things, encourages states to reduce this effective tax rate on child support payments by low-income NCPs. For a more detailed analysis of the legislation, see Primus and Daugirdas (2000).

Another way to support separated families is to create child support incentives whereby the state would match child support payments with state funds to low-income custodial families. Even when a low-income father pays the full child support owed, the amount paid usually falls far short of the actual costs of raising a child. If states matched a father's payment, it would offer an incentive to pay and would result in more support for the child.

Finally, as discussed in the previous section, employment services are needed for fathers. The labor force participation rate of young African-American men (age 20 to 24) declined between 1993 and 1999, while it increased significantly during that time period for Black women of the same age. Fathers need access to an array of employment and social services.

The services provided to NCPs should not be more generous than, or come at the expense of, programs for low-income custodial parents. As this chapter demonstrates, separated single-parent families are most in need of financial support, and increasing the earnings of the noncustodial father is an important way to get extra dollars to the mother and children. But giving employment services to separated fathers could lead to a potentially unfair situation, if his services came at the expense of custodial families. At the same time, many cohabiting or married-parent families also need extra employment help.

Ensure That Separated Families Receive the Supports They Need

As the analysis described earlier in this section has shown, when the impact of all low-income programs are taken into account, separated families do not fare as well financially as married or cohabiting families for a wide variety of income combinations. Given the large financial incentives for living together, we should ensure that separated families have the economic supports they need. The analysis in the previous section demonstrates that additional services and economic assistance can be provided to both mothers and fathers in separated families without creating marriage penalties. Many single-parent families do not receive all the benefits and services for which they are eligible.

Research evidence indicates that declines in welfare caseloads are also driving down participation rates in food stamps and Medicaid (Zedlewski & Brauner, 1999).[18] When families are no longer receiving cash assistance, they may be unaware of, or not informed of, their continued eligibility for food stamps and Medicaid. Indeed, the declining participation rates among eligible families is a central problem and must be addressed in food stamps and TANF reauthorization. States have discretion to make TANF policies that increase the ability for single-parent families to access services—and they should take advantage of that flexibility. Additionally, states should ensure that more separated families have access to

---

[18] The Clinton administration recognized the problem of declining participation rates in Medicaid and took aggressive measures to reverse this trend. The latest data suggest that Medicaid participation rates are once again rising.

child care services (Sweeney, 1999). States should re-engineer their welfare offices to accommodate better the needs of working poor. Some suggestions include giving families access to all benefits (cash assistance, food stamps, child care, health insurance, child support, and advance EITC payments) in one place, extending the office hours, simplifying applications, and allowing applicants to apply by phone, mail, or Internet. States should revisit their asset tests, lengthen certification periods, and use community-based and faith-based organizations to assist in outreach.

Additionally, several improvements could be made to the EITC to support low-income working families. Families with annual earnings around $12,000 face very high marginal tax rates: that is, they keep a relatively small portion of each additional dollar they earn because the increase in income results in higher taxes and lower benefits. If the EITC plateau were lengthened so that it began to phase out at a higher income level, these marginal tax rates could be decreased, families would have a stronger incentive to continuing earning, and more families with children would be lifted above poverty (Ellwood & Liebman, 2000).

Likewise, a third tier—or higher benefit level for families with three or more children—should also be added to the EITC. Currently, there are two "tiers," or maximum benefit levels, in the EITC: one level for families with one child, and a higher level for families with two children. Families with three or more children have higher poverty rates than smaller families, and have experienced more difficulty moving from welfare to work in recent years. Although the combination of minimum wage work, the EITC, and food stamps raises a family of four with a full-time year-round minimum wage worker close to the poverty line, it leaves families of five or more well below the poverty line. Adding a third tier to the EITC would help address this problem.

In general, tax policy has appropriately awarded custodial parents most of the tax benefits from children. The custodial parent receives the child tax credit, the EITC, the dependent exemption, and benefits from the fact that child support payments are not treated as income. If the tax treatment of families of children were to be reviewed in a comprehensive manner, one might also want to examine whether child support payments should be allowed as a deduction from income for families who pay child support. Most tax analysts would argue that if it is allowed as a deduction to one family it should be treated as income in the other family. However, given the diseconomies of scale in maintaining two households, one could argue for simply allowing child support payments as a deduction and not having it count as income by the receiving household. All other things being equal, families who pay child support do not have the same level of income as those families who do not pay child support.

Provide Health Coverage to All Low-Income Children and Their Parents

Providing health care coverage to all low-income children and their parents, including NCPs, is another step that would both reduce marriage penalties and improve the well-being of children in low-income families. Providing additional health care coverage, especially to the parents of low-income children, would reduce marriage penalties because families would no longer fear losing coverage if they were to marry.

Research has shown that family-based Medicaid expansions that include parents can increase Medicaid enrollment among children who already are eligible for Medicaid but are not enrolled. Securing health care coverage improves the well-being of low-income children and adults: recent studies in Tennessee and Oregon demonstrate that newly covered people make greater use of preventive health services, have fewer unmet medical needs, and have better continuity of medical care than do similar individuals who lack medical coverage (Ku & Broaddus, 2000).

CONCLUSION

For couples with children in common, this chapter has demonstrated that the conventional wisdom that low-income married families face marriage penalties is wrong. In fact, cohabiting families generally are treated similarly to married families in the transfer system and that both of these family types are economically ahead if they stay together. It is also true that in certain circumstances the cohabiting family is better off than the married family under federal tax laws. But this advantage could be removed quite easily, if the tax code recognized a cohabiting family with common children and treated them similarly to that of a married couple.

The major problem facing two-parent families is that these families do not participate in means-tested programs and therefore do not take economic advantage of these benefits. Although the precise reason for this lack of participation is unknown, states must assist these families to a much greater extent in moving into the labor force and obtaining a livable income. Additionally, these fragile families should be given additional services and information so that more of these relationships could endure. TANF's emphasis on work should allay old concerns about creating dependent two-parent families, and given the state flexibility that now exists, much more attention should be given to serving these families. Additionally, NCPs should also be given additional assistance—their child support could be matched or at a minimum their entire child support payment could be passed through to the custodial family without fears that the single-parent family has been treated too generously.

This chapter has ploughed new ground by carefully defining what a marriage penalty is and has presented many examples of how separated fragile, cohabiting families, and married families are treated given identical earnings of the mother and father in these separate family constellations under the combination of low-income programs that are available. One of the reasons the conventional wisdom is wrong is because the child support program is typically not included in the analysis. Child support is key to making the tax and transfer system work. Ultimately, each couple is going to have decide what kind of family they wish to create. Regardless of the parents' decision, the child should receive as much support as possible from its biological parents before looking to government for support. We believe the suggestions we have made to the current tax and transfer system move in that direction. Government cannot force to people to love each other forever in a permanent relationship even if at one point that relationship produced progeny. What government can do is provide encouragement for the relationship to last and if it does not, insist that both parents continue to emotionally and financially provide for the child(ren).

Finally, the chapter has primarily focused on couples with children in common. We recognize that we have not prescribed as completely rules for new relationships that do not have children in common. In reality, these relationships vary considerably, are even more complicated to analyze, and also any policy would seem difficult to administer on a consistent basis.

ACKNOWLEDGMENTS

This chapter does not necessarily reflect the views of the Center on Budget and Policy Priorities. We gratefully acknowledge Kristina Daugirdas for her invaluable (and cheerfully given) assistance in creating tables and editing, and acknowledge Allen Dupree and Mandy Lackner for their help in compiling Tables 12.1, 12.4, and 12.5. Also thank you to Shawn Fremstad, Theodora Ooms, Dottie Rosenbaum, Paula Roberts, Barbara Sard, and John Wancheck for their helpful comments.

REFERENCES

Behrman, R. E., (Ed.). (1999). *The future of children*. The David and Lucile Packard Foundation. Volume 9, No. 1.

Bumpass, L., & Lu, H-H. (2000). Cohabitation: How the families of U.S. children are changing. *Focus, 1*, 5–8.

Dickert-Conlin, S., & Houser, S. (1999). *EITC, AFDC and the female headship decision*. Unpublished manuscript.

Duggan, A., McFarlane, E., Windham, A., Rohde, C., Salkever, D., Fuddy, L., Rosenberg, L., Buchbinder, S., & Sia, C. (1999). Evaluation of Hawaii's Healthy Start program. *The Future of Children, 9*, 66–90.

Edin, K. (1999). *What do low-income single mothers say about marriage.* Unpublished manuscript.

Ellwood, D. T., (1999). *The impact of the earned income tax credit and social policy reforms on work, marriage, and living arrangements.* Unpublished manuscript.

Ellwood, D. T., & Liebman, J. B. (2000). *The middle class parent penalty: Child benefits in the U.S. tax code.* Unpublished manuscript.

Evenhouse, E., & Reilly, S. (1999). *Pop swapping? Welfare and children's living arrangements.* Unpublished manuscript.

Garfinkel, I. (2001, February). *Assuring child support in the new world of welfare.* Paper presented at The New World of Welfare, Washington, DC.

Horn, W., & Bush, A. (1997). *Fathers, marriage, and welfare reform.* Indianapolis, IN: Hudson Institute.

Johnson, E. S., Levine, A., & Doolittle, F. C. (1999). *Fathers' fair share.* New York: Russell Sage Foundation.

Johnson, J. M. (1999).Testimony before the Subcommittee on Human Resources of the Committee on Ways and Means, October 5.

Knox, V., Miller, C., & Gennetian, L. (2000). *Reforming welfare and rewarding work: A summary of the final report on the Minnesota family investment program.* New York: Manpower Demonstration Research Corporation.

Ku, L., & Broaddus, M. (2000). *The importance of family-based insurance expansions: New research findings about state health reforms.* Washington, DC: Center on Budget and Policy Priorities.

McLanahan, S., Garfinkel, I., & Carlson, M. (2000). The fragile families and child wellbeing study baseline report: Baltimore, Maryland. Available online at opr.princeton.edu/crcw/ff/

McLanahan, S., & Sandefur, G. (1994). *Growing up with a single parent: What hurts, what helps.* Cambridge, MA: Harvard University Press.

Moffit, R. A. (Ed.). (1998). *The effect of welfare on marriage and fertility: What do we know and what do we need to know? Welfare, the family and reproductive behavior.* Washington, DC: National Research Council, National Academy of Sciences.

Moffitt, R. A., Reville, R. T., & Winkler, A. E. (1994). State AFDC rules regarding the treatment of cohabitors. *Social Science Bulletin, 4.*

Morgan, L. (1999). The duty of stepparents to support their stepchildren. Published online at www.SupportGuildelines.com/articles/archive.html.

Ooms, T. (1998). *Toward more perfect unions: Putting marriage on the public agenda.* Washington, DC: Family Impact Seminar.

Pate, D., & Johnson, E. S. (2000) The ethnographic study for the W-2 child support demonstration evaluation: Some preliminary findings. *Focus, 21*(1), 18–22.

Primus, W., & Daugirdas, K. (2000). *Improving child well-being by focusing on low-income noncustodial parents in Maryland.* Baltimore: The Abell Foundation.

Rosenbaum, D. T. (2000 May). *Taxes, the earned income tax credit, and marital status*. Paper presented at the ASPE/Census Bureau Small Grants Sponsored Research Conference, Washington, DC.

Steuerle, E. C. (1997 June). *The effects of tax and welfare policies on family formation*. Paper presented at the Conference on Strategies to Strengthen Marriage: What Do We Know? What Do We Need to Know? Washington, DC: Family Impact Seminar.

Sweeney, E. (1999). *Windows of opportunity: Strategies to support low-income families in the next stage of welfare reform*. Washington, DC: Center on Budget and Policy Priorities.

U.S. Department of Health and Human Services. (2000). *Temporary assistance for needy families (TANF) program: Third annual report to Congress*. Washington, DC.

U.S. House of Representatives. (1996). *Green Book*. Washington, DC.

Waller, M., & Plotnick, R. (1999). *Child support and low-income families: Perceptions, practices and policy*. San Francisco: Public Policy Institute of California.

Zedlewski, S. R., & Brauner, S. (1999). *Declines in food stamp and welfare participation: Is there a connection?* Washington, DC: The Urban Institute.

13

Federal Social Policy, Cohabitation, and Marriage

Ron Haskins

Brookings Institution and Annie E. Casey Foundation

As the chapters in this volume amply demonstrate, family arrangements in the United States, like those in Europe, have changed dramatically. The trends are toward less marriage, more divorce, more illegitimacy, and more cohabitation.

Until recently, marriage rates had been in decline for nearly half a century. In 1950, 65.8% of all females over age 15 were married. The rate decreased steadily to 55.9% in 1994, at which point it increased slightly before dropping again. By 1998, the female marriage rate stood at 54.8%, down by well over 15% since 1950 (U.S. Bureau of the Census, 1998).

One cause of the decline in marriage has been rising divorce rates. In 1950, only 2.4% of females over age 15 were divorced. By 1998, that rate had increased by more than a factor of 4 to 10.2%, although the rate of increase slowed considerably starting in the 1980s (U.S. Bureau of the Census, 1998).

The propensity to have children did not decline apace with the propensity to be single. On the contrary, until very recently the birth rate to unmarried women had been increasing steadily since the beginning of World War II. Between 1940 and 1994, the nonmarital birth rate rose from 14 per 1,000 unmarried women aged 15 to 44 to 46.9 per 1,000, the highest rate ever. Happily, after nearly six decades of relentless increases, the rate has now fallen in 4 of the last 5 years. Trends for the illegitimacy ratio (number of unwed births divided by number of total births) follow a similar pattern, although conspicuous increases do not begin until around 1960. Even so, like the illegitimacy rate, the illegitimacy ratio rose steadily until 1994, at which point nearly one third of U.S. children were born outside marriage, and then flattened out (Ventura & Bachrach, 2000).

Changes in the U.S. rate of cohabitation are covered well by Smock and Gupta (chap. 4, this volume). In 1990, about 3.5% of children were living in a household headed by cohabiting parents. This relatively low figure is misleading, however, because there is great churning among cohabiting households. As a result of this churning, Bumpass and Lu (2000) estimated that nearly 40% of children will spend part of their childhood in a cohabiting household.

Here then is the new family environment provided for children: about one third are born outside marriage, a little less than half will live through the divorce of their parents, and about 40% of all children will live with cohabiting parents. Many children experience two or more of these disruptive and difficult life events.

Since publication of McLanahan and Sandefur's (1994) masterful survey of the evidence on being reared by a single parent, virtually no one denies that the effects of single parenthood are bad for children; being born to a never-married parent is associated with even more negative effects on children (Duncan & Brooks-Gunn, 1997). Now researchers are beginning to find, although the evidence is not yet very strong, that the effects of cohabiting, as compared with being reared by two married biological parents, are also bad for children.

If social science research is taken seriously, one can conclude that, on average, America's children have more mental health problems, learn less in school, drop out of school earlier, engage in teen sex earlier and more often, get pregnant as teens more often, and are involved in more crimes than they would if a higher percentage of them were being reared by both of their natural, married parents. To paraphrase the famous *Nation at risk* report on education from two decades ago, if a foreign power were responsible for our falling marriage rate and high illegitimacy, divorce, and cohabitation rates, we would declare war on them.

Because we can't declare war on ourselves, let us do the next best thing and examine the nation's public policy to determine what could be done to slow or reverse the trends that are harming our children. What follows is an agenda that should be debated if we are serious about fighting the demographic trends that many social scientists and others seem to view as implacable.

LEGISLATION TO PROMOTE MARRIAGE AND TWO-PARENT BIOLOGICAL FAMILIES

The legislation would begin with a brief summary of Congressional findings showing that family forms inimical to the interests of children and the nation; namely, divorced, never married, and cohabiting parents, have been increasing, whereas the two-parent family form that is good for both children and adults has been declining. Taken together, these developments signal an important national problem. The legislation would then state its purpose; namely, to increase the number of children being reared by their married biological parents and to discourage all other family forms, especially among the poor. There would follow a host of provisions that reform many social programs to achieve this legislative purpose.

Welfare Programs: TANF and Medicaid

As Primus and Beeson (chap. 12, this volume) show in convincing detail, the Temporary Assistance for Needy Families program (TANF) in most states allows two-parent families to qualify for benefits roughly on the same basis as single-parent families. Regardless of type, if two-adult families meet the income requirement, the family qualifies for TANF benefits. However, in 17 states the TANF program has a bias against two-parent married families because one parent must be disabled or unemployed for the family to qualify for benefits. In addition, although every state counts the income and assets of resident biological fathers in calculating TANF eligibility and benefit levels, many states do not count the income and assets of either stepparents or cohabiting adults.

In both of these cases, the TANF program is more lenient in its treatment of single parents, stepparents, and cohabiting adults than of married couple families. Similarly, married parents in 17 states lose eligibility for TANF if they work more than 100 hours per month. If the goal is to remove bias against marriage from welfare programs, action must be taken to change TANF rules in most states. Changing TANF eligibility and benefit rules, however, raises a serious issue. Since 1996, TANF has been a block grant. As a result, states have great flexibility in designing their own TANF program. If the federal government, in the interest of promoting marriage, were to require states to adopt specific TANF policies, the states and their powerful interest groups in Washington would strongly resist. At least for the foreseeable future, it seems unlikely that this resistance could be overcome. Thus, another approach would be for the federal government to offer some type of bonus or reward to states that adopt particular pro-marriage policies. Serious consideration should be given to appropriating funds to provide financial incentives for states that agree to remove all bias against married-couple families from their TANF rules. Given the similarity in eligibility requirements between TANF and Medicaid, particularly in states with the 100-hour rule, federal policy should also contain financial incentives to provide Medicaid to married couples on the same basis as other two-parent and single families.

Welfare Programs: Food Stamps

There is only a slim chance that nonmarital families with two adults would receive more food stamps than married-couple families. The only way for this unusual situation to occur would be for nonmarital couples to apply separately for food stamp benefits on the highly implausible grounds that they prepare food separately. As Primus and Beeson point out, the complexity of the food stamp application process, which includes providing documents and periodically updating eligibility, often by making trips to a food stamp office, would seem to involve enough hassle that dual applications by nonmarital couples is unlikely. Thus, no policy changes in the food stamp program seem necessary to remove discrimination against married-couple families.

Welfare Programs: Housing

Federal housing policy presents interesting possibilities for promoting marriage over cohabitation. Although current housing law contains no disincentive for marriage as against cohabitation, two changes in policy could provide clear incentives for marriage. First, local housing authorities could be required to give priority to married-couple families in a certain percentage of both their public housing and voucher programs. For example, if a local housing authority controlled 50,000 units of public housing, the authority could give first priority to married couples in 20,000 units while maintaining their current priority system for the remaining 30,000 units. In order to avoid removing any current recipients from their units, housing authorities could be given 5 or more years to complete the transition to the new policy. Second, the current policy of barring units to adults with a felony drug conviction could be modified so that the bar would be removed from married couples with a single conviction. Both couples that married after and before the drug conviction would be eligible for the exemption as long as they were married at the time of application and benefit receipt. The policy could also include expulsion from public housing if the couple divorces.

CHILD SUPPORT

For those who wish to promote marriage, child support may be the most important program on which to focus the attention of policymakers. Established in 1975, the federal-state child support program was substantially reformed and strengthened by Congress in 1984, 1988, and 1996. The outcome of these reforms has been to greatly increase the mechanisms for locating and seizing the money and property of noncustodial parents, to create uniform and often nonjudicial (therefore more streamlined) procedures in every state, to build huge databases of information, including information on everyone with a job in the United States, and to improve collections in cases in which the children live in one state and the noncustodial parent (NCP) in another state.

Until recently, the child support program existed exclusively to collect child support payments from NCPs, usually fathers. From the perspective of fathers, the exclusive focus on collecting money meant that other, perhaps equally important issues, were ignored. For purposes of this discussion, let us posit the existence of two types of fathers, those with regular employment and those who are erratically employed. Fathers in the former group tend to have higher incomes and some assets and to have been married to the mother of their children. Those in the latter group have little money, few if any assets, and often had their children outside marriage.

Public policy should draw a sharp distinction between these two groups. For fathers with regular attachment to the labor force, child support is an inevitable part of post-divorce life. Even in the case of this group, however, some modifications of child support policy seem justified. Given the level of difficulty faced by some divorcing couples, it makes sense for local government to offer counseling, dispute resolution, and visitation assistance programs to divorcing couples who want it. Federal legislation includes funds for such programs, and some states have combined federal funds with their own money to operate larger scale programs. On balance, it is probably a good thing that many state and local governments are now beginning to expand their child support enforcement efforts to include these relatively new types of programs that attempt to smooth relations between divorcing parents. But these programs do little to promote marriage.

In addition to these new state and local family policies, there is a nascent movement to help poor fathers who have never been married to the mother of their children. These fathers are often unemployed or underemployed, usually have spotty labor force attachment, and often have ongoing problems with the law. Recent evidence suggests that, at least in big cities, nearly half of nonmarital births occur to cohabiting parents and an even higher percentage, perhaps more than 80%, of these parents are involved in an exclusive relationship that both the mother and father hope will become permanent. In most of these cases, the fathers fall into the group of poor and marginally employed men (McLanahan, Garfinkel, Reichman, & Teitler 1999).

As described by Manning (chap. 8, this volume), research on parents who have babies while cohabiting shows that more than half of these unions end in marriage by the time the child is 5. However, this research was conducted on a broad cross-section of cohabiting couples, including many working- and middle-class couples who in previous generations would have been married at the time of the birth. That representative samples obscure what is happening among poor fathers is suggested by research conducted by Rangarajan and Gleason (1998) on the fathers of teen mothers on welfare. This study found that at 2 to 5 years after the birth, only 7% of the fathers lived with the mother and half the fathers had no consistent contact with their children. This picture is, of course, very different than the one portrayed by research on nationally representative samples.

If Rangarajan and Gleason's study is correct, there is dramatic instability in living arrangements and a huge deficit in father contact among poor children born outside marriage. Again, from the perspective of public policy, it seems necessary to draw sharp distinctions between types of cohabiting parents who have children. Even if births to cohabiting couples occur all along the income distribution, it is nonetheless clear that there is a large group at the bottom who are poor or near-poor and who live in neighborhoods and kin networks in which marriage is the exception and illegitimacy the rule. What is the role of child support within this group?

In the last several years, researchers, Congress, child support administrators, and fathers' and even mothers' advocacy groups have started to show concern for how poor fathers are treated by the child support program. The most direct indication of this concern was House passage in both November 1999 and September 2000, by overwhelming bipartisan majorities, of legislation that encourages states to work with poor fathers to promote marriage, better parenting (including payment of child support), and employment. As part of this legislation, Congress encourages states to work with fatherhood projects in the public and private sector to, in effect, renegotiate the child support contract. Many of these young fathers have incurred child support arrearages of $5,000 or $10,000, often during periods of unemployment, which they simply cannot pay. If they agree to a child support order that is sustainable given their income, to make a serious attempt to remain employed, and to pay child support on a regular basis in the future, their arrearages would be temporarily set aside as long as they maintain the new payment schedule. This is a reasonable approach and even enjoys support from groups that represent custodial mothers, as long as these programs do not represent an attempt to permanently terminate arrearages for a mere promise to pay in the future.

But it does not solve one of the dilemmas raised by Primus and Beeson; namely, whether cohabiting couples should pay child support. Both Primus and Beeson as well as McLanahan and her colleagues (1999) assert that fathers in cohabiting couples should not be required to pay child support. But if promoting marriage is the goal, public policy should not relieve cohabiting fathers of their responsibility to pay child support. Child support should be suspended only for married fathers who reside with the mother and children. Moreover, as an additional incentive for marriage, child support arrearages should be suspended for as long as the mother and father are married and live together. In most cases, this policy will impose a cost on both federal and state governments because child support claims are assigned to government while mothers are on welfare and most of these mothers and children have been on welfare. But government should forego these child support payments as an additional incentive for marriage.

EARNED INCOME TAX CREDIT (EITC)

The EITC is an exemplary program in two respects (Haskins, 2001). First, it provides benefits only to working parents; second, it greatly improves the financial status of millions of working parents. All workers with children earning below about $10,000 receive additional payments from the EITC for every hour they work. The payments are then flat, neither increasing nor decreasing, between $10,000 and approximately $13,000. Above this level, the benefit begins to phase out and disappears, in the case of families with two or more children, at around $30,000. The EITC has a powerful effect on the income of less affluent working families because, after large increases under Presidents Reagan, Bush, and Clinton, it provides such a generous cash benefit—up to $4,000 to families with two or more children and $2,300 for families with one child. In fact, the EITC has a notable impact on child poverty, especially among children in female-headed families. According to data from the Current Population Survey, mothers in the bottom fifth (income of less than $11,800) of the income distribution of female-headed families with children increased their EITC income from $209 in 1993 to $716 in 1999, an increase of nearly 250%. Mothers in the second fifth (incomes between $11,800 and $17,250) increased their EITC income from $678 to $1,973, an increase of nearly 200%. Not surprisingly, in 1999, even after the effect of social insurance, means-tested cash benefits, and means-tested noncash benefits have been factored in, the EITC reduced child poverty by 10% (Haskins, 2000, 2001).

Unfortunately, the EITC contains a marriage penalty. Assume that a mother with two children earning $10,000 married a man earning $18,000. At an income of $10,000, the mother would receive the maximum EITC of nearly $4,000. But once she marries, the combined income of the mother and father would be $28,000 and the EITC would fall to under $800. On the other hand, the couple would enjoy some economies of scale, the father—if he is the father of children living in the household—would no longer be responsible for payment of child support, and the combined income of the family would be quite substantial.

Even so, reducing the marriage penalty in the EITC is an important goal. To achieve this end, it is simply necessary to lengthen the phaseout range by granting married couples what amounts to an income disregard. The effect of this policy is to allow married couples to enjoy higher income before the phase-out range begins and ends. Congress has already enacted such legislation, widely agreed to on a bipartisan basis, but the legislation was vetoed by President Clinton (although he supported the expanded EITC for marriage, he opposed other provisions of the tax bill which contained the EITC fix). It seems virtually certain that if Congress passes tax legislation in the 107th Congress, reduction of the EITC marriage penalty will be a part of the final law.

CONCLUSION

Although many scholars and other observers seem to regard the unfortunate demographic trends that now characterize adult living arrangements in the United States as implacable, something is at least neutralizing the movement toward more divorce and illegitimacy. The divorce rate has been steady for well over a decade, the illegitimacy rate and ratio have been nearly stable for the last 5 years, teen pregnancy has been declining sharply for nearly a decade, and the fall of marriage rates may be slowing. The evidence on cohabitation rates in recent years is not clear one way or the other.

Given these hopeful trends, now is the perfect time to align our public policies on the side of marriage and children. If we overcome our willingness to accept demography as destiny, all of us—children, adults, and society—will be better off.

REFERENCES

Bumpass, L. L., & Lu, H. H. (2000). Trends in cohabitation and implications for children's family contexts in the United States. *Population Studies*, *54*, 29–41.

Duncan, G. J., & Brooks-Gunn, J. (1997). *Consequences of growing up poor.* New York: Russell Sage.

Haskins, R. (2000, November 13). Work works: The verdict on welfare reform. *Weekly Standard*, *6*(9), 20–21.

Haskins, R. (2001). The second most important issue: Effects of welfare reform on family income and poverty. In R. M. Blank & R. Haskins (Eds.), *The new world of welfare*. Washington, DC: Brookings.

McLanahan, S., Garfinkel, I., Reichman, N., & Teitler, J. (1999, May). *Unwed parents or fragile families? Implications for welfare and child support policy.* Princeton, NJ: Princeton University, Bendheim-Thoman Center for Research on Child Well-being.

McLanahan, S., & Sandefur, G. (1994). *Growing up with a single parent.* Cambridge, MA: Harvard University Press.

Rangarajan, A., & Gleason, P. (1998). Young unwed fathers of AFDC children: Do they provide support? *Demography*, *35*(2), 175–186.

U.S. Bureau of the Census. (1998, March). Marital status and living arrangements: March 1998 (Update). *Current Population Reports*, Series *P20–514* (and earlier reports).

Ventura, S. J., & Bachrach, C. A. (2000, October 18). Nonmarital childbearing in the United States, 1940-99. *National Vital Statistics Reports*, *48*(16; revised). Hyattsville, MD: National Center for Health Statistics.

14

The Complexity of Tax and Transfer Program Rules Regarding Cohabitation: Challenges and Implications

Anne E. Winkler
University of Missouri-St. Louis

The increased prevalence of opposite-sex cohabitation in the United States has opened up a host of research questions. First, there is the question of the factors underlying this trend, and whether cohabitation will eventually replace marriage, or if it is another step in what has been termed a "family-building process" (see, e.g., Brien et al., 1999; Bumpass & Lu, 2000; Kiernan, chap. 1, this volume; and Smock & Gupta, chap. 4, this volume). Second, there is the question as to the effects of cohabitation on children's well-being, both developmental and economic (see, e.g., Manning, chap. 8, this volume). Another question of interest, which is the focus of chap. 12 by Primus and Beeson, is how current government tax and transfer policies treat cohabiting couples with children vis-a-vis married-couple families with children and single-parent families.[1]

Primus and Beeson clearly show that disposable income can differ considerably depending on one's family structure and prevailing tax and transfer program policies. They also point out that tax and transfer policies provide differing and often conflicting incentives regarding a range of family structure decisions, including whether to marry, cohabit, or have children outside of marriage. The research evidence to date is varied, but it appears that welfare likely affects these decisions (see, e.g., Moffitt, 1998; Moffitt et al., 1998). Nevertheless, welfare cannot explain the decline in marriage or the rise in nonmarital fertility that began in the 1970s (Moffitt, 1998). There is also evidence that tax policies such as the Earned Income Tax Credit (EITC) have modest effects on the decisions to marry and divorce, as well as on the timing of births (see, e.g., Alm et al., 1999). Tax and transfer policies also influence decisions regarding paid work, though that is not the focus here (see, e.g., Eissa & Hoynes, 1998; Moffitt, 1992; Wolfe, 2000).

In evaluating the relationship between government tax and transfer programs and family structure, at least four questions arise: (a) What are the programs' rules regarding family structure?; (b) How does disposable income vary by family struc-

---

[1] As in Primus and Beeson (chap. 12, this volume), this discussion focuses only on cohabitation arrangements that include children. Furthermore, following their terminology, cohabiting parents refer to two unmarried adults living together who have a child in common, whereas cohabiting partners refers to two unmarried adults living together with a child present, but only one of the adults is the child's parent.

ture given prevailing rules?; (c) What are the potential incentive effects of the rules on family structure decisions?; and (d) Do the stated rules actually affect family structure decisions, and if so, to what degree?

Analyzing the rules and incentive effects of government tax and transfer programs is far more difficult than an average reader, who is not immersed in this literature, might suspect. Early research focused on only a single or a handful of programs at the exclusion of others. But, data on program participation indicate that a sizeable number of individuals receive benefits from several programs, so no single program can be regarded in isolation when considering effects on outcomes such as family structure and work incentives. Consequently, recent research has focused on analyzing multiple transfer programs and taking account of how they interact. Moreover, the relative importance of safety net programs has changed in recent years, altering the nature and scope of the analysis. For instance, as a result of legislative changes made since the early 1990s, the EITC has become the largest means-tested cash transfer program in the United States. This has led to considerable interest in understanding its effects on poverty alleviation and behavioral incentives (see, e.g., Blank, 2000; Dickert-Conlin & Houser, 1998; Ellwood, 1999; Liebman, 1998). Additionally, the federal welfare legislation of 1996 replaced Aid to Families with Dependent Children (AFDC) with a new program called Temporary Assistance for Needy Families (TANF). One other major change is that paternity establishment and child support enforcement have been considerably stepped up in recent years (Institute for Research on Poverty, 2000).

Until the mid-1990s, researchers analyzing the incentive effects of tax and transfer programs on family structure ignored cohabitation as an outcome, but this is no longer tenable in light of the increasing frequency of this living arrangement. Research on the effects of government tax and transfer policy on cohabitation include Winkler (1995); Moffitt et al. (1998); Dickert-Conlin & Houser (1998); Alm et al. (1999); Evenhouse & Reilly (1999); Dickert-Conlin (1999); Ellwood (1999); and London (2000), among others. These studies each focus on only a handful of the potential living arrangements of women and children, including cohabitation, rather than the full array. For instance, some studies (e.g., London, 2000) look at cohabitation as a choice for single mothers, along with living with relatives or living alone. Other studies look at marriage, headship, and cohabitation, but do not analyze doubling-up with relatives (e.g., Moffitt et al., 1998). Although limiting the number of living arrangements analyzed considerably simplifies the empirical analysis, one consequence is that it makes it difficult to compare the effect of program rules on different living arrangements. Studies have also generally failed to address the new reality that increasing numbers of individuals, both adults and children, experience transitions and disruptions in their living arrangements (Bumpass & Lu, 2000). This fact has implications not only for children's well-being, but also in considering how policies should be structured and how they might affect individuals and families.

Primus and Beeson's chapter is directed at the first three questions raised earlier. As compared to other studies on cohabitation, they more closely consider the exact rules regarding the EITC's treatment of cohabitors and their implications. Along with the EITC, they also consider AFDC/TANF, food stamps, and child support, with emphasis on how child support policy interacts with TANF. Of particular note, Primus and Beeson observe that recent changes in child support policy have served to encourage marriage among low-income couples relative to incentives in the past (see also Nixon, 1997). After reviewing effects on disposable income and potential incentive effects, Primus and Beeson bring to bear what social scientists have thus far learned about the nature of cohabitation and offer a detailed set of policy recommendations.

It has often been the case that program rules have been misunderstood by researchers or only incorporated in limited fashion, although researchers have made increased efforts to get the rules right. This is important for assessing the effects of policy on economic well-being, analyzing incentive effects, and formulating meaningful policy. Earlier studies by Winkler (1995) and Moffitt et al. (1998) clarified AFDC program rules, noting that the fundamental distinction for eligibility in the basic AFDC program and unemployed-parent program was whether the unit was a one- or two-parent family, regardless of marital status. Specifically, single mothers who cohabited with a boyfriend were effectively treated as a single-parent family, whereas those who cohabited with their children's father were assumed to fully share income and were treated as a two-parent family. The new TANF program classifies one- and two-parent families similarly. Primus and Beeson examine the EITC at this same level of detail. What is generally known about the EITC is that it depends on absolute earnings, and for married couples, the distribution of earnings between husbands and wives. Another major factor affecting the size of the EITC received is the presence and number of children. However, far less attention has been paid to the rules that apply to households comprised of two or more unrelated adults and a child. These rules have been modified several times in recent years. As of tax year 2000, if a single mother lives with her boyfriend, then only the single mother can claim the EITC on behalf of her dependent child (her boyfriend cannot).[2] On the other hand, if the single mother lives with the child's father, then the EITC rules *require* that the parent with the higher adjusted gross income claim the child.[3] Hence, the EITC treats different kinds of cohabitors differently.

A number of recent studies have incorporated these types of program details into their analyses (see, e.g., Dickert-Conlin & Houser, 1998; Evenhouse & Reilly, 1999) but one notable recent exception is Ellwood (1999). Ellwood made no dis-

---

[2] Previously, the EITC rules required that the boyfriend claim the children in the household if he lived there for the whole tax year, cared for the child as he would his own, and had higher adjusted income, as compared to the mother's (Internal Revenue Service, 1999). Under the previous rules, the value of the EITC potentially depended on the duration of cohabitation as well.

[3] As of 2001, either unmarried cohabiting parent is able to claim the credit.

tinction between cohabiting partners and cohabiting parents on the grounds that actual practice likely differs from the aforementioned rules (see Ellwood, 1999, footnote 19). Although the rules regarding the EITC, for instance, may not be followed precisely, a non-negligible fraction of individuals claiming the credit seek the help of tax preparation professionals, who are presumably familiar with the rules and are under obligation to follow them. To the extent that rules *are* followed, they may have considerable effects on disposable income and poverty alleviation, as demonstrated by Primus and Beeson. Furthermore, an examination of the precise details is valuable because it shows the full range of potential (dis)incentives and "loopholes" that might be taken into account in revising and rethinking existing policy. Nevertheless, as Ellwood correctly observed, whether or not the rules actually affect individual decisions very much depends on whether recipients themselves know what they are and how to use them to their best advantage. Certainly, one direction for future study would be to investigate the extent to which program rules are known and correctly understood, and the ways in which this information is disseminated.

An interesting exercise that Primus and Beeson undertake is to examine the ways that disposable income might differ, depending on how one's family is configured (or perhaps how it is reported on a tax form or application) for two hypothetical couples. From their analysis, it is clear that seemingly modest differences, such as whether or not a live-in boyfriend is included in the food stamp unit, have a considerable impact on economic well-being.[4] We should be particularly concerned to the extent that information on program rules is not fully understood, so individuals fail to participate in safety net programs available to them that could improve their incomes. Primus and Beeson observe that this is very much the case for poor two-parent families; their participation rate in TANF is far lower than the rate for poor single-parent families. Furthermore, we should be concerned to the extent that individuals misreport themselves, when, with full information they would act differently. On the other hand, if program rules are fully understood, then those who do not follow them are at their own peril.

A further issue raised by this chapter that has received insufficient attention is who is the appropriate benchmark or comparison group. Or, perhaps there is more than one. For instance, in computing a marriage penalty, the alternative might be that the individuals cohabit or it might be that they live separately. Furthermore, a single mother, for instance, might cohabit with her children's father or with a boyfriend. As Primus and Beeson observe, living separately leaves the individuals worse off than if cohabiting or married, holding all else constant, simply because they are unable to benefit from economies of scale. To date, this point has been acknowledged by researchers, but its ramifications have not heretofore been worked out. Taking economies of scale into account is a valuable contribution. On the other hand, given the mixed research evidence to date, I am wary of the im-

---

[4] In the cases shown, disposable income is higher if the boyfriend is not included.

plicit assumption made in the empirical analysis that cohabitors, both those with and without children in common, pool all of their income.[5] By its very nature, cohabitation is different from marriage and cohabitors differ from married couples (Smock & Gupta, chap. 4, this volume; Manning, chap. 8, this volume). Most notably, cohabitation arrangements tend to be of relatively short duration and cohabitors do not have the same legal protections as offered by marriage, which would suggest that cohabitors, in general, may be less likely to pool income.[6]

Although the analysis in Primus and Beeson is quite valuable, it is limited in at least one important way. Most notably, it only demonstrates the magnitude of penalties (bonuses) for a limited number of hypothetical families of given size and earnings. What is the fraction of families who actually face a marriage penalty or realize a marriage bonus, and what is the average magnitude of these effects, given the actual distribution of earnings and assets of individuals or couples? Previously, Dickert-Conlin and Houser (1998) and Alm et al. (1999) conducted simulations to compute such magnitudes using information on earnings, assets, and tax and transfer program rules. They came to the conclusion that the tax and transfer system, as a whole, imposes a sizeable "average net marriage penalty" for a considerable fraction of low-income families. However, their analyses failed to include child support. Given that child support enforcement tends to work in the opposite direction and encourages marriage over other alternatives, I would be interested in seeing these same type of simulations undertaken, with child support taken into account.

A critical assumption made in calculating marriage penalties and bonuses by Primus and Beeson and the aforementioned studies is that labor supply is fixed. Although this is a useful starting point, it is important to keep in mind that there are substantial differences in women's labor force participation, depending on the presence and ages of children, and marital status (see, e.g., Blau, Ferber, & Winkler, 2002). Hence, from a practical standpoint, earnings and penalties (bonuses) are likely to differ if behavioral responses are taken into account. As just one example, Table 12.7 assumes that a mother with two children who earned $7,500 prior to her separation will continue to have the same earnings afterwards. It is possible, however, that she may respond by working additional hours, which in turn will affect her tax liability and transfer benefits. In summary, an important direction for future research is to explicitly incorporate behavioral responses into such analyses.

---

[5] This can be seen by the fact that in calculating cohabitors' economic well-being, they sum up the income sources for both partners and then divide total income by the poverty line for the social family.

[6] Winkler (1997) examined income pooling by drawing inferences from a generalized model of labor supply and found that cohabitors, overall, do not pool income. However, the null hypothesis of pooling could not be rejected for cohabiting parents and for those cohabiting for an extended period of time. In other work, Landale (chap. 2, this volume) provides some evidence that that income pooling is less likely for cohabiting parents than for married couples. This is clearly an important issue that merits further study.

The research evidence from this and related studies clearly indicate that programs rules are often unclear and confusing for researchers, policymakers, and recipients alike. Moreover, tax and transfer policies provide conflicting incentives regarding family structure. In rethinking policy, there are at least three possibilities: (a) improve information dissemination and increase take-up rates given existing program rules; (b) change specific aspects of programs to meet certain goals; and (c) make comprehensive changes and integrate programs. Clearly, the most modest policy recommendations are to simply try to make existing programs more effective. For instance, Primus and Beeson suggest that the federal government should undertake policies to encourage states to raise the participation rates of two-parent families in TANF. However, even with such efforts, participation rates may still remain fairly low due to the program's especially strict work requirements for these families. In terms of specific program changes, Primus and Beeson recommend that all states make eligibility rules for two-parent families in TANF identical to those for single-parent families, which is currently not the case in a number of states. Easing these rules should help needy families and, at the same time, should not raise any concerns about dependency, since TANF benefits are time-limited.

Primus and Beeson make other valuable recommendations as well, such as paying greater attention to improving the employment and income prospects of low-income fathers. Furthermore, the current 100% tax on child support payments made by noncustodial parents to children in TANF families provides an enormous disincentive for them to formally contribute, and it may have negative repercussions on their relationships with children. Their suggestion to increase the disregard should be strongly considered.

Another specific change they recommend is to create a new tax filing category for cohabitors with children in common called "cohabiting couple, filing jointly." They argue that this change would place these families on equal footing as married couples. This recommendation, although seemingly modest, would affect taxpayers up and down the income distribution, not just those at the lower end. Hence, any incentive effects and revenue implications would be magnified. Furthermore, this change in the tax code would face stiff political opposition by some groups because it would appear to further legitimize cohabitation.[7] For this latter reason alone, I do not think that this suggestion is politically viable.

Even modest changes to the EITC can have unintended effects. For instance, Primus and Beeson also recommend that the rules be changed so that the EITC could always be claimed by a low-income non-custodial parent, regardless of the

---

[7] There is also the issue of whether this would apply to same-sex as well as opposite-sex couples. Another option, which does not currently have much support, is to return to a system of individual taxation, as was the case prior to 1948. Among the advantages, taxes paid would be independent of family structure, and unlike the current regime, the tax structure would not discourage the entry of secondary earners in married couple families and there would be no marriage penalties in the tax system. However, this change would be strongly opposed by traditional married couple families, and would not encourage marriage per se.

[8] This is among the changes in the EITC signed into law by George W. Bush in spring 2001.

earnings of the other adult, if it was more financially beneficial.[8] In terms of poverty alleviation, this recommendation makes good sense. However, it should be noted that this change, alone, would increase the benefits of cohabitation to marriage in some instances. As just one example, consider the situation of a single mother earning $10,000 currently living with her child's father, who earns $25,000. The value of the EITC to this family would be considerably increased, and hence the cohabitation bonus would be increased, if the mother could claim it since she could receive the maximum value whereas the father would receive a much smaller credit. This discussion suggests that even changes made on a piecemeal basis must be carefully evaluated. Additionally, in making any changes to programs, policymakers also have to consider effects on work incentives, along with interactions between family structure and paid work.

Policymakers face a considerable challenge in the 21st century. In thinking about structuring policies they face even more complications than those posed by the classic "iron triangle of welfare." The iron triangle of welfare points to the fact that it is not possible to provide work incentives, provide a benefit level sufficient to alleviate poverty, and keep costs down, all at the same time. Added to this, policymakers must try to design policies that seek to financially support a variety of families including "fragile families" (unwed parents who have recently had a child), single-parent families, and low-income married couple families and, at the same time, they must consider the incentive effects of rules on family formation decisions. As noted earlier, there is some evidence that traditional welfare programs like AFDC have had a statistically significant, albeit quantitatively modest, negative effect on marriage. In addition, AFDC has also been found to discourage work. Even more recent policies that focus on *low-income working families,* such as the EITC, pose similar concerns for some individuals as a result of the fact that benefits are eventually phased-out as family earnings increase. As Ellwood (1999) observed, the EITC provides incentives for an employed single parent to remain single and provides the secondary earner in married couples, typically the wife, with a disincentive to work (see also Eissa & Hoynes, 1998).

Realistically, any set of policies that are adopted will have disincentive effects of some kind. As a result, this study, which seeks to identify potential incentive effects, is only a first step. Next, we must discern which effects are "statistically significant." From there, we need to determine the *magnitude* of the identified effects. Information about magnitudes is critical in determining which incentive effects to worry most about. Additionally, we need to have a fuller understanding about the effects of cohabitation on children's outcomes as compared with the effects of growing up with a single parent or with two married parents. Finally, it is important that such analyses distinguish among different types of cohabitors, that is, whether they are cohabiting parents or cohabiting partners.

In conclusion, Primus and Beeson demonstrate the complexities of federal policies with respect to cohabitation. Furthermore, they make a convincing argument that analyses of economic well-being and (dis)incentives of the tax and transfer system should take into account the role of child support. Additionally, policies have to take account of the difficulties faced by noncustodial fathers and those in two-parent families with low potential earnings. Primus and Beeson's recommendations are a useful starting point because they take into account recent changes in the structure of many U.S. families and the challenges faced by these families. It is also clear that the task ahead for policymakers is not an easy one.

REFERENCES

Alm, J., Dickert-Conlin, S., & Whittington, L. A. (1999). Policy watch: The marriage penalty. *Journal of Economic Perspectives, 13*(3), 193–204.

Blank, R. M. (2000). Fighting poverty: Lessons from recent U.S. history. *Journal of Economic Perspectives, 14*(2), 3–19.

Blau, F. D., Ferber, M. A., & Winkler, A. E. (2002). *The economics of women, men and work.* Saddle River, NJ: Prentice-Hall.

Brien, M. J., Lillard, L. L., & Waite, L. J. (1999). Interrelated family-building behaviors: Cohabitation, marriage, and nonmarital conception. *Demography, 36*(4), 535–552.

Bumpass, L. L., & Lu, H. H. (2000). Trends in cohabitation and implications for children's family context in the United States. P*opulation Studies, 54*(1), 29–41.

Dickert-Conlin, S., & Houser, S. (1998). Taxes and transfers: A new look at the marriage penalty. *National Tax Journal, 51*(2), 175–217.

Dickert-Conlin, S. (1999). EITC, AFDC and the female headship decision. Mimeo, Syracuse University.

Eissa, N., & Hoynes, H. (1998). The earned income tax credit and the labor supply of married couples. Mimeo, University of California at Berkeley.

Ellwood, D. T. (1999). The impact of the earned income tax credit and social policy reforms on work, marriage, and living arrangements. Mimeo, Harvard University.

Evenhouse, E., & Reilly, S. 1999. Welfare and children's living arrangements. Mimeo, Vanderbilt University.

Institute for Research on Poverty. (2000). Child support enforcement policy and low-income families. *Focus, 21*(1), 1–4.

Internal Revenue Service. (1999). *Publication 17.* Washington, DC: Author.

Liebman, J. (1998). The impact of the earned income tax credit on incentives and income distribution. In J. Poterba (Ed.), *Tax policy and the economy* (pp. 83–119). Cambridge, MA: MIT Press.

London, R. A. (2000). The interaction between single mothers' living arrangements and welfare participation. *Journal of Policy Analysis and Management, 19*(1), 93–117.

Moffitt, R. A. (1992). The incentive effects of the U.S. welfare system: A review. *Journal of Economic Literature, 30*(1), 1–61.

Moffitt, R. A. (1998). The effect of welfare on marriage on fertility: What do we know and what do we need to know? In R. A. Moffitt (Ed.), *Welfare, the family and reproductive behavior* (pp. 50–97). Washington, DC: National Research Council.

Moffitt, R. A., Reville, R., & Winkler, A. E. (1998). Beyond single mothers: Cohabitation and marriage in the AFDC program. *Demography, 3*, 259–278.

Nixon, L. A. (1997). The effect of child support enforcement on marital dissolution. *Journal of Human Resources, 32*(1), 159–181.

Winkler, A. E. (1995). Does AFDC-UP encourage two-parent families? *Journal of Policy Analysis and Management, 14*(1), 4–24.

Winkler, A. E. (1997). Economic decisionmaking by cohabitors: Findings regarding income pooling. *Applied Economics, 29*, 1079–1090.

Wolfe, B. (2000). *Incentives, challenges, and dilemmas of TANF.* Working Paper No. 1209-00. Madison, WI: Institute for Research on Poverty.

15

The Economic Rights and Responsibilities of Unmarried Cohabitants

Margaret M. Mahoney
The University of Pittsburgh School of Law

This chapter explores the current state of the law regarding several important financial issues that arise between members of the nontraditional family headed by an unmarried cohabiting heterosexual couple: the child support obligations of the unmarried partners to their children, the economic rights of the partners when they dissolve their relationship, and the rights of the surviving partner and children following the death of one partner. Many legal issues affecting such nontraditional families are not discussed herein including the child support responsibility of one partner for the children of the other, economic issues involving third parties such as creditor claims, and noneconomic issues within the family such as health care decision making. As to each topic discussed, the current rules are analyzed in terms of the various policy goals of the state that operate in the field of family law.

Historically and today, a key policy that has informed lawmakers in their treatment of nontraditional families is the preference for marriage and the related preference that children be born and raised in families headed by married parents. This is the same policy concern highlighted by Primus and Beeson (chap. 12, this volume) in their discussion of safety net programs for low-income families. In each context, a policy operates along with other important concerns of state and federal lawmakers when they undertake the regulation of family economic rights. Furthermore, the question whether the rules of law actually affect private decision making about family matters remains a speculative one, whatever the context in which it is posed.

An important aspect of private family relationships is the mutual economic responsibility of adult family members for each other and for their children. Every state in the United States has embodied the economic rights and responsibilities of husbands and wives in a series of legal doctrines that include spousal support, child support, inheritance rights, and the sharing of assets between spouses in the event of divorce. This chapter explores the extent to which the economic rights, responsibilities, and protections of the traditional family have been extended, as a matter of state law, to nonmarried couples and their children. Generally speaking, the state legislatures and courts have not extended their recognition and treatment of the family as an economic unit to the adults living in nontraditional families.

The children of unmarried parents fare somewhat better than the adults, although their legal status in some ways is still not on a par with the children of married parents.

STATE LAW POLICY CONCERNS

State lawmakers have given various explanations for their failure to recognize the family headed by an unmarried couple as an economic unit, depending on the specific issue at hand and the time and place of the inquiry. For example, a preference for marriage over cohabitation, coupled with a belief in some instances that the law can shape individual behavior in this regard, has supported the denial of various legal benefits over time to the members of nontraditional families. At one time, but no longer, this rationale was used by many states to deny child support rights to nonmarital children (Clark, 1988, pp. 149-150). Currently, in some but not all states, the rationale is still used to deny property rights to the economically dependent partner when a couple terminates their cohabiting relationship (Raggio, 1994, pp. 65-30–65-32). Thus, the vitality of this particular rationale has varied depending on the particular issue being analyzed (child support, property rights, or something else), and the particular jurisdiction and the time in history that provide the analytical context.

A second rationale for refusing to attach legal significance to the relationships of unmarried couples involves a stated respect for the autonomy of the individuals who enter into such unions. Here, an assumption is made that heterosexual couples who are legally free to marry signal a mutual desire to be left alone by the state when they elect to cohabit. The assumption is made that these individuals do not want the state-designed marriage contract imposed on them. Even if one partner later changes his or her mind and seeks the benefit of a support or property order, the state courts, in applying the principle of autonomy, look to the earlier and established intention of the couple and deny all claims between them (Seff, 1995, pp. 154-156). The intention of the parties generally does not, however, control the legal rights of their children.

Notably, the doctrine of common law marriage, which applies in cases where couples have failed to comply with the formal requirements (licensing, ceremony) for marriage, is similarly respectful of the autonomy of the partners. The key element of proof in establishing a common law marriage is the intent of the parties to be married and to be regarded as wife and husband, despite the absence of any marriage license or wedding ceremony (Clark, 1988, p. 48). When a common-law marriage, based on the intent of the parties, is established, the partners are spouses in the eyes of the law for all legal purposes. The doctrine has fallen into disfavor in modern times and is only recognized now in about a dozen states (Krause, 1996, p. 69). In any event, the element of intent plays a similar role in the context of lawmaking for nonmarital partners, where their intent not to be treated like a married couple is respected by the legislatures and courts.

An additional rationale for denying any legal status to cohabiting couples involves the problem of definition. That is, if certain rights should in fairness attach to the cohabiting relationship, then how should cohabitation be defined for this purpose? Unlike marriage, there is no public record that provides the easy identification of each and every eligible couple. The need to formulate and apply standards to determine who is in and who is out has discouraged many lawmakers from attempting to elevate cohabitation to the level of a legal status.

Finally, additional concerns unique to each specific legal issue incline lawmakers away from the legal recognition of the nonmarital family. For example, a crucial underlying policy of the probate system involves the need for certainty and efficiency in the probate process in order to avoid lengthy periods of time when the ownership of property is uncertain. Consistent with this policy, many states have restricted the types of proof that can be introduced to establish paternity following the father's death, thereby denying inheritance rights to nonmarital children in some cases even when the parents have lived together prior to the father's death (Brashier, 1996, pp. 103–147).

The remainder of this chapter reviews the current state of the law regarding financial rights within the nontraditional family in light of these various policy concerns.

CHILD SUPPORT

Current U.S. child support laws provide that every biological or adoptive parent owes a duty of financial support to his or her minor children (Krause, 1996, p. 182). The right to support is extended evenhandedly to all children, whether or not their parents have married or have ever lived together. This evenhanded treatment of nonmarital children is a constitutional mandate. In 1973 in the case of *Gomez v. Perez*, the U.S. Supreme Court ruled that state laws that denied support claims for nonmarital children violated the Equal Protection Clause. Notably, the old laws were premised in part on the desire of state lawmakers to send the message that marriage was the preferred context for bearing and rearing children. Although the Supreme Court accepted this preference as a proper goal of the state lawmakers, the justices believed that the denial of parental support to children was not an acceptable method of promoting the goal (*Gomez v. Perez*).

Whenever the child and both parents reside in the same household, the courts generally refuse to entertain a child support suit by one parent (or another representative of the child) against the other parent. Thus, the only enforcement of support duties in the intact family takes place when a third party, such as the welfare authority or another creditor who provided necessary support to the child, seeks to recover from the obligated parents (Krause, 1996, p. 182). By way of contrast, once the parents have separated, or if they never resided together, the noncustodial parent's (NCP's) support duty is enforceable in court by the custodial parent.

The question of properly identifying the father, which may be raised as an issue in support proceedings for nonmarital children, rarely arises in cases involving married parents where the strong (at times, conclusive) legal presumption exists that the child born to a married woman is also the child of her husband. As to nonmarital children, the rules of evidence in paternity proceedings initiated during the father's lifetime flexibly permit evidence of cohabitation along with other forms of evidence including blood test results to resolve the factual question of parenthood (Krause, 1996, pp. 253–254).

In each child support case, the court must determine the amount to be paid by the NCP. Congress has mandated that every state (under the threat of losing federal funds) must adopt quantitative guidelines for determining child support amounts. The guidelines, which may entail a calculation as simple as the multiplication of a stated fraction against the gross income of the parent, must be applied in every case (Melli & Oldham, 2000, pp. 113–116). Within this framework, there is reason to anticipate that the amount of child support awards will not be affected by the marital status of the parents. The residual discretion reserved for judges under the state guidelines leaves some room for continuing unequal treatment in setting the amounts of support for children from their NCPs. Still, the guidelines on their face embody the same determination made by the Supreme Court in the *Gomez* case that whatever the societal view of cohabitation, the law of child support is not a proper vehicle for expressing a preference for marriage.

PROPERTY RIGHTS UPON DISSOLUTION

In the event that a cohabiting couple (with or without children) ends their relationship, the question arises whether the law will recognize and enforce any post-dissolution financial claims between the two adults. A natural point of reference is the law of marriage dissolution which, in every state, authorizes the designated court to make a fair distribution of the parties' assets, however they are owned and titled at that time, and also to enter spousal maintenance orders in certain circumstances for the future support of one party (Krause, 1996, pp. 149–172). State lawmakers have never extended these doctrines to unmarried cohabiting couples. Nevertheless, the recurring claims of partners for economic relief from the courts have produced a different set of doctrines reflecting a special set of state policy concerns.

The development of the law in this area is quite recent. Historically, very few cases were reported that involved financial claims by former cohabiting partners. Until just a few decades ago, the judges who heard these occasional cases were very intolerant of the former partner seeking relief. Their intolerance stemmed from the viewpoint that cohabitation was morally wrong, illegal in many states, inconsistent with the state's preference for marriage, and not to be encouraged through rules that rewarded either participant for such conduct (Seff, 1995, pp. 149–151). Of course, this approach produced great hardship for individuals who had become financially dependent in long-term nontraditional family relationships.

During the past three decades or so, the courts and legislatures in a number of states have taken a new approach to this issue as they seek to balance the equitable considerations raised by the financially dependent former cohabitor against the competing traditional state policies. Rather than formulating a rule of law similar to the law of equitable distribution or alimony applied in divorce proceedings, however, the recent trend purportedly relies on general principles of contract law to resolve the economic claims of cohabitors. In other words, the dependent partner must allege and prove the existence of an agreement between the partners that includes a promise regarding post-dissolution financial rights. In the case of a written contract signed by both parties, the theory is very workable. In many cases, however, there is no such document and the claim is based on either a verbal promise or, even more tentatively, a so-called "implied contract" arising from the course of conduct between the parties during the period of cohabitation (Raggio, 1994, pp. 65-29–65-30).

The doctrinal focus on contractual principles enables the legislatures and courts to maintain that the state is not favoring cohabitation choices, as it does marriage, by raising such relationships to the level of a legally protected status. Furthermore, because the results under this approach turn in particular cases on the intention of the parties, personal autonomy in family matters is protected. Currently, some states enforce only written contracts; others enforce both written and oral agreements; still others include the implied contract theory in their state doctrine (Raggio, 1994, pp. 65-29–65-36). Critics of the latter approach argue that post-relationship property claims based on a pattern of financial sharing and other common family behaviors are not really contract-based claims but rather a means of elevating cohabitation to a protected status for this purpose (*Morone v. Morone*).

Although the financial issues arising at the time of dissolution directly affect only the two partners, the potential indirect consequences for children of the relationship are obvious. In cases where the financially dependent partner becomes the primary custodian of the children following dissolution of the cohabiting relationship, the failure to make economic provision for the custodial parent has inevitable consequences for the children in his or her care.

PROPERTY RIGHTS AT DEATH

The state laws regulating the distribution of a deceased person's estate have two main functions. First, the laws are designed to make sure that the decedent's property passes to his or her intended beneficiaries. Where a will has been executed, the property is distributed to the named beneficiaries, subject to the exception created by the so-called elective share statutes (Johnson & Robbennolt, 1999, pp. 423–425). The elective share statutes embody the second goal of the state in this context: the economic protection of surviving family members. These statutes enable the surviving spouse to "elect against" the will and take a designated share, which is frequently stated as a fractional one half or one third of the property, when the decedent has failed to adequately provide for the surviving partner. There is no counterpart in the law designed to protect children. Furthermore, cohabiting partners do not enjoy elective share rights. As a result, when parents cohabit but do not marry, the decedent's wishes control the distribution of assets, and no claim to the estate can be made by the surviving partner or children who were not provided for in the will. Thus, the state goal of protecting surviving dependent family members is ignored in the nontraditional family.

In cases where an individual dies without a will (intestate), his or her assets will be distributed to the surviving relatives who are identified in the state intestacy statute (the heirs). When the decedent leaves a surviving spouse and/or biological or adopted children, they are the sole heirs. The state legislatures have created this substitute estate plan for individuals who have not made their own plans, based on the assumption that surviving spouses and children are the natural objects of bounty of most persons. Notably, a surviving cohabiting partner is not regarded as an heir and does not inherit any portion of the estate (Dukeminier & Johanson, 2000, pp. 71–75). The exclusion of the cohabiting partner from both the elective share legislation and the intestacy statutes of every state reflects several policy concerns of the state lawmakers. The traditional preference for marriage is coupled here with a reluctance to view cohabiting partners in general as likely "objects of bounty," and a refusal to complicate probate proceedings by requiring judicial inquiries into the actual nature of the relationship in each case.

The claims of nonmarital children are subject to a more complicated set of rules that allow their inheritance claims in many but not all cases when the parent dies without a will. Historically, there was a blanket exclusion of nonmarital children from the category of children who inherit from their fathers under the laws of many states. In 1977, the U.S. Supreme Court ruled that such laws discriminated against the excluded children in an unconstitutional manner (*Trimble v. Gordon*). However, the Court did not require, and many state laws still do not create, an unrestricted right of inheritance for nonmarital children. The limiting concern is the question of proof of paternity and the desire to avoid claims in the probate court that are false or difficult to prove.

Children born to a married mother are presumed to be the children of her husband, and few questions arise about paternity and inheritance rights in this context (Brashier, 1996, pp. 117–134). Where there is no marriage, however, the various states have formulated different tests to establish paternity and the right of a child to inherit from a deceased man (Hauser, 1997, pp. 931–957). Thus, many states recognize the child as an heir if the decedent informally acknowledged the child as his own during his lifetime. The biological or adopted children of unmarried cohabiting parents would likely succeed in inheriting from the father who died without a will under such a standard. On the other hand, in a case decided just one year after *Trimble v. Gordon*, the Supreme Court upheld the constitutionality of a state law that allowed inheritance from an unmarried father only if paternity had been established by judicial decree during the father's lifetime (*Lalli v. Lalli*). The obvious potential for the exclusion of deserving children from inheritance under this standard was thought to be justified by the competing goals of efficiency and accuracy in the probate process.

Of course, the unmarried property owner need not and should not rely on the laws of intestate distribution to benefit his or her loved ones at death. A simple will leaving assets to the surviving partner and children is the only method of assuring post-mortem economic security in the nontraditional family.

CONCLUSION

This chapter has surveyed and analyzed the current legal treatment of three important financial issues in families headed by an unmarried cohabiting couple: child support, property rights upon dissolution of the cohabiting relationship, and property rights at death. The legal recognition and protection extended to such nontraditional families falls far short of the legal status established for the traditional family. Various state policies underlie the governing rules of law, including the well-established preference for marriage over cohabitation. In recent decades, the burden of this preference has been reduced in the context of issues directly affecting children (child support, inheritance rights of children). By way of contrast, the rules of law governing the economic rights and responsibilities between the adults in the cohabiting partnership continue to embody the traditional reluctance to elevate cohabiting relationships to the level of a legally significant status.

ACKNOWLEDGMENTS

I acknowledge the valuable contributions of my research assistant, Allisha Chapman, University of Pittsburgh School of Law class of 2001, in the preparation of this chapter.

REFERENCES

Brashier, R. C. (1996). Children and inheritance in the nontraditional family. *Utah Law Review*, 93–225.

Clark H. H., Jr. (1988). *The law of domestic relations in the United States* (2nd ed.). St. Paul, MN: West Publishing.

Dukeminier, J., & Johanson, S. M. (2000). *Wills, trusts, and estates* (6th ed.). New York: Aspen.

Gomez v. Perez, 209 U.S. 535 (1972).

Hauser, K. (1997). Inheritance rights for extramarital children: New science plus old intermediate scrutiny add up to the need for change. *University of Cincinnati Law Review*, *65*, 891–963.

Johnson M. K., & Robbenolt, J. K. (1999). Legal planning for unmarried committed partners: Empirical lessons for a preventive and therapeutic approach. *Arizona Law Review*, *41*, 417–457.

Krause, H. D. (1996). *Family law* (2nd ed.). St. Paul, MN: West Publishing.

Lalli v. Lalli, 439 U.S. 762 (1978).

Melli, M., & Oldham J. T. (2000). *Child support: The next frontier*. Ann Arbor: University of Michigan Press.

Morone v. Morone, 413 N.E.2d 1154 (N.Y. 1980).

Raggio, G. H., Jr. (1994). Unmarried cohabitants. In A. H. Rutkin (Ed.), *Family law and practice* (pp. 65-1–65-64). New York: Matthew Bender.

Seff, M. A. (1995). Cohabitation and the law. In L. J. McIntyre (Ed.), *Families and law* (pp. 141–168). New York: Haworth Press.

Trimble v. Gordon, 430 U.S. 762 (1977).

16

What Does It Mean to Be "Just Living Together" in the New Millennium? An Overview

Lynette F. Hoelter and Dawn E. Stauffer
The Pennsylvania State University

The role of cohabitation in family formation has recently emerged as an interest of social scientists and policymakers alike. Rising divorce rates have drawn attention to the shift in family forms, and increased rates of cohabitation have been cited as one possible indication of the "breakdown" of the traditional family (e.g., Bumpass, Sweet, & Cherlin, 1991; Glenn, 1996; Popenoe, 1988). The chapters in this volume, however, indicate that cohabiting unions are neither new nor necessarily negative in terms of their influence on the well-being of individuals and families involved. Each chapter in this volume addresses a particular aspect of cohabitation and the role that this type of union plays within the larger society; however some common themes emerge throughout.

One theme that cuts across all chapters is the idea that cohabiting unions do not represent a unitary phenomenon. There are variations in cohabiting unions that are often given only cursory treatment in research and discussion of the topic. Although most cohabiting unions are short-lived, a number last for 5 years or longer, and this is not insignificant as these unions are likely to be qualitatively different than their short-term counterparts. Variability is also present in that, for some, cohabitation is viewed as an alternative to marriage, whereas others view it as a prelude to a marital union or a response to the dissolution of a marriage. Diverse cultures and subgroups within a larger society also hold different ideas about cohabiting. All of these possible differences in the cohabitation experience must be kept in mind in discussions of research about the topic. It seems that family researchers have barely scratched the surface when thinking about what the experience of cohabitation *means* for various couples. The differences in meaning are likely to be related to differences in actual experiences within such a union.

Another theme emerging from the chapters is that cohabiting unions are difficult to study because of the same factors noted above. Defining and capturing the nature of cohabiting unions statistically is not an easy task given their transitory nature. Likewise, social scientific research typically involves comparing one group of individuals to another. It is unclear, though, to whom cohabitors should be compared. General comparisons to married couples tend to oversimplify the diversity within both types of couples (e.g., step- versus two-biological parents, children involved or no children involved, etc.). Such a comparison also tends to start with the idea that there will be something lacking in cohabiting relationships as marital unions are used as the standard against which other unions are compared. Authors in this volume note that this idea of "deficiency" may be true statistically when comparing first-married families to cohabiting unions, but it is less obvious once factors such as ages of the adults and children involved and distribution of income among family members are considered. Additionally, comparisons between those in cohabiting unions and those in single-parent families are likely to yield quite a different picture, one that does not seem as negative for cohabiting unions. The comparison between cohabitors and their never-married, non-cohabiting counterparts is, at present, lacking in this research. This is a significant omission that deserves attention in future research.

A final theme evident in the chapters in this volume is that of cohabitation as an "incomplete institution" (Cherlin, 1992). The role of cohabitation within western societies is changing and the understanding of that role is continually evolving. The lack of readily defined roles, and indeed rules or laws, for cohabitors likely adds to the diversity of such unions. Both the causes and the responses to individuals' choices to cohabit should be studied within this context. Additionally, institutional (non)response affects research by influencing the way data on union formation are collected and utilized. Therefore, the research based on these data captures a snapshot within an experience that is much more fluid than might be indicated. Conversely, individuals for whom cohabitation is a very real part of their lives may have negotiated roles and patterns of behavior that are missed in current research because the right questions have yet to be asked. Although this is the case for most social research, the point is especially important when examining something as "process-oriented" as union formation. Thoughts about the relative benefits of marriage and cohabitation are also situated within this framework such that one is left comparing a union that is a "complete institution" to one for which the "rules" are still evolving.

We now turn to a discussion of the major sections within this book, always keeping an eye toward the themes presented here.

HISTORICAL AND CROSS-CULTURAL TRENDS IN COHABITATION

Individuals making the choice to live together without the legal recognition of marriage have always existed in some form or another. Kiernan (chap. 1, this volume), Landale (chap. 2, this volume), Brines (2000), and Hunter (chap. 3, this volume) take on the difficult task of setting out historical and cross-cultural patterns in cohabitation as a form of union formation. This task is a daunting one because data on cohabiting unions are not always readily available. When such unions are not recognized by the society as "legitimate," they are not recorded in official data. Even when they are legitimated, the short duration of most cohabiting unions makes them difficult to capture statistically. Additionally, as Kiernan,

Hunter, and others demonstrate, cohabitation as a type of union formation is generally more prevalent among subpopulations within a society, and these are often the same subpopulations that are underrepresented in social research. Such limitations not withstanding, these authors are able to present a picture of the "state of cohabitation" both historically and cross-culturally.

The focus of Kiernan's (chap. 1, this volume) work is on historical and current European trends in union formation. She proposes that the type of cohabiting union common today actually represents a "new form" of cohabitation in that the cohabiting union precedes or replaces marriage. In fact, in several European countries, the most common first union formation is now cohabitation rather than marriage. She argues that in the past, cohabitation was often the result of marriages that had ended due to separation or divorce or the death of one spouse. One should note that individual countries are not all at the same point with regard to occurrence and acceptance of cohabiting unions; cohabiting prior to marriage is much less common in countries in southern Europe than in other European countries.

Following from the trends she identifies in the state of cohabitation in Europe, Kiernan sets forth a "stage theory" of the role of cohabitation in a society. Briefly, her stages are as follow:

1. Cohabitation is "deviant" and practiced by only a small minority within a society.
2. Cohabitation serves as a "test" of a relationship prior to marriage but remains a short period in which childbearing is rare.
3. Cohabitation becomes as accepted as marriage and fulfills the same position within society (e.g., childbearing and parenting occur).
4. Cohabiting and marital unions are largely interchangeable.

Even in countries that reach the latter stages of this model where cohabitation is accepted and childbearing occurs within such unions, cohabiting unions still differ from marriages on at least one key issue. That is, the stability of cohabiting relationships does not generally reach the level that it does for marriages. Regardless of duration, relationships beginning with cohabiting unions are often at higher risk for dissolution than are those relationships beginning with marriage directly. Cohabiting unions that never convert into marriages have the highest dissolution rate of any union type (Jayakody & Cabrera, chap. 5, this volume; Kiernan, chap. 1, this volume; Landale, chap. 2, this volume).

Landale and Hunter (chaps. 2 and 3, this volume, respectively) argue that the dichotomization of cohabitation into "old" and "new" forms as Kiernan sets forth may be oversimplifying reality because this model uses the northwestern European example as the foundation for studying family patterns. Northwest Europe could be more unique in its approach to family formation than it would seem on the surface, thus making the comparisons exaggerated and similarities in cross-cultural cohabitation experiences muted. For example, cohabitation has existed as an alternative to marriage for decades among subgroups of Latin American, Caribbean, and North American populations. Hunter notes that cohabitation has played a slightly larger role in family formation among African Americans, particularly in terms of childbearing, possibly stemming from a time when legal marriages among African-American slaves were not recognized by the larger society.

The comparisons not only across countries but also between marriage and cohabiting unions within a single society may also be misunderstood. The key issues for both Landale and Hunter seem to be who chooses informal unions over marital unions and the ways in which cohabiting unions function in comparison to marriages. Largely, poorer subgroups within Latin and North America seem to be the ones for whom cohabitation is an attractive alternative to marriage (see also Jayakody & Cabrera, chap. 5, this volume). This is particularly true for Kiernan's "new" form of cohabitation where cohabitation is preceding or replacing marriage. A significant proportion of individuals of all socioeconomic statuses choose cohabitation after a failed marriage.

In addition to knowing who cohabits, patterns of relating within different union types also deserve further attention. In her sample of Puerto Rican individuals, for example, Landale (chap. 2, this volume) found that those who cohabit have very different mechanisms for sharing income than do those in married- or single-parent households. That is, females in cohabiting relationships were more likely to get an "allowance" or an occasional purchase or payment for expenses from their partners than were married women; whereas married women were significantly more likely to have income from their husbands put into a "common pot" from which household expenses could be paid. This finding underscores the importance of learning more about the meaning of cohabitation in relation to other types of unions using qualitative approaches that tap individuals' subjective understandings of family phenomena. Additionally, such studies of the differences between types of unions should be done without assuming "pathology" in the less traditional family forms (e.g., Hunter, chap. 3, this volume).

Thus, although a range of family formation behaviors exists within societies, the arbitrary distinctions between these types may be imposed by social scientists and demographers, rather than by the members of the couples themselves. The transition between union types may not be as meaningful for the participants in the relationship as the "events" are to those who study them, yet evidence suggests that differences in expectations for each union type do exist. It is important, therefore, to study union formation as a process rather than as a series of events.

Causes and Consequences of Cohabitation Patterns

Within their discussions of patterns in cohabitation, the authors in this volume suggest both macro- and micro-level factors relating to the current and historical trends.

At the macro level, patterns corresponding to the rise of cohabitation in Western cultures include the increasing instability of marriages that creates a desire to know more about one's future partner prior to committing to marriage, women's roles in the economic and social milieu becoming more equal to those of men, and the generation of "baby boomers" going through the educational and labor market systems (Brines, 2000; see also Hunter, chap. 3, this volume). The intersection of power and status differences caused by both structural (labor market, income differences between men and women) and attitudinal factors appears to be key to decisions to cohabit versus to marry. Cohabiting unions occur when the "benefits" to marriage are lower—that is, when women can support themselves outside of such unions and/or when marrying a low-income partner, particularly an unstably employed male, would become a burden to the household unit rather than an asset (Brines, 2000; Jayakody & Cabrera, chap. 5, this volume; Landale, chap. 2, this volume). Additionally, attitudes of equality in gender roles are associated with choosing cohabitation over marriage. There is evidence, however, that once cohabiting unions convert to marriage or childbearing unions, couples have a tendency to revert to more stereotypical gender role patterns (e.g., Brown, 1998). The most egalitarian relationships, at least in terms of household division of labor, however, are cohabiting unions formed post-marriage. Other societal factors that influence the decision to cohabit include weakening ties with traditional religious belief systems and the experience of a parental divorce within one's own family of origin (Kiernan, chap. 1, this volume).

One micro-level factor that seems to be related to the rate of cohabitation is a desire for marriage to be truly long term; that is, individuals who prefer the ability to get out of a relationship that is not beneficial are likely to chose cohabitation (Jayakody & Cabrera, chap. 5, this volume). Autonomy and independence, in addition to commitment to the relationship, are significant concepts for these individuals. For example, Hunter (chap. 3, this volume) notes that African Americans value marriage as much as Whites do; however, the difference appears to be that, for African-American women, the idea of one's own identity above and beyond the role of wife and mother seems key to waiting for the "right" relationship before settling into marriage (see also Landale, chap. 2, this volume). The mother–child bond is thus seen as more important in terms of "family" than a marital union, meaning that individuals are inclined to do what is best for themselves and their children rather than following what society calls "ideal." Johnson (1991) also proposed that the identity that comes from being in a lasting relationship may be one of the factors keeping individuals committed to a particular relationship. Therefore, the decision to marry might be seen by some as more "sacred" and better reserved for "sure" relationships.

Although these factors are arguably causal in affecting the rates of cohabitation, the consequences of rising rates also fall along the same lines. Largely, the increase in childbearing within cohabiting unions and the greater instability of these unions is related to increased female-headship of families. Female-headship is correlated with higher rates of poverty. So, not surprisingly, childbearing in these unstable unions is related to increased risks of living in poverty. There also seems to be, at least at some level, a questioning of the value of marriage over other family forms. This is not to say, however, that marriage is weakening as an institution. In the United States, evidence shows that marriage is still a goal of most individuals and the rates of ever marrying have not dropped significantly (Cherlin, 1992). Nevertheless, it is likely that the shift in family forms as individuals adapt to changes in society will continue.

THE ROLE OF COHABITATION IN CONTEMPORARY NORTH AMERICA FAMILY STRUCTURE

As evidenced by the focus of this volume, cohabitation has rapidly gained research attention as an emerging type of co-residential union in both the United States and Canada. In general, there is basic agreement among researchers and policymakers that cohabitation represents an increasingly common approach to first (and subsequent) union formation in North America. However, its increasing public presence as a type of coresidential union is also a source of research controversy and bewilderment because in some instances cohabitation closely resembles marriage, but in other instances cohabitation uniquely diverges from its more traditional counterpart to represent a conceptually undefined union type. Thus, researchers including Smock and Gupta (chap. 4, this volume), Coley (chap. 6, this volume) Jayakody and Cabrera (chap. 5, this volume), and Le Bourdais and Juby (chap. 7, this volume), have sought to identify and clarify the nature, role, meaning, and diversity of this "newly" recognized family form.

Smock and Gupta, in their comprehensive review of *Cohabitation in Contemporary North America*, contend that cohabitation is increasingly posing a threat to marriage, and thereby is challenging the very basic conceptions of family structure. To support their assertion that cohabitation represents a retreat from marriage, they provide evidence of rapid increases in both Canada and the United States in terms of the number of individuals who will ever experience a cohabiting union, the percent of first unions that are formed through cohabitation, and the number of children born into cohabiting unions. Even more intriguing, as Smock and Gupta point out, is that the reality of these dramatic changes in union formation has outstripped knowledge, as social scientists struggle to empirically measure and document social changes that have already occurred.

Although research may lag in documenting changes underway in demographic categories and statuses (especially rises in cohabitation), the meaning of increases in cohabitation rates may have little to do with marriage per say, and what is framed as a "retreat," and more to do with broad scale structural changes taking place across the globe. Contextualized in what Stacey (1990) referred to as the *postmodern family*, cohabitation trends may provide evidence for the thesis that family life is continuing to evolve into an indeterminate variety of forms, as change in both family roles and arrangements draws our attention to "the family" as an observable site of social and economic change.

Apart from the social meaning of such demographic shifts, increases in cohabitation rates have also challenged researchers to reconsider static conceptions of family structure (Brown, chap. 11, this volume; Manning, chap. 8, this volume; Smock & Gupta, chap. 4, this volume). In noting the dynamic nature of cohabitation, and defining it as more of a process-oriented rather than stable event, Smock and Gupta argue for revising measurements of marital status and transitions as indicators of family structure, noting that demographic categories such as "single," "married," or "divorced" may be oversimplified and mask important features of relationship formation, and the contexts in which they take place.

Conceptualizing cohabitation also poses a challenge to social scientists because the nature of cohabitation continues to evolve. The nature of cohabiting relationships seems to be even more fluid and diverse than that of other family forms (Le Bourdais & Juby, chap. 7, this volume; Smock & Gupta, chap. 4, this volume). Given this "messiness," the question as to whether cohabitation represents an alternative to marriage is difficult to answer with any degree of certainty. As the work in this volume attests, the answer can depend on a variety of structural, cultural, and individual-level factors (Coley, chap. 6, this volume; Jayakody & Cabrera, chap. 5, this volume; Le Bourdais & Juby, chap. 7, this volume).

Moreover, the question of whether cohabitation represents a retreat in marriage may not be the most pressing or even relevant question in understanding the current demographic trends. As Smock and Gupta (chap. 4, this volume) indicate, the relationship between marriage and cohabitation has changed (cohabitation is no longer always a precursor to marriage), and there appears to be a dichotomization occurring within cohabiting unions. In general, cohabiting unions are increasing becoming more unstable, short-lived, and less likely to end in marriage. However, there is also a growing segment of cohabiting unions that are of longer duration, and "marriage-like" in quality with children increasingly involved.

The apparent dichotomization among types of cohabiting unions is addressed by Coley (chap. 6, this volume), who argues that this trend is part of broader change taking place in family life where roles and relationships are increasingly polarized. She cites "father involvement" as an example of this broader trend, noting that some fathers are taking a more active and nurturing role in the lives of their children, while other fathers are ignoring their parenting responsibility and having minimal contact with their children.

The apparent polarization in family life, and concomitant dichotomy in cohabiting unions, creates difficulty in classifying cohabitation, in terms of its role or meaning as either a stable or unstable union, or as precursor or alternative to marriage. As Le Bourdais and Juby (chap. 7, this volume) state, cohabitation is unlike marriage, and thus any simple comparisons between the two are essentially irrelevant because cohabitation represents a variety of intentions and arrangements that are in part determined by socioeconomic and cultural factors.

Diversity in Cohabitation

Smock and Gupta (chap. 4, this volume) address diversity in the role and meaning of cohabitation as it varies across social class and culture. To illustrate the role of culture in producing variability in the experience of cohabitation, they point to Quebec as a region in Canada that is conspicuous for its marriage-like quality. As Le Bourdais and Juby discuss, "cohabitation has become a socially acceptable alternative to marriage as the context for family life." Compared to other regions of Canada, Quebec as a primarily French-speaking cultural region, has embraced cohabitation as "a way of life," with 80% of all co-residential first unions forming through cohabitation, and with a remarkable 43% of all children born to cohabiting couples (as reported by Smock and Gupta).

   In contrast to Canada, Smock and Gupta report that in the United States, cohabitation tends to be selective of those with lower education and income, and plays a more prominent role in the lives of African Americans and Hispanics. In seeking to explain these macro-level trends, Jayakody and Cabrera and Coley examine the role that social class and culture play in shaping gender attitudes and relationship choices at the micro-level. In culturally reframing the question that Smock and Gupta pose as to whether cohabitation represents a threat to legal marriage, Jayakody and Cabrera ask "what are the alternatives?" for low-income African-American single mothers. Jayakody and Cabrera, citing the work of Wilson (1987), suggest that poor economic and employment prospects for African-American men make marriage and quite possibly cohabitation an unrealistic and even undesirable choice for Black mothers. African-American mothers often choose to remain single rather than risk the well-being of a household that may arise from the emotional and economic strain that may arise with the presence of an unemployed male.

   In explicating the meaning of these choices beyond economic considerations, both Jayakody and Cabrera and Coley, elaborate on the work of Edin (2000), suggesting that there is a movement away from marriage and relationship formation due to a "culture of gender distrust." They argue that women, and in particular single mothers, are increasingly likely to forego relationship formation not only due to a shortage of what is termed *marriageable men*, but also because there is a general distrust of the opposite sex and a concern that many fathers will be unable to remain faithful, supportive, and responsible.

   Examining how women incorporate beliefs such as a general distrust of the opposite sex into a broad schema of relationships, Coley and Chase-Lansdale (cited in Coley, chap. 6, this volume) interviewed single mothers about the messages they conveyed to their daughters about men and heterosexual relationships. Although mothers' messages to their daughters were what Coley and Chase-

Lansdale termed *complex and multidimensional*, there was a great deal of negativity about men, which was often conveyed directly or indirectly through warnings to be cautious and to choose partners wisely.

Both the works of Coley (chap. 6, this volume) and Jayakody and Cabrera (chap. 5, this volume), in addition to examining gender attitudes as factor precipitating relationship decisions, challenge dominant cultural paradigms of relationship formation, noting that neither marriage nor cohabitation may be viable options for certain groups of women who may choose to remain single, even when children are involved. Of course, the concept of "singleness" and living alone may not adequately capture the quality of one's life, as certain single mothers may have the social and economic support of kin and extended kin to provide them with certain options and freedoms when deciding on forming a union. It is these same groups of women, women of color and the poor, who Coley and Jayakody and Cabrera suggest may forego relationship formation, who are also paradoxically those very groups most likely to form a cohabiting union, and to have children within the boundaries of a cohabiting relationship (Smock & Gupta, chap. 4, this volume).

Thus, the work of these researchers suggests that many paradoxes and inconsistencies still remain in our understanding of cohabitation in the United States, especially among the poor, single mothers, and people of color, the groups most likely to diverge from dominant conceptions of family and family life. Illuminating trends in cohabitation conceptually and empirically poses a particular challenge to researchers who are forced to grapple with its diverse, transitory, and rapidly changing nature. To unravel the complexity of cohabiting union formation, many in this volume suggest the need for qualitative research, to get at the micro-level experience and meaning of cohabitation. Researchers should consider expanding the range of research questions to include "why" and "how" people are choosing, forming, and remaining in cohabiting unions.

Finally, the increasing intersection of this union with childbearing poses additional research questions that have yet to be answered. More specifically, increases in the number of children who will ever live in a cohabiting union begets the question of how cohabitation will impact and shape children's lives and development (Manning, chap. 8, this volume; Smock & Gupta, chap. 4, this volume).

THE IMPACT OF COHABITATION ON CHILD WELL-BEING

It is clear from the chapters in this volume that the question "What is the impact of cohabitation on child well-being?" is a complex, multilayered question that requires further conceptual elaboration and theoretical specification before definitive conclusions can be reached. Manning (chap. 8, this volume), Brown (chap. 11, this volume), and Kalil (chap. 9, this volume) each acknowledge that empirical research addressing this question has largely been descriptive and constrained by data limitations. Thus, there is a paucity in the understanding of what is important about cohabitation in producing child outcomes and of the mechanisms and processes that bridge the relationship between family structure and child development.

In an effort to disentangle the complex relationship between cohabitation and child well-being, Manning summarizes the empirical literature and argues that more subtle distinctions need to be made among cohabiting families in terms of parental marital status and the biological relationship between parent and child. More specifically, she suggests that we need appropriate comparisons groups in order to understand how family structure may influence child development (e.g., two-biological parents married versus two-biological parents cohabiting; stepfamilies married versus stepfamilies cohabiting).

Both Manning's literature review and Brown's findings attest to the diversity that exists among cohabiting unions, and to how diversity in familial arrangements differentially influences child functioning. In general, socioemotional and academic outcomes among children differ according to the type of cohabiting union they reside in (e.g., two-biological parents cohabiting, stepparent cohabiting union), with children living in a two-biological parent, cohabiting union fairing better than their peers in cohabiting stepfamilies and single-parent families (Brown, chap. 11, this volume; Manning, chap. 8, this volume). The literature also suggests that biological parentage rather than marital status is more important in determining child well-being (Manning, chap. 8, this volume). Although some studies have found differences in children's well-being between those living in biological married versus those living in a biological cohabiting relationship (Brown, chap. 11, this volume), this research is far from conclusive.

Absence of a biological parent, in particular the lack of biological father involvement, in a child's life (a primary concern of social policymakers) is addressed by both Ellis (chap. 10, this volume) and Kalil (chap. 9, this volume). Ellis proposes that children's biological relationship to parents is a powerful determinant of later development. Noting that children in cohabiting unions are at increased risk for the absence of a biological father and the presence of a stepfather, he uses an evolutionary model of psychosocial functioning to examine the impact of family arrangement and functioning on girl's pubertal timing (early pubertal timing among girls is associated with poor developmental outcomes). His findings suggest an association between the presence of a stepfather in a girl's life and early pubertal maturation that he speculates is mediated by the exposure to the pheromones of a biologically unrelated male in the household.

In a similar vein, Kalil, in examining the role of "social fathers" (boyfriend or male relative) versus biological fathers in children's lives, found that the presence of mothers' boyfriends lowered the emotional well-being of children in African-American communities (Jayakody & Kalil, 2000). Jayakody and Kalil speculate that the presence of what they termed a *social father*, could potentially limit the biological father involvement in the lives of their children, and thus impede emotional adjustment. Although the absence or presence of social or biological fathers in the lives of children and youth may provide but one indicator of the context in which children develop, additional studies are needed to examine not only fathers' time and economic contributions, but also the "quality," emotional closeness, and support of these relationships as they relate to cohabitation and child well-being.

What Is It About the Context of Cohabitation That Is Detrimental to Children?

Manning (chap. 8, this volume) notes that what is detrimental is driven by the assumption that cohabiting unions are qualitatively different from marriages. In theorizing why cohabitation may create a less than optimal environment for children, instability of the union is often referred to as salient factor. Research reporting cohabiting unions as unstable, short-lived unions ending in marriage or separation is overly simplistic and begets the diversity in cohabitation, the fluidity of its form and the actual duration of the parental relationship. Currently, there is little known about the duration of cohabitation for those couples with children (Manning, chap. 8, this volume). Manning acknowledges that this is a "key limitation" in understanding how cohabitation impacts children's lives. She argues the need for measures that capture when parental relationships end (couple-based measure) as opposed to when the cohabiting union ends (union-based measure).

Evidence suggests that family environments may be different for children living in cohabiting unions versus children living with married parents due to important differences in economic status, parenting, and psychological well-being among parents in each union type. Using data from the National Survey of American Families (NSAF), Brown (chap. 11, this volume) found that cohabiting parents are more likely to be in poverty, to be psychologically distressed, and to experience more parenting aggravations than married parents. Moreover, her findings identify mechanisms through which cohabitation might deleteriously affect child well-being.

In addition to Brown, Kalil (chap. 9, this volume) and Ellis (chap. 10, this volume) also theorize the role that cohabitation plays in producing child outcomes, proposing specific mechanisms and mediating factors that may elucidate the relationship between cohabitation and child well-being. Recognizing the importance of differentiating among "types" of cohabiting unions, these researchers shift the focus of analysis from a strictly demographic and descriptive level of analysis (e.g., family structure), to a more process-oriented, micro-level of analysis (e.g., parenting behaviors) that addresses the proximal determinants of child outcomes.

Kalil (chap. 9, this volume), in theorizing within a psychologically oriented paradigm, suggests several interrelated pathways that mediate the relationship between cohabiting unions and child well-being including family interactions, variation in cohabiting unions, and individual differences among children. In taking an individual difference approach that emphasizes what the child contributes to the family environment, Kalil argues that the affects of cohabitation on child well-being are likely to vary depending on the characteristics of the child such as gender, race/ethnicity, temperament and developmental age.

Kalil's research proscription to address individual differences among children to more fully understanding the role of cohabitation in producing child outcomes is compelling given that a majority of children in cohabiting unions are under the age of 5, and that few studies to date have assessed developmental outcomes among this age group (Brown, chap. 11, this volume; Manning, chap. 8, this volume). Furthermore, studies assessing development outcomes for children living in cohabiting unions have only tapped a narrow range of developmental indicators. Additional measures are needed in order to document which features of development are impacted by cohabitation (Brown, chap. 11, this volume; Manning, chap. 8, this volume).

In summary, research examining the relationship between cohabitation and child well-being is in its infancy, and there is much to be discovered about the experiences of children in cohabiting unions and how variability in union type and among children interact to impact children's development. Furthermore, certain demographic trends highlight the necessity, if not the urgency, for scholarly research in this area. Demographic research suggests that children are increasingly likely to experience cohabitation before the age of 18 (Manning, chap. 8, this volume; Smock & Gupta, chap. 4, this volume). Additionally, children living in cohabiting unions are more likely to be African American or Hispanic, and to be poorer than their counterparts living in married families (Manning, chap. 8, this volume); thus they resemble children residing in single–mother families in terms of their demographic characteristics (Brown, chap. 11, this volume).

Each of these trends draws attention to diversity in the experience of family life, especially among those who are members of disadvantaged populations, that has important implications for social policy regarding the future of children and families. Because cohabitation lacks widespread social recognition and institutional support, social policies have yet to address this union type, even though it appears that cohabitation may be quite common among those who qualify for or receive social welfare services. "Should cohabiting couples be treated as their married equivalents?" or "Should parental biological relationships to children determine the level of benefits and services?" are just some of the social policy questions related to children that Manning (chap. 8, this volume) suggests warrants our attention. Such questions are critical to current social policy issues such as welfare reform, and the related emphasis on father involvement in family life, that have direct and indirect relevance to the lives of children in cohabiting unions.

POLICY ISSUES

The concern for child well-being underscores the importance of social policy that addresses cohabitation. Furthermore, one of the recurring themes throughout the chapters in this book is the issue of whether cohabitation is a threat to marriage. This is perhaps nowhere more apparent than in the discussion of current policy relating to today's family forms. It should be noted that much of the legislation and public policy explicitly relating to cohabitation exists outside the United States and has typically been in response to pressure for recognition of homosexual partnerships (Kiernan, chap. 1, this volume; Le Bourdais & Juby, chap. 7, this volume). Within the United States, laws have been slow to recognize cohabitation as a legitimate family form. For example, inheritance and property rights among cohabiting partners must be spelled out in formal contracts and documents such as a will in order to be enforceable in the court system (Mahoney, chap. 15, this volume).

In general, cohabiting partners are strangers in the eyes of the law—unless children are present. The presence of children raises greater questions of outcomes and general well-being for these younger members of society, which leads to greater concern from policymakers. In the cases where children are present, and the members of the couple are their biological parents, the children are treated the same way they would be if the union were a marriage (Mahoney, chap. 15, this volume; Primus & Beeson, chap. 12, this volume). That is, if such a cohabiting union broke up, the custodial parent would be entitled to child support from the other parent. One difference involving children is that in a marital union, a stepparent can claim any children present as dependents for tax purposes but that is not the case for unrelated partners in cohabiting unions (Primus & Beeson, chap. 12, this volume).

Although the United States is somewhat "behind" on legislation and policy officially relating to cohabitation, Primus and Beeson set out to answer the question that is often in the forefront of the media, policymakers, and public alike—are there benefits (financial) to remaining "single" in the eyes of the law by living in a cohabiting rather than a marital union? The authors detail the programs and benefits available to low-income families, many of which are "blind" to marital status, and then examine the effect of living in a cohabiting versus marital union on the receipts from each. Even though it makes calculations and prediction more difficult, it is essential to look at these programs and all possible combinations of filing statuses simultaneously because their effects are typically interrelated. One striking point emerging from the comparison is that the government does not seem to notice cohabiting unions until children are involved because many of the programs for low-income families deal with children's well-being (Mahoney, chap.

15, this volume; Primus & Beeson, chap. 12, this volume; Winkler, chap. 14, this volume). The use of programs for low-income families or individuals is a response to the fact that cohabiting families, especially when children are involved, have rates of poverty similar to single-parent rather than two-parent families. The major finding presented by Primus and Beeson is that, overall, cohabiting couples may benefit from the current policies, but the benefits are most likely to be seen when comparing them with separated or single-parent families rather than married couples. Additionally, one of the "benefits" to cohabitation—as compared to living as a single parent—is the idea of economies of scale. That is, the difference is in the cost savings of maintaining one household rather than incurring the doubled expense of two households. Therefore, Primus and Beeson suggest that maybe cohabiting is not such a bad idea in terms of policy because it is often easier to get individuals into shared households through cohabitation than it is through marriage. They suggest, then, that to answer the question of whether there are economic benefits to cohabiting, one should look at the "progression" of benefits awarded for each family type rather than narrowing the comparison to cohabiting and married couples.

Haskins (chap. 13, this volume), on the other hand, advocates policies in which benefit comparisons do follow the cohabiting versus married status differences. He suggests that because children are likely to be harmed by living in an arrangement other than the traditional two-biological parent family, an argument not necessarily shared by others in this volume (see e.g., chapters by Brown, Manning, and Kalil), individuals should be benefited by choosing marriage. Haskins notes that these benefits could come in the form of housing preferences, Medicaid, and the like in addition to the tax and transfer programs discussed by Primus and Beeson and Winkler.

Loopholes in Policy

One of the problems with public policy relating to cohabitation is the lack of knowledge about specific programs and rules on the part of those who might be eligible. A push for educating individuals about their eligibility for tax and transfer programs, as well as the rules that govern such programs, is essential (Primus & Beeson, chap. 12, this volume; Winkler, chap. 14, this volume). Families also need to be made aware of the differences in the amount of assistance granted that can occur with minor differences in how family situations are reported because these can have sizable impacts on disposable income in some cases.

Legislation also falls prey to the same difficulties confronted by family researchers because of the problems inherent in establishing a straightforward definition of "cohabiting unions" (e.g., no official record to signal the start and end of such a union) and the diversity within these unions once identified. Perhaps this is one reason why legislation is still fairly rare. This could also be why other countries, such as Canada and some European countries, conceptualize the parent-child relationship as the root of public policy and use that relationship as the starting point for programs and legislation (Kiernan, chap. 1, this volume; Le Bourdais & Juby, chap. 7, this volume). Indications are that the United States may be following suit. The emphasis placed on the two-parent, first-married family as the ideal is still quite strong in the United States; to create legislation or policy relating to cohabitation is likely a larger challenge to the social structure than most care to attempt (Haskins, chap. 13, this volume; Mahoney, chap. 15, this volume).

Finally, cohabiting families are much more diverse than the current policies imply. For example, short- and long-term cohabiting unions might be quite different in their needs for and responses to assistance programs. An emerging theme with regard to legislation surrounding cohabitation is that some people are choosing to cohabit rather than marry for the very reason that they do not want the legal rights, recognitions, and responsibilities which accompany legal marriage bestowed upon them (Mahoney, chap. 15, this volume). If that is the case, no amount of "marriage benefit" is likely to entice them into a marital union. Besides, the difficulty in knowing and understanding the rules relating to such policies make it unlikely that the decision to marry or cohabit will be based solely on weighing the costs and benefits of governmental assistance.

CONCLUSION

The authors in this volume present convincing evidence that cohabitation is a family form that is "here to stay" and deserves to be recognized as such. Norms are changing so that cohabiting is becoming an alternative to either remaining single or moving into marriage for many individuals. Whether the types of cohabiting unions present in western societies today represent a "new" form or a continuation of old patterns may not be a question with a definitive answer (Kiernan, chap. 1, this volume; Landale, chap. 2, this volume). Noting the ways in which cohabitation has arisen as a family form in other social and historical contexts is one way of understanding the patterns present today. However, while learning from the past is important, families also need to be met where they are today (e.g., Hunter, chap. 3, this volume; Le Bourdais & Juby, chap. 7, this volume). Thus, an examination of union formation patterns for various subgroups of the population is also important. Especially important when thinking about the "hows" and "whys" of union formation is keeping an eye toward policy implications for meeting families where they are (Haskins, chap. 13, this volume; Mahoney, chap. 15, this volume; Primus & Beeson, chap. 12, this volume).

The chapters in this volume underscore that cohabiting unions are no less diverse than any other social grouping. Therefore, true understanding of the cohabitation experience should involve examining the variability within cohabitation (e.g., long- versus short-term relationships, pre- versus post-marital cohabiting unions, and two-biological parent versus stepparent relationships). Questions about trends, outcomes for various family members, and policy implications must all consider the ways in which cohabiting unions, like all family forms, may differ from one another. It is also important to shift focus away from the zero-sum argument of "cohabitation versus marriage." As has been true in the past, it is likely that different family forms meet different needs for their participants (Hunter, chap. 3, this volume; Le Bourdais & Juby, chap. 7, this volume).

It is clear from the chapters presented here that the study of cohabitation as a family form is in its initial stages—the stages where often more questions than answers result. The possible directions for future research on cohabitation are many. Perhaps a start would be to build an understanding about the decisions individuals and couples make with regard to union formation. That is, what does it mean to the people involved when they choose to remain single, form a cohabiting union, or enter into marriage? Do the different family forms carry with them different connotations and, possibly, benefits that are not being captured by standard research questions. The mere fact that researchers use marital status as a starting place for comparisons between families clouds the findings. To what extent is the diversity within each type of family greater than the differences between family types? This is not to suggest, however, that differences between union types are not present. Evidence shows that there are differences in behaviors, attitudes, and beliefs for individuals in different types of relationships. Researchers just need to be able to capture those differences (e.g., Jayakody & Cabrera, chap. 5, this volume; Landale, chap. 2, this volume). Brines (2000) noted many factors associated with the rise in cohabitation rates; it is vital to follow these trends over time. For example, as the roles of men and women continue to become more egalitarian, how will this affect decisions about union formation? Additional research should also stem from an interdisciplinary approach—to date, demographers and sociologists seem to be at the fore with cohabitation research. It is essential to have developmental psychologists, family therapists, life-course scholars, and others involved as well because each would bring to the research a unique perspective on the causes and consequences of family behaviors.

REFERENCES

Brines, J. (2000, October). Paper presented at "Just living together: Implications of cohabitation for children, families, and social policy," National Family Issues Symposium, State College, PA.

Brown, S. L. (1998). *A prospective analysis of cohabitation: Union dynamics and their meanings for men and women*. Unpublished doctoral dissertation, The Pennsylvania State University, University Park.

Bumpass, L., Sweet, J., & Cherlin, A. (1991). The role of cohabitation in declining rates of marriage. *Journal of Marriage and the Family, 53*, 913–927.

Cherlin, A. (1992). *Marriage, divorce, remarriage.* Cambridge, MA: Harvard University Press.

Edin, K. (2000). Few good men. *The American Prospect, 11,* 26–31.

Glenn, N. (1996). Values, attitudes, and the state of American marriage. In D. Popenoe, J. Elshtain, & D. Blankenhorn (Eds.), *Promises to keep: Decline and renewal of marriages in America* (pp. 15–34). Lanham, MD: Rowman & Littlefield.

Jayakody, R. & Kalil, A. (2000). *Social fathering in low-income African American families with preschool children.* Manuscript in preparation.

Johnson, M. P. (1991). Commitment to personal relationships. In W. H. Jones & D. W. Perlman (Eds.), *Advances in personal relationships* (Vol. 3, pp. 117–143). London: Jessica Kingsley.

Popenoe, D. (1988). *Disturbing the nest: Family change and decline in modern societies.* New York: Aldine de Gruyter.

Stacey, J. (1990). *Brave new families: Stories of domestic upheaval in late twentieth century America.* New York: Basic Books.

Wilson, W. J. (1987). *The truly disadvantaged.* Chicago: University of Chicago Press.

Author Index

Subject Index

A

Adoption, 73
AFDC, *see* Aid to Families with Dependent Children
African American
  cohabitation among, 41, 44, 258
  decline in marriage among, 85, 87, 100
  gender relations among, 44
  improvisions in family organization by, 43
  increase in nonmarital childbearing in, 91
  influence on family pattern of, 46–47
  marriage among, 44
  out-of-marriage parenting among, 44, 63
  subversion of social/legal convention by, 44
African American child
  family living arrangements of, 46, 123, *see also* child; cohabitation, and child outcomes
African American women
  messages to daughters on biological fathers, 100–102
  messages to daughters on men, 102–104, 262
  on marriage, 45
  on motherhood, 45
Age
  and first birth/partnership type in Europe, 21–22*t*

distribution of, NSAF project, 183*f*–184
effect on cohabitation tendency, 11
Aid to Families with Dependent Children (AFDC), 141, 194, 238, 239
Alberta, child support obligation, separating cohabiting couple, 109
Assortive mating study, 68
Australia, 6
Austria, *see* western Europe
Autonomy, 45, 259

B

Belgium, *see* western Europe
Biological parent family, 122–123
  behavior/emotional outcome for child in, 134
Black, *see* African American
Black matriarchy, 44
Black-White marriage rate, difference in, 41–42

C

California, TANF benefit in, 216
Canada
  attitude toward cohabitation in, 110, 111
  child in cohabiting household in, 58, 61, 67, 111
  cohabitation as precursor to marriage in, 66